HOGS, MULES, A

Hogs, Mules, and Yellow Dogs

Growing Up on a Mississippi Subsistence Farm

JIMMYE HILLMAN

WITH A FOREWORD BY ROBERT HASS

THE UNIVERSITY OF
ARIZONA PRESS

TUCSON

The University of Arizona Press
© 2012 Jimmye Hillman
All rights reserved

www.uapress.arizona.edu

Library of Congress Cataloging-in-Publication Data
Hillman, Jimmye S., 1923–
    Hogs, mules, and yellow dogs : growing up on a Mississippi subsistence farm /
Jimmye Hillman ; with a foreword by Robert Hass.
        p. cm.
    ISBN 978-0-8165-2991-9 (pbk. : alk. paper) 1. Hillman, Jimmye S., 1923–
2. Agricultural economists—United States—Biography. 3. Farms, Small—
Mississippi—Greene County—History—20th century. 4. Subsistence farming—
Mississippi—Greene County—History—20th century. 5. Greene County (Miss.)
—Social life and customs. I. Title.
    HD1771.5.H55A3 2012
    338.1092–dc23
    [B]

                                    2011040707

Manufactured in the United States of America on acid-free, archival-quality paper
and processed chlorine free.

17   16   15   14   13   6   5   4   3

To my parents, Bud and Agnes Hillman, and
to Helen Hillman, my wife of sixty-five years

Contents

Illustrations

Foreword

ROBERT HASS

IT'S IN THE NATURE OF THINGS that whole worlds disappear. Their vanishings, more often than not, go unrecorded or pass into myth, just as they slip from the memory of the living.

This book ensures that one of those worlds survives by setting it before us in its vivid lived life. It does for one patch of ground what historians, centuries after the fact, hunger for; it makes a memorable portrait of what a very particular world was like, how its people lived, and how they invented their world in the pungent language of a place.

Its author, Jimmye S. Hillman, has had a distinguished career as an economist specializing in agriculture, economic development, and international trade. After serving as a young officer in the US Army during the Second World War, he received his doctorate from the University of California at Berkeley. In the early 1950s he supervised Green Revolution projects in Brazil and later in the Cape Verde Islands. He taught courses in the economics of agriculture and international trade at the University of Arizona, advised the Portuguese government on agricultural policy when it was preparing to enter the European Union, wrote a number of books on tariff and trade policy, served as executive director of the President's National Advisory Commission on Food and Fiber during the Johnson administration, and was a Research Fellow at Oxford University and a Fulbright Fellow at Christchurch in New Zealand. He was elected to lifetime membership in the International Association of Agricultural Economists and served as president of the American Association of Agricultural Economics. When he retired from the University of Arizona, Hillman fellowships were established in his and wife Helen's names, which allow young scholars from all over the world to study economics and international trade in the United States.

An admirable career. But before that he was a boy on a subsistence farm in the depths of the Depression in the sandy pine country of coastal southeastern Mississippi. His parents were itinerant school-teachers. When the salaries townships gave to teachers became a paper scrip and negotiable only as long as the landlord or the grocer extended credit on the basis of its intangible promise, they homed to the family farm, taught school for scant salaries, and raised food for the table. You have to imagine a world without electricity, indoor plumbing, hot-water heaters, and telephones, though the telephone did come while Hillman was still a young boy, and so did the radio and the phonograph. And there were trains, so it was possible to go by a wagon pulled by mules or by motorcar (if you had one) to a train station and take a train to Gulfport or Hattiesburg and see a motion picture (if you had the cash). Until he was nine—in a world rich in story, rich in characters and gossip and Sunday preaching and church choirs and long tales spun from family genealogies, and droll humor laced with Biblical allusion (and in his family because they were book-reading people, allusion to Shakespeare and Milton and the Romantic poets)—he lived as most humans had lived since the Sumerians began to grow wheat and raise domestic animals twelve thousand years ago.

"What did you have for breakfast?" I asked him once, when we were talking about food. I knew he was writing about his childhood.

"Well," he said, "nothing special. We had chores to do and we ate for fuel."

"But what?" I had asked.

"Grits for sure, 365 days. And biscuits. Most mornings, biscuits. And tea."

"Your mother baked the biscuits in the oven?"

"A wood-burning oven, and the wood had to be cut, and it came from the woods on the property."

"And the flour?"

"It came from the general store in town, and the family traded sides of pork to the storeowner for the account on which we bought the flour and tea."

"And what about the biscuits? Did you eat them with butter and jam?"

"With molasses."

"And where did the molasses come from?"

"Well, we grew the cane, and once a year ("I have been writing about this," he would say) Cynt (Cynthia) Bradley came around with her sugarcane mill paraphernalia that chewed up the cane in a crusher powered by a mule. The juice was cooked over a large wood-burning apparatus that turned it into syrup." Cutting the cane was a nasty business. He worked at it with his brothers and his father, and the leaves were razor-sharp.

"How did you pay Aunt Cynt?"

"Usually with hog parts." So it was in part a barter economy, and it seems to have been founded on pigs.

"Where did you get the pigs, and how did you go about raising them? And where did the pigs come from?" This must have been 1930, and it must have been a hundred years before, around 1790, when white people from Europe came into that country—driving before them, in William Faulkner's telling, their livestock, their African slaves (perhaps African-born, perhaps American-born, and not many: if you had a lot of slaves back where you came from, you weren't out adventuring in a wilderness), and hauling their goods, their womenfolk and children, and seed corn behind. So there is the story to tell of the Hillman clan, without slaves, of the boy's father, the principal of the school at Neely and occasional alderman of Greene County, and the story of his father's father, Charles Hillman, and how he came to own the Hill Farm and how the farmhouse came to be built—no mansion but an owned property and considerable enough for there to be stories of its building and alterations and tributary tales about a Hillman cousin's wife and her resemblance to a woman of questionable character in the Book of Kings.

And there were all the stories about the pigs. Of course, pig stories are everywhere in literature. Hadn't Odysseus the moment he returned to Ithaca paid his first visit to the loyal swineherd? And hadn't the Prodigal Son worked at that trade? And hadn't the Lord driven a flock of devils into a herd of swine? And wasn't there that amusing story by Wordsworth's friend Charles Lamb about how the Chinese discovered roast pork? In Greene County there was an abundance of hog stories, and they turned on the local method of hog-raising—which was to mark your piglet, once it had been fattened a bit and could stand on all fours, with a distinctive cut on the ear—an earmark, that's where the word originated—and then turn it loose into the swamps and the pine wood where it—and everyone else's hogs—could forage and grow large and feral (at no cost to the farmer) and where—hogs being territorial creatures—you could go hunt one, when you needed meat. No stock law. So there were the stories of legendary hog hunts in that backwoods common and stories of the magical, canny, and ruthless hogs that could not be caught.

Readers of Hillman's hog stories may be put in mind of Faulkner's "The Bear," the epic tale of hunting the dwindling Mississippi wilderness. But Faulkner's Mississippi is, I gather, a very different world from Hillman's Greene County. Faulkner's Mississippi is the world and culture of the Delta, of western Mississippi with its cotton plantations, its affluent planter culture, and its enslaved and then tenant-farming African-American majority, the legendary country of the big river and big cotton and the blues. In fact, most of the very rich culture of Mississippi writing comes out of the Delta culture. Not only Faulkner but Eudora Welty, Tennessee Williams, Elizabeth Spencer, Ellen Douglas, Walker Percy, and Barry Hannah come out of Delta culture.

Greene County in southeastern Mississippi belonged to the coastal plain of longleaf pine forests, small rivers, and lowland swamps that, before the coming of Europeans, stretched from southeastern Louisiana through coastal Mississippi and Alabama to southern Georgia and the Florida panhandle. Before the coming of Europeans, it was the second largest forest in what is now the United States—after the great hardwood forest to the north that extended from the Atlantic to the Upper Mississippi. The people who came into that country came either to cut trees for the wood and turpentine businesses or to clear land for farming its sandy and not especially rich soils. It was a land home to one of the richest temperate forests on earth, with an abundant fauna and more endemic species of animals and plants than anyplace else in the United States except California. And by the time Jimmye Hillman's story begins, the timber boom was over and the forest was gone. Ninety-eight percent of it was clear-cut by 1920, replaced by small pine plantations and small farms.

It was not, or seems not to have been, a world of Sartorises and Snopeses. There were about 10,500 people in all of Greene County in 1930 and no one seems to have had much money. There was no educated class who had grown up in affluence and learned to read Latin in school and had gotten their fatalism from reading French decadent poetry out of school, and so there were no corresponding Snopeses either, to trade horses and watch the decline of the planter class and to keep their eye on the main chance. That may have been one of the points of contrast. If Oxford was a world of carriages and thoroughbred horses, Greene County was a world of wagons and mules. The educated class was people like the Hillmans who had given their children as much education as they could afford and kept books in their houses and taught school. Readers will notice that when the family sends the precocious young Jimmye Hillman off to school (on a train), he goes to Mississippi State, the land-grant university in the northeast, and not to Ole Miss, the university of the wealthy planters' sons in the Delta.

How much Greene County was a world stranded by the end of the timber boom and how much a world hit by the Great Depression it would probably be hard to say. One way or another, the world described here so richly was hard, and its most striking characteristic seems to have been that, though its people had not much money, they had language and stories to tell and family genealogies to rehearse and the rich language of the King James Bible to roll on the tongue and a taste for both irony and eccentricity that may have come in part from the contrast between the grandeur of that language and the actual daily world they found themselves attending to. It's why one of the treasures of this book—a small miracle of recuperation—is Hillman's "Greene County Dictionary." It's there that he gives us so much of the pungency and humor and invention of speech in a particular place and a particular time that—along with the legends of the Widow Smith's Blue Boar and the Suddy Sow and the No-yer'd Bar—most completely brings that place and its people alive.

Jimmye Hillman left Greene County when he was just fifteen years old. And the family moved from the coast to the village of Avera, if I read the chronology right, when he was seven years old. So the extraordinarily rich world evoked in these pages is, in fact, the memory of about seven or eight years in the life of the place from the point of view of a boy who was going to leave it quite early. It is a moving feat of memory, and readers, reading it, are apt to feel the power of memory and the equally extraordinary fragility of our daily world. Czeslaw Milosz, in his great poem "From the Risings of the Sun," ponders his effort to reconstruct the world of his grandparents' manor farm in an obscure district in Lithuania across which great wars would roll, and writes about what he has been attempting to do, trying to remember the names of the children of the farmworkers, the nickname given to a crossroads market. He addresses himself to an old priest who was a chronicler of local customs:

> It was, to make a comparison, like trying to tear a cloud apart.
> Human ways trick us with their warmth and their bubbling laughter.
> That isn't the truth of the earth that we know in our flesh and blood.
> I had the memory of many lives, so I was not defenseless.
> And I understood enough to choose what was small and local
> Because the great names and events pass in just the same way.
> So I hope to put my books on the shelf where your proverbs are
> On shelves smelling of wild ginger, by the Lithuanian statutes.

Hillman's book belongs on some similar shelf of Mississippi writers, a shelf smelling of—I guess—loblolly pine and of a smokehouse where a side of boar is curing; it could settle in next to an old Bible and his mother's worn copies of the poems of Tennyson and Keats.

Acknowledgments

FROM MY DEN IN TUCSON, I look out over the Sonoran Desert to the Santa Catalina Mountains on the northern skyline, and I consider how fortunate I am to have lived these many years in two wondrous places. Although southern Mississippi and southern Arizona differ in many ways, there are striking similarities. Each has a rich natural endowment, from the stately longleaf pine and saguaro cactus to the earth-rummaging woods hog and javelina. And each has a rich cultural endowment as well, stemming from a long history rife with human exploit and struggle for a country promising a full agricultural cornucopia. It is at this intersection of people and land that Mississippi and Arizona aren't so very different after all.

I owe much to the long train of my Scotch-Irish ancestors and their penchant for storytelling. I am grateful to my father and mother, who encouraged me to tell my own stories, which I finally began to put down in my eighth decade. My childhood brain-disk had only to harvest the gossip and the goings-on and to store them, which it did for my first fifteen years, becoming a kind of historical repository of Mississippi's Old Washington church, school, and community.

My poet-daughter and Tucson native Brenda Hillman urged me to set down these words and images. Many others provided support, including my sons Brent and Bradley Hillman, grandchildren Elizabeth and Thomas Hillman and Louisa Michaels, my sister Lora Jean Allgood, and nephew Dr. Henry Hillman. Norman Austin, Harry Ayer, Charlotte Cardon, Thelma and William Cooper, John Ferres, Roger Fox, Jean Garretson, Jane Greer, William Howard, Charles Ingram, Fred Karamar, Ann Kirkland, Zohreh Ladjevardi, Joyce Lowrie, Jane Meedal, Richard Newcomb, James (Rusty) Newman, and Richard Shelton. Robert Schreiber and Russell Turner all read selected stories and made helpful comments. Other friends and acquaintances gave encouragement in my effort to paint the chasm between existential modern America and earlier times: Herman Kohlmeyer made invaluable suggestions about literary matters; Elbert Hilliard of the Mississippi Department of Archives and History offered specific encouragement; and former governor William Winter added cultural backdrop.

I am especially indebted to Ken Lamberton for his prodigious and meticulous efforts in helping me edit this volume.

Thanks are due the editors and staff of media in which some of these stories have appeared: the *Arizona Daily Star*, *Gastronomica*, the *Greene County Herald*, the *Iowa Review*, the *Lone Star Iconoclast*, and the *New Harmony Journal*.

Finally, I am most grateful for the tolerant listening, steady love, and companionship of Helen, my wife of sixty-five years.

Beginnings

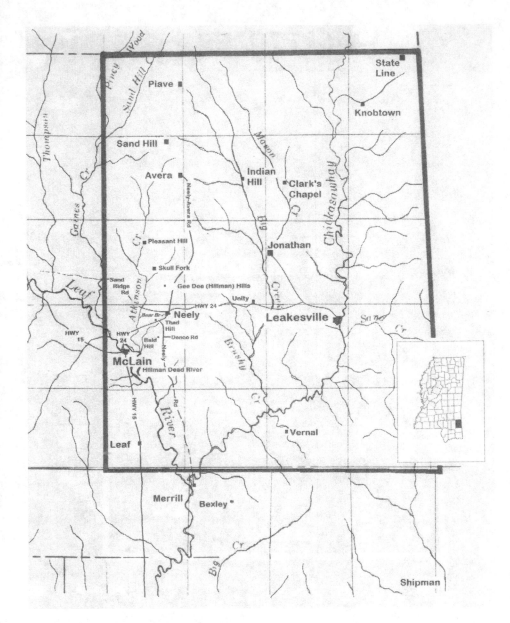

Map of Greene County, 1930.

The Suddy Sow

The horses of Achilles are said to have wept when they saw Patroklos
dead, their immortal natures outraged. So why can't a porcine sow
lament her own heritage and destiny?

HIS EYES WERE SHARPLY FOCUSED on the objects of a lifelong avoca-
tion, which had, in the Great Depression, become a source of family
subsistence and income. The hogs' wary eyes reciprocated his focus.
Both sides, having made their calculations, appeared content with
this moment of mutual accommodation.

His cracked and calloused hands shelled corn, which he had
shucked at the farm crib. He tossed the empty cobs into a bucket,
so they could be used later in our outhouse as the next best substitute
for the Sears and Roebuck catalog. With one strap from his Big Ben
overalls unbuttoned and the bib folded open, he shelled the corn
alternately with right hand and left, scattering it in a circular pattern.
The hogs were gathering, some in the bush well away from us, others
in front on a grassy knoll in the clearing. The horn of our Ford Model
A had brought the hogs running. The honking always started, and
continued intermittently, as we descended the hill through the blackjack oaks, dodging stumps and an occasional sinkhole. The horn had
replaced his vocal chords as hog-caller, penetrating more effectively
into the woods and the far reaches of hog habitat. It got the attention
of every hog within earshot. *Sound equals food*, they quickly learned,
for hogs are the brightest of farm animals.

That day, a Sunday afternoon in September 1935, a large herd had
sensed that a good feeding awaited them. It had been a long, hot,
and dry summer in Greene County, Mississippi. Wild food was scarce.
We could see that several sows had brought with them their late
summer pigs and spring shoats, which dodged the aggressions of two

young boars. The boars fought for turf and advantage. Hogs are very knowledgeable about power and strictly respect its use. Being semi-wild, most were cautious about coming close to us. Occasionally, he tossed a whole ear into the bush to one of the larger animals. One sow seemed to be his favorite, the one he called the "Suddy Sow."

This is one of my most vivid images of Joseph Levi Jefferson Hillman, my father, known locally as "Bud" Hillman. (How those beautiful given names got exchanged for "Bud" I did not know and still don't.) While feeding his hogs, he appeared almost transfixed, studying each animal, its size, shape, coloring, markings, including earmarks, even its eating habits and personality. Sunday afternoon hog feeding was part of a weekly routine that had evolved over the years for males in the clan of Charles Hillman, my grandfather. (Such feeding escaped the Victorian condemnation of Sabbath violation accorded to playing sports or shopping or going to the movies. Whenever we had to catch a hog on Sunday, my father would say, "The ox is in the ditch," and we did it.) My father's capacity for recording details about hogs was the keenest in the community. Each was an individual to him, often with a name, or a descriptive reference, and in many cases there developed a certain symbiosis between man and animal.

Hillman hog tales grew naturally out of particular animals and incidents. The Suddy Sow became a part of our hog lore mosaic, along with others like the "Listed Shoat," the "Spotted Gilt," "Widow Smith's Blue Boar," and the "No-yer'd Bar." Several years later in some idle conversation during my animal husbandry class at Mississippi State College the Suddy Sow came to mind. I wanted to know what breed or type she was, other than a "Bear Branch" hog, but the professor couldn't determine it from my description. I was confused about the word "Suddy." It wasn't in the dictionary, and only after I asked Father about it that Christmas did I get an explanation. "Aw! You remember!" he said. "She was that old gray-black sow that we fed for many years at the foot of the hill of Sand Ridge. The old Suddy Sow—a real rakestraw, not an easy-living swamp hog like the No-yer'd Bar. No bloodline, but always dependable for a litter o pigs. Finally, she was about worn out and we trapped and spayed her, put her over in the potato patch and fattened her." I surmised the rest. Her fate was the same as the Blue Boar and the No-yer'd Bar.

That was when I remembered: "Suddy" meant "sooty," as trans-literated into Mississippi-Hillman lingo used exclusively for hogs. Among them, the Suddy Sow, an ashen-charcoal breeder, stood out, even if she had "no blood," meaning she was without pedigree characteristics. She ultimately took her place in the Hillman pantheon (and pantry) of swine, though possibly less conspicuously. Like them, she made the supreme sacrifice, after a few months sumptuous living among sweet potatoes.

The Suddy Sow was a descendant of the hogs that accompanied European settlers across the North American continent: over the Appalachian Mountains, through the ports of Charleston, New Orleans, and Galveston, among other places. Polynesia, Australia—wherever colonizers went, they carried hogs, *Sus scrofa* (European) and *Sus cristatus* (Indian). This animal, which for millennia was considered a scavenger, the Chinese discovered three thousand years ago to have edible flesh. In America we introduced it into a new environment with seemingly limitless resources.

The hogs that "jumped ship" escaped a domesticated farm life and took to the woods and river swamps of North America. These feral wanderers played a crucial role in the development of the South. Though their fate was the same as that of their city cousins—those dwellers in close-quarter fattening pens—the relationship with people was vastly different. They squealed in a different milieu. They were more than objects of hedonic pleasure, gluttonous enjoyment, and economic profit. They were often considered part of the rural culture, and backwoods family, even part of the *Other*, philosophically. So it was with the Suddy Sow.

I have an image of my father as a repository for animal fat. All the bits of fat had been carefully carved from the lean meat by us children at meals. I see him yet at the table, after downing our greasy remnants, commenting, "There ain't nothin like the taste of hog fat!" Perhaps all that fat had something to do with his perennial digestive problems, and with the colon cancer that eventually killed him.

Fat came mostly from large "meat hogs," as my father dubbed them, and the Suddy Sow had a disproportionate amount of it after we put her in the potato patch. We butchered such animals into hams, sides (pork bellies in market terms), shoulders, even jowls, then salted and smoked them with hickory wood. Finally, we packed the meat in large crates or wooden barrels for long-term use. We singled out backbones for special treatment and, with the offal, exchanged them on a barter basis for day labor or special jobs my mother needed around our house. Fresh meat of any type came at a premium, so it was easy to get Earl or Felder to put in time raking, hoeing, chopping, or being at the behest of "Miz Agnes." It was the Depression; labor was cheap. No price was agreed upon for the labor or the meat; everything was just a "deal." When time came to kill a hog, Father would say, "Come over to the house, Felder, and get yourself a piece of backbone. You and Agnes can work out an arrangement."

By the age of thirteen, I knew the anatomy of a hog like a practiced surgeon. I was adept at farm butchery. Disjointing legs and the head from a hog torso had become second nature. With my eyes closed, I could carve around cartilage without severing ligaments or crosscutting a muscle. Today, seventy-five years later, with severe osteoarthritis in my hips, knees, and shoulders, I know exactly what is occurring in my joints, but the surgeons won't follow my instructions as to a remedy.

I could also make sausage, tossing the small lean bits of meat into a hand-operated grinder. (We never put offal parts in sausage.) Then I flavored the ground-up meat with salt, black pepper, and a hint of sage (*Salvia officinalis*), stuffing it in a casing of hog gut for the smokehouse. Less desirable, or fatty, ground meat, we fried and preserved in Mason or Kerr quart-size jars. (We called them "fruit jars," although we put up all kinds of vegetables and meat, even sausage.) Mother served Hillman sausage on Sundays and special occasions with eggs, homemade biscuits, sugarcane molasses, and that ubiquitous Southern dish, grits.

We rendered lard from excess fat that we diced up and dumped into a giant iron pot in the backyard, where heating separated the liquid from the rubbery mass. This so-called wash pot was the same vessel we used for boiling dirty farm clothes on Saturdays. It was well past World War II before any cooking fat, other than lard, entered our house. Like many Southern families, we fried everything in lard.

Lard rendering left a residue called "cracklings," which we ate directly or mixed with cornbread. (A form of cracklings is pork rinds, or fried hog skin, a favorite of former president George Herbert Walker Bush.) Crackling bread was a specialty of my grandmother, Ginny. She had her own secret recipe, which I remember as being a heavy and rich cornmeal-based pone, and full of calories. We used to substitute "cracklin" for "shortnin" in the ditty "Shortnin Bread":

> I'm so glad the little dog's dead
> Mamma's gonna make some cracklin bread

Although it was rarely on my mother's menu, chitterlings was part of our local cuisine. Many times I assisted Mary A. Hestle, our live-in maid, to "rid guts," inverting the hog's small intestine and thoroughly cleaning it, including a final scalding. Lest this delicacy raise eyebrows, you can rest assured that fried "chittlins" are a delicacy with a distinct flavor. When I think about chicken gizzards, oysters, and goose livers, then chittlins appear absolutely respectable. Chitterlings and collard greens combine to make a special treat.

The Suddy Sow also contributed a favorite of mine: hogshead cheese, or souse. In this I shared the palate of England's Richard III, who loved boar's head. Hestle made souse for us by thoroughly boiling the feet and head parts, not including the brain and eyes. She then picked out the bones and pulverized all meat and skin, seasoning it with minced onion and sage. Gelatin from the joints and cartilage allowed the mix to gel into a quivering mass, which we could slice and eat on bread. The hog's brain often ended up mixed with scrambled eggs for supper.

I was unprepared for the recent apparent commercial success of certain body parts of the Suddy Sow and her kind. On a recent trip to Greene County with my daughter Brenda, we entered a village market and discovered shelf after shelf of quart-size jars containing pig lips—pickled in water, vinegar, salt, cayenne pepper sauce, and paprika. I paused and thought: *The old order changeth, yielding place to new . . . Lest one good practice should corrupt the world.* Lord Tennyson brought to mind by pig lips.

The Suddy Sow lived in the branches surrounding Sand Ridge, yet another Hillman hog universe. Though less than ten miles from other hog landmarks such as Bald Hill, the Leaf River swamp, and

Atkinson Creek near Pleasant Hill as it looks today.

the Hillman Dead River, Sand Ridge was a world apart as to geology and provenance. To approach Sand Ridge, we had to go to the rear of the farm fields and connect to the Old Mobile Road that ran parallel to the fence on the north side of the former Thaddeus Green homestead.

Now largely abandoned, the Old Mobile Road made it easier to get to the backcountry and woods that lay beyond the old homestead,

Denco Road to the Old Turner Place and hog-hunting heaven.

what we called Thad Field. A half mile to the west of the juncture of "Old Road" and Highway 24, a fork ran through the woods and ultimately wound down the Sand Ridge. Rough debris, washouts, and trees choked the road, and we always stopped the Model A near where Bear Branch joins Atkinson Creek. This route was the traditional approach to the habitat of what my father called his "Bear Branch hogs."

This was a very different hog habitat, with very different hogs. The relative scarcity of natural foods, a more open terrain, and their more frequent molestation by man and dogs kept the hogs always on the move. They ranged wider for acorns and roots, and were more dependent on supplemental feed. To me they appeared not quite so wild, and I was never afraid when Father fed them.

Hogs in this area resembled what people commonly called razor-backs, though we never referred to them that way. To us, they were rakestraws, piney-woods rooters, and woods hogs, and in many years of associating with them I can't remember if a purebred animal, male or female, ever altered the mix. We traded boars with neighbors on occasion, but the Bear Branch breed remained an invariable homogeneous taxonomy. Once my father approached a vocational agriculture teacher, Mr. C. P. "Tub" Barker, about getting a purebred boar to improve the Bear Branch hogs. Barker said, "Ah, Mr. Bud. He'd probably starve to death out there."

Sand Ridge is part of the Atkinson Creek watershed, which originates near the community of Sand Hill at the northern border of Greene County. (One could walk into the woods at any point along Atkinson Creek and find the same general soil type: sandy loam.) In the days of early European settlement, the creek was a route for small canoes and exploration. Midpoint on the creek is Skull Fork, the place where my great-grandfather, Pinckney George Hillman, settled in the 1840s.

From Sand Hill, the creek flows through Pleasant Hill, a church community, then Skull Fork and Harvison Bridge, on a narrow sandy road just west of Neely, formerly called Old Washington. The old wooden bridge was about a hundred yards upstream from the "baptizing hole" where all those who joined Old Washington Baptist Church during revival meetings were "ducked."

Sand Ridge, a few miles south of Harvison Bridge, was a secret world the Suddy Sow shared with me. At the brink of the ridge, I often mounted a large tree stump, or climbed an oak, and looked due west over Atkinson Creek valley toward De Soto National Forest in Perry County. A clear fall day gave me a magnificent vista of color: the greens of pine, magnolia, and live oak, mixed with variegated yellows, browns, and reds of oak, dogwood, poplar, and gum. To the far horizon, this panoply spread itself before my eyes, which were born to fantasy and escape. All my forbears, the Chickasaws and Choctaws, and early white European settlers, no doubt, must have experienced the same emotion in this place.

My retreat to this part of the Hillman property depended at first on Father's frequent hog-feeding sashays, but in the summers I often ventured there barefoot and alone. Those days gave me an exhilarated sense of pleasure and isolation. At an early age, I became rich by mining the ores of nature and of sentiment.

Like certain deserts of the world, Sand Ridge surprised you with its biological diversity. Bird life did not attract very much attention in our community, yet it was there in abundance. Bluebirds sang and hunted insects among the pines. Woodpeckers (downy, red-headed, yellow-bellied sapsuckers) noisily hammered dead oak limbs from dawn to dusk. Blue jays fed on acorns and ears of corn, often sitting on scarecrows in Thad Field. The yellow hammer, a local name for the flicker, competed for woodpeckers' nesting cavities in dead pine trunks. The ubiquitous mockingbird lived a life of luxury. Father forbade us to shoot them with our slingshots. The mocker earned his keep by chasing off chicken hawks. Turkey vultures, what we called "buzzards," were also sacred to us because they cleaned up our own farm animal slaughter.

Late evenings along Sand Ridge, lightning bugs glowed in beautiful phosphorescence. Although deer no longer stepped quietly through the pines because of overhunting, rabbits, possums, skunks (polecats), gray fox, and both gray and red squirrel still foraged along the creeks and hollows. Yellow jackets and ants constantly harassed us. Fire ants had spread across the South from their Argentine origins, and to counteract the plague we imported armadillos from west Texas. Ultimately, the cure became worse than the disease, as the armadillos rooted up and tunneled through acres and acres of pasture and cropland.

Gopher tortoises also caused problems with their tunnels. When one appeared in a field, Father would yell, "Git that dadgum gopher outta here. I don't want him diggin up my potatoes." Hands who came to the farm from McLain at cotton harvest trapped tortoises by digging a hole at the burrow entrance, placing a large bucket in the hole, and masking it with grass. The tortoise tumbled in as it ventured forth. Father allowed the workers to believe that he was doing them a favor. There was a saying in the Depression that anything moving was in danger of being eaten.

Lest one think of Sand Ridge and its reaches as a universe of agrestic repose, where a dreaming teenage lad wandered about, and where hogs ranged before joining us at the Hillman dining table, there was a lot of action going on. It escaped the attention of everyone except the most observant. Just behind Thad Field there was a spot on the Old Road where some giant oaks grew. A thick screen of pine saplings had sprung up under the oaks, which from within gave an illusion of privacy. For reasons mysterious to us, this spot had become a trysting place.

Lovers from both directions on Highway 24, sensing that they may have discovered *the spot*, would turn off at the Old Mobile Road, gear down the engine, and quietly park. The favorite time seemed to be late Saturday afternoon and early evening. In any season couples might rendezvous, church-going adulterers from Neely or McLain. At one summer twilight, returning from Sand Ridge, I observed the lovemaking between two well-known Neely citizens: in the raw, fornicating in the brush. I was very surprised, but the dramatis personae have forever remained my secret.

The story of the Suddy Sow begins with the European settlement of North America and ends with my childhood at Thad Hill. In all the lore and song of the new land—"Canaan's fair and happy land" to many an Irishman and Scot—little was said about the role of the hog. Much was made of cattle, horses, mules, mares, chickens, roosters, even turkeys and ducklings in early American folk music, but hogs? "One spotted hog" in "Sweet Betsy from Pike," and a bit of oink in "Old MacDonald Had a Farm" are all that come to my mind.

There were other sows among Bud Hillman's Sand Ridge hogs— one black listed (striped), another white, and several motleys—but the Suddy Sow was my father's favorite. Why didn't he treat her differently, show her preference and put her to pasture like horses are retired to stud, or to foal? Even in her final days, he didn't show a sentimental gesture. It would have been sacrilegious for him to make any ceremony, as an Arab might bless the camel before he eats the friend who has served him so long and faithfully. Perhaps it was the perennial hard times that Father, like others, had inherited from frontier living and the Depression. No doubt, the daily scramble for survival had inured him to having compassion for the Suddy Sow.

Farmers like my father avoided personalizing a relationship with slaughter animals, but there were occasional exceptions. When we moved to Thad Hill, we children adopted two orphaned lambs we named "Lamikin" and "Ramakin" and raised them to adulthood with bottle-feeding and loving care. The orphans became so much a part of the family that they lived out their lives, yielding only wool at the annual shearing. Then there was "Little Boy," a bull calf with pink eye (conjunctivitis) that my mother and father in their later years raised to an animal weighing nearly a ton. They cried when they could no longer care for him and had to give him away to a friend. His greatest sacrifice had been servicing heifers that strayed into his pasture.

Father had no such consideration for the Suddy Sow. Year after year, we methodically harvested her progeny in their semi-wild state among the other Bear Branch hogs. Then one day in late October the bell tolled for her as well.

Her capture began with a simple deception: the trap pen. My father's routine feeding of the Bear Branch hogs, season after season, had been part of his design to add the Suddy Sow's carcass to that great meat-hog parade into the Hillman smokehouse. Those Sunday afternoons shelling corn not only sustained the hogs but also baited them. Noise from the Model A resonated down Sand Ridge, through trees and bushes, extending to the far reaches of Atkinson Creek. A honk from the horn brought them running, mouth agape, innocent, and believing.

Instead of removing her by rope or by a quick grab of an ear or leg, as he had with other hogs, Father decided to employ a special contrivance. "Bo," his younger brother, had designed and perfected it to avoid injury to the animals. The trap was a simple thing to build. The basic material included panels of heavy wire fence, six to eight feet high, which Bo and I stretched and wove and double-layered through a dense thicket of trees enclosing the feeding site. We then nailed the panels with heavy-duty staples to secure them against the impact of an excited two-hundred-pound hog. Father always insisted that we construct the trap in situ in a fashion that would not disturb the undergrowth. We added a camouflage of grass and gave the animals time to become accustomed to the structure.

For a few weeks, we gave the hogs free ingress and egress to the snare, lulling them into false security with corn scattered within and without the pen. We had built a strong jamb fitted with a heavy wooden door that dropped like a guillotine blade. But the success of the trap depended on the trigger, in this case, a latchstring of strong cord, tied at one end to a hook atop the trapdoor, pulled upward to a pulley on a tree limb and then to the rear of the enclosure to the "trettle," where an ear of corn was tied. Our trettle was a forked dogwood branch with its prongs driven into the ground. With the trap door pulled up, the cord stretched tightly to the ear of corn held by the trettle, the hog trap was set.

We took care to hide the bait under some oak leaves. We didn't want the trettle to release the corn too quickly because few hogs would have entered the enclosure. Experience had taught us that once the hogs began to attack the bait, the trigger would release the door too quickly. This was the only major hitch in Bo's trap, assuming that all the mechanics worked perfectly. We could never be too sure we would capture the desired hog. If an occasional stray fat shoat showed up in the trap, we'd take him home for pork. But sometimes we would have to release piglets and old and unfit hogs, which meant we had to start over at rebuilding the trust of the herd, giving the skittish animals time to forget the experience of the trap.

We caught the Suddy Sow on the first setting of the trettle. Father, my older brother Bill, and I discovered her and a couple of shoats in the pen on a September Saturday. It was a special catch, fulfilling my father's plan. Leaving Bill with the hogs, we hurried home, geared up the mules, hitched them to the wagon, and put a hog box on it. Father put me in charge of slowly retracing our path down Sand Ridge with the wagon. He followed in his Model A. By dark, we had delivered the sow to the common hog pen beyond the corncrib in the pasture.

The following week, we moved her to a patch of ground from which we had dug most of the sweet potatoes. There she gleaned potatoes until we returned her to a corn diet in the fattening pen. During the Suddy Sow's last days, I spent lots of time feeding her and her companion meat hogs. On those quiet occasions, I'm certain I knew what she was thinking:

They think that I don't think and don't know. But I sense it all, the Before and the After. Here I await my fate, not so much in a state of anger but in disappointment. Disappointment at the faulty philosophy and hypocrisy of Homo sapiens *and his "double-speak." Even disappointment at the inability of my own master and caretaker during my life's service to him to express his feelings to me. Rather it was corn and more corn, automobile horn-honking, his pleasant but penetrating stare during those weekly visits through the years—deceptions all—until the trap door fell. He is such a gentleman!*

I came into existence as a piglet there in the Bear Branch, and in short order was singled out for breeding rather than eating. Master took a liking to me, and I to him, though from the beginning there was always mutual suspicion. Cunning man, vigilant beast. He knew who he was, but I also knew who he was, and who I was.

Year in and year out, I produced shoats to be harvested. Why, in my motherhood, did I permit myself the illusion of being any different, a special hog, the master's favorite? Why did I dream of immortality?

Now, here comes the master, axe in one hand, his butcher's knife to draw my blood. His expression aglow, and his countenance strange—you might surmise that he thinks he is doing me a favor.

The night my father decided to kill the Suddy Sow, I became engulfed with apprehension and foreboding. In a state of disquietude, I tossed in bed trying to think of reasons and excuses to single her out for exclusion. For me, she had been a diversion and pleasure and, I presumed, for Father as well. I considered briefly a prayer, but animals don't have souls and aren't Christians. Morpheus soon assuaged my conscience.

That was in the mid-1930s, and no one had yet heard of "animal rights." And, even so, the humane treatment of animals probably wouldn't have applied to wild savages such as the Suddy Sow, who had abandoned her domesticated life and turned feral. As Father had so often said, she was a rakestraw, a piney-woods rooter, implying she deserved no consideration.

I arose from bed that January day cold but more composed. Father had preceded me at breakfast, so I gulped down some grits and eggs, took one of Mother's large biscuits, punched a hole in it, poured it full of sugarcane molasses, and dashed toward the big red oak. Already, Father, Bo, and Felder had killed and scalded two hogs, one of which had no ears, and had hung them naked and steaming from the tree's limbs. Seeing this, I rushed to where we had penned the Suddy Sow and looked down at her. She grunted as if to say, "It's okay."

My father hurried toward the pen, axe in one hand, knife in the other, to stun, stick, and bleed her. He seemed agitated, uncontrolled emotionally. Our eyes met, and as he was yet some distance away, I sensed a miracle. Suddenly his face brightened, and I imagined Moses descending Mount Sinai carrying the tablets of God's commandments. He mumbled something unintelligible and then ran to the pen and looked at her.

"Jim," he said in a calm voice, turning toward me. "I ain't gonna do it. We ain't that bad off for meat. Run, and tell Bo I said come ere, quickly."

Bo, who implicitly obeyed his older brother, was almost reverential in his walk. Father's command left no doubt about his wishes: "Bo, load this sow and take her over to Bill Lambert's widow. She and her hungry children need meat and they need this hog more than we do. Anyway, I don't ever want to see or hear tell of this Suddy bastid again!"

My father, Joseph Levi Jefferson Hillman, master to the Suddy Sow, had read Greek as a young man and, no doubt, at one time was familiar with Heraclitus. Thus, he was aware that *change* is the essence of the universe in which he lived. A thing *is*, and it is always *becoming*. But culture and life moved slowly in his post–Civil War world of Greene County, Mississippi. His was a closed society. He could not disregard custom, lest he be branded as "different." Father could not have flung open the pen gate and liberated the Suddy Sow back to the wilds of Bear Branch for fear his neighbors would have said, "Bud's crackin up in his old age."

At the same time, my father could do what he was noted for in his community: helping a needy human being. Platitudes like "It is more blessed to give than to receive" and "Inasmuch as ye did it unto the least of these . . ." dominated his thinking. Taking care of widows and orphans was as important to my father as feeding his own children.

It was a natural act for my father to relieve his conscience of the guilt of killing the Suddy Sow, to dissolve the long relationship between the two, by doing a good deed and allowing someone else to be her executioner. Feeding the Lambert family was sufficient balm for his conscience. But for his son many questions remain about the kinship between hog and man.

The Easiest Way
to Pineville

THE SEARCH FOR MY OWN HUMAN KINSHIP began with the place of my origins: Pineville. And getting there meant going through New Orleans.

On a recent day in April, I flew to the airport named for Louis Armstrong, for the Satchmo himself, after the Crescent City had for years ignored his contribution to its image in the world of jazz. In New Orleans, I rented a car, drove through the city, took Interstate 10 east, crossed Pearl River, and stopped at the Mississippi Welcome Center. A young volunteer was of little help in answering questions about history, and in particular had never heard of Pineville. I was shocked, as it is but a few miles from the Welcome Center, just inland from Pass Christian (pronounced locally as "Pass Christy Ann"). His map didn't help either of us. Just as I was leaving, a man in line behind me volunteered, "Mister, the easiest way to Pineville is when you come to Exit 24 off Interstate 10, turn right and head south on Menge Avenue, cross the river, then start asking questions." Good instructions. Within an hour I was parked in front of Pineville Elementary School.

This short drive through the piney woods had already launched me back in time to the place about which so much lore had been recounted in my family over the last eight decades. Crossing Wolf River wrought magic. Though housing development has changed things, the woods, the rural ambience, and the river itself were just as I remembered them. My image of that quiet village of 1920s fortune-seekers was well preserved by family oral history, and for the moment I prepared to put the puzzle together. Familiar place-names abounded, and the Universal Map of Gulfport-Biloxi provided cartographic detail.

Pineville schoolchildren with Principal Hillman in front of Ford Model T school bus, ca. 1920.

Finding the school office was easy, and as I entered I heard a voice and someone appeared from down the hall. "I'm Jimmye Hillman," I introduced myself, "and you are?"

"Jackie Graves, the principal. You must be the man who has been inquiring about the school's history, who wrote the county superintendent? And your sister, Jean Allgood, you say, has been active in Gulfport schools and social life for almost fifty years?"

"Yes, ma'am!" We connected immediately. "My father was principal here in the early years, about 1920–26, I believe. I began life here. We lived out in the country on Red Creek Road near Wolf River." The conversation became easier, and Jackie, as I was permitted to address her, kindly assisted my search.

She said, "The two-storied wooden structure was a small high school, but after World War II the present building replaced that and we are now a sixth-grade elementary school and part of the Harrison County system."

My conversation with Jackie, and my recollection of those childhood days, created instant excitement. Fragments from Hillman family files, and the tattered memories of three ninety-year-old former Pineville students, whom I affectionately call "nonos" (for "nonagenarians"), gave me valuable material to begin some fragile reflection.

Jackie Graves was a very impressive black woman and teacher. She won me by her knowledge of the school's history. Old pictures of horse-drawn and Ford Model T school buses, the children's school choir of the 1920s, and of individual teachers during that era grace the walls of her office and the halls. She assisted me in regaining insight into the heritage of Pineville School, Harrison County, and the surrounding area. Her parting words to me that day were, "I am very honored to follow in the footsteps of some very important people, your father included. And I endeavor to maintain the rich culture and charm of this little schoolhouse."

Without doubt, Pineville is in good hands.

Timber and turpentine barons led the boom on the Mississippi Gulf Coast through the turn of the century and World War I. Land promoters sold plots for pecan and satsuma orange orchards, later for tung oil farms, arable agriculture being unprofitable on these coastal meadows. My father, Joseph L. "Bud" Hillman, young and recently widowed, came to the Gulf Coast in 1920, but left a baby boy in Neely in the care of grandparents. A veteran of World War I, and graduate of Clarke College, Mississippi, he took a job at the relatively new school on Pineville Road, five miles inland, equidistant from Pass Christian and Long Beach. It was a high school then, though student numbers were sparse in the upper grades. He taught arithmetic to ninth through eleventh graders and became its principal in 1921.

Agnes Butler had just received her teaching certificate from Georgia State Normal. Answering an advertisement in a teachers' magazine, she took a position at Pineville and began teaching English and substituting in the elementary grades.

Within a few months, Miss Butler began visiting the principal's office quite often. In the evenings, Mr. Hillman appeared to have lots of business at Myrtle Grove. Rumor became fact, romance was in the air, and Mr. Hillman quietly sought the hand of his new Georgia teacher. She accepted, and a June 1922 wedding took place in a small northeast Georgia church. Perhaps it was the principal-teacher relationship, or the Victorian culture, but she addressed him as "Mr. Hillman," and he called her "Agnes," the rest of their lives.

Bud Hillman with children, baby Bill in arms, a nephew and niece, Uncle Bo looking on, ca. 1921.

Agnes Butler at Gulfport near Pineville School, ca. 1921.

They returned to Pineville—not much more than a schoolhouse, store, and post office—which at the time was called Cuave, a derivative of a famous Spanish family name, Quevas. It was located on Bayou Portage, and today there is a Pass Christian address and appropriate zip code. Mr. and Mrs. Hillman began a schoolteaching life together at Pineville. But schoolteachers are often busy at matters other than teaching; and I was born in March 1923.

Now, eighty-plus years later, I still remember the names Bell, Cross, Choate, Dubisson, Ladner, Lamb, LaSabe, Lessere, Necaise, and others, the majority of which came from French stock, descendants of original settlers along the coast and bayous. My three "nonos" are among these: Annie Ruth Carr, known as "Pete," Paul Parker, and Artlisa Basch Rouse.

Several years ago, when I was visiting her in Mobile, Alabama, my ninety-four-year-old cousin Pete Carr rekindled my interest in Pineville. For my first five years, I was *her* baby, so to speak, because of the family relationship. My father and mother lived in the Carr guesthouse cottage, just off Red Creek Road, near the Wolf River. "Jim," she joked, "I bounced you around on my knee. Your feet seldom touched the ground because we carried you all the time!" She talked of teenage trysts in De Lisle, going to see Rudy Valentino in the silent pics at Pass Christian, and doing the Charleston, all with the idea of keeping up with her older siblings, Alton, Louise, and Devan, and her cousin Matilda Jones. It was the Roaring Twenties, even in the piney woods of Harrison County, and teenagers from a few prominent families led the charge. The rumble seat was in vogue for those who could afford an automobile, and chaperoned dances were held every Saturday night at De Lisle, across Wolf River. Those rich enough built houses just off the beaches; the water was shallow and warm. In fact, southern Mississippi appeared to have been infected with a giddy flapper and Charleston mentality, and even my mother was infatuated with Theda Bara.

Pete introduced me by correspondence to Paul Parker, now living in Water Valley, Mississippi. His family came to Pineville in 1920. The Parkers and their Myrtle Grove estate held a special place in my mother's memory. They were friends to an insecure young lady, far from home. Paul's unpublished memoirs contain a chapter about school days and the details of community life there. He writes of primitive school buses and river ferries, outdoor toilets in the pines where boys smoked on the sly, baseball and basketball on dirt courts, games of marbles, lunch pails and the eating habits of rural school kids, even lovemaking. While reading his manuscript and letters, and talking with him on the phone, I recalled those years of my beginning.

Parker describes his life as a teenage boy in Pineville and surrounding villages along the Gulf Coast during the 1920s. His

Agnes Butler with schoolchildren at Pineville School, ca. 1922.

exploits reminded me of Mark Twain. He talks of fishing in Wolf River, sailing to Ship Island, shucking the large, plentiful oysters found off the coast, and even helping his dad run the family business, which involved driving their new Ford Model T. Trips to Gulfport and Biloxi and occasional visits to New Orleans added spice to his adventures. In his midnineties, his memory is acute, and his positive manner assisted in recapturing what life was like for me as a child. Paul's mother was one of those competitors for my presence, and she babysat me while my mother taught school.

Paul told me that once Miz Agnes, my mother and an avid basketball fan, had said to him, "It was worth coming all the way from Georgia to see Pineville beat Quarles!" Quarles was another elementary school near Long Beach.

My parents had spoken of the Rouse family, but I didn't remember them. It wasn't until Paul Parker told me about Artlisa Basch Rouse and sent me an old picture of her and other schoolchildren at Pineville that I was able to associate people with events. I phoned Artlisa, and despite our aging voices and ears we had several good conversations. Our memories hadn't dimmed. She sent me the only picture I have of Pineville School from 1920. Ms. Gladys Freeman

Agnes Hillman with Ms. Parker and Jimmye at Myrtle Grove, ca. 1924.

Lindsay, a young second-grade teacher, stands in a fur-lined, low-belted, long winter coat at the fence in front of the building.

Artlisa left Pineville after being promoted to the tenth grade in 1926. She recounted the days she played hooky and went to the beach, the time she and the other "big girls" would try to catch the new teacher, Miss Butler, in an error in English, and her delight at getting married at fifteen and quitting school. Like so many "teeners" in every age, the principal objectives seemed to have been escape and adventure. When she graduated from Pineville School, she traveled to the four winds, to places like California. The Depression, however, put an end to her—and many others'—wanderlust.

Artlisa presently lives in Baytown, Texas, and she remembers many childhood friends, playmates, and school incidents. During our last visit, she mentioned a trip she was taking with her daughter back to Gulfport by automobile along Old Highway 90. From a laboring class, she was representative of many children during that rapidly changing era of the 1920s, and in that evolving piece of geography, the Mississippi Gulf Coast. As with Paul Parker, I have never met her in person, but we have become "Artlisa" and "Jimmye." We talk at length about the old times in Pineville. She confirms stories about the joy everywhere when I arrived as everyone's baby.

These three nonagenarian voices, Pete Carr, Paul Parker, and Artlisa Basch Rouse, are a common thread running through my parents' lives at Pineville School, Harrison County, Mississippi, there on the banks of Wolf River in 1923.

One other name creeps from my Pineville memory closet: Ralph Bonine. Father told of coming to school one day and "inheriting" a young lad whose father had abandoned his mother. She had asked my father, "Mr. Hillman, will you help find a home for my boy?" Ralph wound up staying with us and doing chores for my parents, including babysitting me. My mother adored him, but it is one face I barely remember. He stayed with us all those Gulf Coast years. He was in his early teens when my father gave him the option of moving with us to Neely. He chose instead to go to Pittsburg and live with his grandparents. We lost track of him, but for years we wove stories about him around the supper table.

His was a Horatio Alger story. One day in 1944 Mother got word that Ralph was in New Orleans and was coming for a visit. (How had he found us? Why had he chosen to come home?) He arrived in the latest Buick and wearing a business suit, and I remember him hugging my mother and saying to her, "I'm sorry I never wrote, Mrs. Hillman." In an aside to us he said, "I could never call her Agnes." Hugging her tightly, he said, "It's sure good to see you again!" He explained that after leaving Gulfport, he had worked in the steel mills, graduated in engineering from Carnegie Tech, and was now employed by Westinghouse. He was in the Crescent City as a "trouble shooter" executive for the company. I happened to be at home from the army and met the man who had changed my diapers. The myth we had spun about him had become reality. He took a picture of our house on Thad Hill and had an enlargement made, which still hangs on the adobe brick walls of my den.

Like dust from Pineville's back roads, a cloud of nostalgia hovered over me as I departed the Gulf Coast for Neely and Greene County. Driving north on US 45 toward our first real home on Thad Hill, nostalgia turned into a *vision*. It appeared before me on the hood of the automobile, just like Moses's burning bush, only I didn't hear any command to remove my shoes. I certainly was not on holy ground. This was the house of Uncle Jim Jones, where the Carrs lived until my older half-brother set fire to it that day in 1926.

Bill, at the ripe old age of six, was supposed to be watching me while our parents were at school. Aunt Nora was picking blackberries along the fencerow outside. We were on the second floor in the master bedroom of the Big House. "Jim, let's build a fire," he said, and wadded up some newspaper and piled magazines on the grate of the fireplace. I was only approaching four, but I recall that when he struck the match I clapped my hands. Flames quickly got out of control, and we tried to quench them with water from Aunt Nora's syringe. Terrified, we tried the slop-jar water, to no avail.

We ran down the stairs, yelling to Aunt Nora, but the house was in ashes within an hour.

That fire, my first disaster. Fear of fire seared my subconscious throughout childhood, replacing my fear of drowning, being kicked by a mule, and of being grabbed by the Devil. Sure enough, there were soon more major family house fires to reinforce my sense of doom.

As the fire in my vision smoldered, cars whizzed by, going and coming. How did I avoid an accident? The Jones house was never rebuilt, and all of what remains of the property is covered by a 1950s housing development. After the fire, Father and Mother were obliged to move out of the Pineville cottage next to the ruins and to relocate to one of Grandpa's properties, the Carr place, in Neely.

Hectic and itinerant years for my parents followed. With three small boys (my baby brother Elmer was born in June 1926), they began immediately to contact school boards and school principals all over Greene, Perry, and Stone counties. During the next three years my father taught intermittently at Avera, Jonathan, Oak Grove, Pine Level, Pleasant Hill, and Progress, all villages in Greene County. Mother filled in temporarily at Neely, and was hired as a regular at Clark's Chapel, where the Presbyterian Church was the location for a four-grade public school. She dressed before daylight, and packed me off to school at four years of age along with my books and lunch pail. Father and Mother borrowed cars or bummed rides for the next few years while commuting to work around the county, dragging me along with them. So began my accelerated experience in public education.

The burning bush on the hood dimmed. Suddenly, I'm at the cutoff for Hattiesburg on my way to Neely. The endless rows of young pine zip by me like stalks of corn.

Discovering Sounds

SHE DIED BELIEVING THERE WAS A BODY in the box. They called it a radio. She departed Earth skeptical of the noises and sounds emanating from that audio device that her husband, Charlie, had slyly deposited in the parlor of their five-gabled territorial-style house, half a mile up the road from Harvison Merchandise in Neely, Mississippi. When that lovely structure went up in flames in 1929 (my second disaster), the box was one of the few items saved from the fire. The radio was an Atwater Kent that Grandpa had bargained from a salesman despite the objections of my Grandma Gin.

In the presidential race of 1928, Al Smith had it that Hoover promised, "A chicken in every pot, and two cars in every garage." Why couldn't we also have a radio in every Southern parlor? American ingenuity was alive and well. Within a few days of its installation, the salesman was back to remove the radio. That "talking machine," Grandma Gin reasoned, was a contrivance that could deliver lightning bolts as easily as its wires could bring voices and noises. News from across the river in McLain was that a woman who had bought one had been killed during a thunderstorm. "The Devil himself," my grandmother told us, "might use this machine to conceal his dirty work." She wanted no part of it. Thus, Charles Hillman divested himself of the radio. It was a luxury the family could live without.

Radio disappeared from my life for another five years, but other media entered. An intrusion of sound came from inviting sources. The phonograph was a critical mechanical diversion in our village. An occasional silent movie was shown at the high school, and the party-line telephone had also made its way to Neely. The emergent radio competed for people's ears, time, and money. There was more time than money; so infant media industries discovered a wide market but few customers in most rural milieus.

Grandma Ginny and Aunt Lora in front of Big House, ca. 1920.

The telephone had its central hub at Albert Harvison's house, and Rachael Breland was its operator. On my first look at the switchboard, I wondered about this toy. She was playing with ropes of spaghetti while cups covered her ears and a knob hung from her lips.

In the late 1920s moving pictures with synchronized sound, or talkies, were shown occasionally in the Neely school auditorium, replacing the silent movies of Charlie Chaplin. But it was the phonograph that became the greatest diversion in our village. Automobiles were scarce, but at least half a dozen families now had a phono. For a period in the late twenties a mild craze set in. Phono mania infected the countryside, and our village was not exempt. The phonograph was a relatively cheap method of entertainment, and was easy to operate. It supplanted the piano in places that had one, and it competed with church music in the home.

My grandpa's desire to have some sort of audio entertainment in the house was not to be denied; nor a salesman his consignation. Soon a Victrola was installed at Old House. The fact that it was advertised as a talking machine didn't provoke the same reaction from Gin as the radio had. Perhaps it was the fact that most of the sounds coming from its speaker were fox-trots. It also played instrumental music and tearjerker songs of pre-WWI vintage such as "A Letter Edged in Black" and "I'm Just Here to Get My Baby Out of Jail."

There were no wires, and no spoken noise came from the phono. Apparently, there was no man in the mahogany box, on top of which sat Nipper, the black-and-white RCA terrier, head cocked, apparently listening to the Victrola from whence came "His Master's Voice." One could identify with the dog, and my grandma accommodated this new contraption with a smile.

When I was not yet six, I was enchanted by the output of the phonograph. Music and song would grow on me, but at this point that little dog aroused my childhood imagination more than the noise. Why did he wear a quizzical look, and why was his head turned sideways? He appeared to be listening intently, but I had never seen one of our yard dogs strike that sophisticated pose. Little did I know then that reality had foreshadowed my fancy. Behind that pose lay the story of Francis Barraud, an English painter, who in the 1880s had often noticed how puzzled his dog Nipper looked, trying to make out where the voice came from. His dog had discovered that the sound came from the phonograph, and Barraud went on to commit this scene to canvas. The famous picture, *Dog Looking at and Listening to a Phonograph* (later renamed *His Master's Voice*), was sold to the Gramophone Company in 1899 for fifty English pounds. Later, this became the trademark of RCA Victor. Of course, few people, let alone a Mississippi child, could know of this and the history-making process before and after.

Childlike, I was impressed by the fact that apparently people were making those vocal projections; it was a human voice coming from the box. "Yes, sir, she's my baby; no sir, I don't mean maybe," and "Yes, we have no bananas" and "Ain't we got fun?" were imprinted on my emerging senses. There were many other tunes in this era of the flappers: for example, "It Ain't Gonna Rain No More." I especially liked being naughty and repeated what I had heard adults say, "How in the *hell* can the old folks tell . . . ?"

On the occasional visits we made to my grandparents' home, I gradually became accustomed to this new piece of furniture in the parlor and to the new world of sound coming from that beautiful mahogany cabinet. There was a little wobbly pine stool I climbed upon to peer into the sunken space where a flat disc was spinning, above which rested a strange looking steel arm separated from it by a shiny needle. A scratchy noise came from the source of direct needle and disc contact, and a jet of music proceeded from the front of the console. Two small doors guarded an opening covered by a protective fabric that muffled the sound. Two larger doors below protected a place for disc storage. The phono embodied a new world, indeed.

Gene Austin was the most popular singer of that era. A high-pitched, mellifluous rendition of "My Blue Heaven" and "My Melancholy Baby" struck my musical fancy. I fell in love with "Ramona," and I still love it in my eighties. It may seem odd that a child that young could have been so attracted to music, but I have a strong Moody heritage. It was said around Neely that the Moodys have music even in their bones, and that they were born humming.

Steel needles, protruding from that heavy arm, pressing against wax records, produced surprisingly pleasant sounds. Frustrating to everyone, however, were the inevitable scratchy and garbled effects that came from poor handling of records, dust, and bad needles. Steel needles dulled after the first few times we cranked the handle, and wax discs warped readily in our warm summers. The phonograph arm was often dropped on the disc, resulting in disconcerting and discontinuous acoustics. What followed was a blurred and horrendous sound, which rose and fell because of the warped record. Too frequently I got the blame for such incidents.

Children weren't allowed to touch the mechanism, so I felt helpless when trouble arose. But it took no genius to discover that the

Aunt Lora, Virginia, and Bubba dressed for a party, ca. 1925.

problem was frequently one of pure mechanics. When the music slowed, it could be remedied by winding that handle sticking out on the side of the console. Nothing, though, could fix cracked and warped discs and worn needles. Grandpa tried to sharpen the needles with a steel file, but it did little good.

Record playing was an integral part of family get-togethers, especially on Saturday nights. (The phonograph was never played on Sundays.) One Saturday, Aunt Lora and her children, Ginny and Bubba, came over to Old House from McLain. Uncle Carr, Aunt Nora, and my teenage cousin Annie Ruth Carr, with her Theda Bara hairstyle, drove up from the Gulf Coast. "Pete" (she hated the name Annie Ruth) tried to do the Charleston to Grandpa's records. But the 4/4 rhythm of the dance didn't fit the music. Cracks in the plank flooring at the old house maddened her by snagging her high heels in the recesses. High heels and dancing at her age were sinful to Grandma. Why couldn't we just listen to the music, sing along with Gene Austin, and contemplate, I wondered? Fortunately, Annie Ruth's visits were always brief, and I could settle back into my cozy world with that intriguing little dog.

After the economic crash of 1929, there was no money for new records and needles, which meant that existing ones got worn and grew dysfunctional. I remember the stacks of scratched and cracked discs. Many needles were lost, the rest useless. The phonograph itself began to malfunction, and finally it was but a piece of furniture in the corner, gathering dust. Gene Austin lay silent.

For several years Charles Hillman's Victrola had been the principal social entertainment of Neely, but those gatherings gradually diminished. The entertainment subsided as the Depression set in. Because of hard times and the solitude and isolation in his heart after Gin's death in 1932, there was never another sound from the box. He closed the lid and lowered the cover, but the bright polished dog always sat there, pondering.

Radio first became part of my limited universe in the late 1920s when one day Father took us to C. J. Neely's to listen to the World Series. What an adventure to be invited to the Neely mansion, a massive two-story columned house built behind a grove of longleaf pines a half mile diagonally across a cotton patch from my grandparents' place! It was a mysterious architectural configuration, but baseball and radio dispelled all of my misgivings.

The announcers' voices surged and faded with the airwaves, often frustrating the all-male audience when an exciting play was in process. Action was described in minute detail. I was unaware that many of

these early baseball broadcasts were recreated in a studio by announcers reading pitch-by-pitch accounts from ticker tapes, using sound
effects and canned crowd noises to simulate live action. An Illinois
boy, who moved to Iowa and read those tapes to create virtual reality,
went on to become the fortieth president of the United States. Along
with Ronald Reagan, radio was carrying me into another world.

As a six-year-old boy, I knew the rudiments of baseball. Connie
Mack was manager of the Philadelphia Athletics and my father's
favorite. I was quick to appropriate Mule Haas, Jimmy Foxx, Al
Simmons, and Lefty Grove as my favorite players. Grove remained
tops with me until Carl Hubbell of the Giants came along. That new
noise and the excitement of a Sunday afternoon in October 1929
were enough to saturate my imagination for hours and to whet my
appetite for baseball for the next seventy-five years. I still prefer a
radio broadcast of a baseball game, à la Mel Allen's voice, to the tele-
vised version, and I still miss the canned crowds and sound effects.

The radio and the World Series were stuck fast to each other,
becoming an annual event in my young life. Worsening economic
prospects removed any hope that my parents could afford a unit of the
wireless wonder. When we moved to Avera the next year, Ed West's
Ford agency was the locale for that fall community gathering where
we listened to the two-league showdown of the national pastime.

During the rest of the year, playmates and I made intermittent
snoops by Mr. West's agency in attempts to catch a sound of the
voices and music coming from his box, listening attentively in an
effort to make sense of the noisy amalgam. I especially wanted to hear
Amos 'n' Andy. Fantasies about having our own radio continued for
several years. It wasn't until we returned to Neely in 1935 that my
dreams finally came true.

My father tentatively announced at supper one night in May that
he was thinking of buying a radio when he finished our house. My
memory of Grandma Gin's reaction to radio was suddenly resur-
rected. Mother and he had discussed it, and since both had tentative
commitments to teach next year, they thought they could handle the
eight dollars per month payment.

Rumors were that John Sprona from the Philco Radio Agency of
Citronelle, Alabama, had contacted several families. His representative was already negotiating with Mr. Neely to replace his current set

with a Philco and to upgrade the reception. Events moved rapidly after that, and in early July a Philco walnut cabinet and its contents were installed by a picture window in the parlor on the northeast side of our new house. It was a safe bet that the new radio would be the center of attention at Thad Hill, the name we gave our home.

Sprona, a small, wiry, and intense young man with quick movements, wasted little time in installing our newfound entertainment luxury. The battery—electricity was still seven years away—the speaker, and the wiring were put in place, and an outside aerial was strung between posts on the east and west gables to ensure better reception. A grounding cable, staked in the earth near the chimney outside, ensured protection from lightning bolts. The radio was operable within an hour. Its installation was high drama, and the entire family and neighbors attended the process. With his job now complete, Sprona handed an operating booklet to Mother and began to instruct us all in the care and keeping of Philcos. (Later, as the inevitable problems with static and poor transmission arose, Sprona became a curse word. Every play we missed during a baseball game, someone would shout, "That damn Sprona. I wish he'd come get his machine!")

Intense competition arose immediately among the children as to who controlled the knobs and selected the programs. The struggle was superficial because none of us had the slightest idea as to what was available from the box. There was no program guide, and we received no daily paper that contained such information. We learned about programs by word of mouth. Our contention over programming was futile anyway because Father and Mother set forth radio hours: occasional mornings, selected evenings, Saturday night, and Sunday when not at church. There was to be no excess diversion during the school days. Even so, not too much time elapsed before the Philco became an instrument of established routine in the Hillman household.

"This is WWL, coming to you from the Roosevelt Hotel in New Orleans," a strong basso voice announced in early morning about breakfast time. With its 5,000-watt station, WWL was the strongest in the region. Such a loud signal dispelled any lingering drowsiness. News and weather were standard, followed by a number of items appealing to city and rural folk, with an occasional advertisement. The one that still rings in my ears from time to time is the Shinola shoeshine jingle. Glistening shoes were part of our culture, when shoes were worn. We usually went barefoot, but when dressing for Sunday, shiny underpinnings were important. Thus, Shinola had a vast market and cultivated it through radio:

> Keep your shoes shined all the time,
> 'Cause all the time is the time to shine,
> So when you hear that familiar chime
> (Bell rings ding-dong, ding-dong) It's time to shine . . .
> S-H-I-N-O-L-A Shinola!

Saturday nights emerged as radio night. After days of hard work and a weekly bath, we ate supper and a freezer of homemade ice cream. Then the WSM Barn Dance and Grand Ole Opry from Nashville, Tennessee, with its innovative country music came on the air. Uncle Dave Macon played "Go Long Mule" on his banjo, and Roy Acuff introduced "The Great Speckled Bird," followed by the Smoky Mountain Boys and Minnie Pearl with her "Howwww-deeee." I had never heard the likes of those rousing voices that created a certain identity. They gave something of a lift and diversion from a drab routine. But with the diversion there was also disturbance of our quiet agrarian rhythm. Alas! Rooster crowing, cow lowing, and sheep bleating eventually became the odd noises.

New competition soon arose for control of the knobs. Among our Saturday night visitors were Uncle Kimmy and Aunt Cannie, who lived down the road toward McLain. They spiced their dull Saturday evenings with visits to see Bud and Agnes. Since Uncle Kimmy and my dad weren't exactly bosom buddies, we children knew that the Kimmy and Cannie visit was an excuse to enjoy the new Philco. Kimmy, a pesky and obstinate little man, insisted on pushing us children aside and taking control of the dials when our parents were not present. Since he was near-sighted, Kimmy had to place his nose near the set, both hands on the knobs, then proceed to vigorously twist them through the static of the numbered spectrum. His favorite comment was, "Damned old stratic. Cain't git nothin."

A periodic interruption of the idle chatter around the Philco came from the voice of Dr. John R. Brinkley and his bizarre brigade. Added to my memory of flappers and flaming youth is his appealing quackery. Brinkley sold pseudo-scientific lectures and high-priced medical treatment from a station across the river from Del Rio, Texas. Singing cowboys, fiddlers, and a Mexican studio orchestra was the backdrop for his hawking of all types of remedies, including a sex-enhancing elixir obtained from goat gonads. It was the greatest apparent sex "fix" until Viagra would come seventy years later.

Children, such as I, listening to the show were impressed only by the music and his theatrics. Though not yet a teenager, I began to wonder what Sprona had wrought. Maybe Grandma was right after all. Radio soon began to compete with reading, the funnies, and what little time we children had after school and work. Our previously uninterrupted daily routines were tempered by diversionary themes from the box.

Idly sitting before the radio evoked a mild guilt complex in me. I wasn't involved in the muscular activity of work, a first principle of Victorian culture. Anything less or different was not work. "An idle mind is the Devil's workshop," my mother admonished. She might have added that an inactive body leads to laziness. The radio of that period didn't activate many brain cells; and the temptation of a tired farm lad was to listen and doze. Gradually I developed an unconscious aversion toward the box, a condition—with the exception of listening to classical music and baseball—I still possess.

Primitive soap operas were scheduled for selected hours. War stories from Ethiopia and Spain began my worries about people killing each other. Why did God allow it? Grandma Gin's fear was always in the back of my mind, that a bolt of lightning might strike the aerial and kill us all. It seems like a silly thought now, but it was real to us then. Still, the radio did allow me to listen to President Franklin Roosevelt's "fireside chats." I still remember his reassuring voice, saying in his first inaugural, "We have nothing to fear but fear itself," which was very comforting to an uneasy rural Mississippi lad.

Grandma wasn't the only one who was suspicious of the radio. There was something fishy and unbelievable about the box. Cousin Chris, a bit backward and unfamiliar with the workings of the radio, was at the house one Sunday. My Uncle Bo, always the practical jokester and cunningly aware of Chris's naiveté, assured him that the communicating process by radio was simple. He told him that there was a man talking from another radio box, and that all he need do was to respond. "Just squat behind the set. I'll connect you, and then you can start talking. People in Hattiesburg and New Orleans will hear you directly. Come on. Do you want to talk to them?"

We watched as Chris squeezed between the wall and radio console. He sat in the corner, unseen by the rest of us as we waited. Bo went to the radio, feigned a switch-on, and told Chris, "It's ready to go; when you're ready, go."

The monologue began: "Good morning. My name is Chris Hillman. I am fourteen years old. I go to Neely school. I'm at Uncle Buddy's house today listening to his radio, and I hope lightning don't strike us." After mumbling a few more words, the broadcast was over. Chris emerged triumphant with his doltish face gleaming, and we rewarded the new believer with applause and approbation.

Such interludes of mirth did not lessen my apprehension of this wireless invader. Moreover, it was just the beginning of a life in which silence and the quiet moment would vanish forever. It had begun in the mid-1920s with Miss Rachael talking into that little button on the wire in front of her lips, and the subsequent ringing of telephones in the few houses of Neely that could afford the service. I still recall that my grandparents' ring was two longs and a short. However, ringing wasn't the principal issue. It was the prattle, juvenile blabber, and local gossip that followed that disturbed the tranquility of many peaceful households. We never had a phone at Thad Hill until well into the post-WWII years. And even in the 1930s, telephone noise ceased to be a problem because most private phone companies went defunct.

How is one to select soothing sounds from the likes of John R. Brinkley or Rush Limbaugh? Should one try? From the vantage point of twenty-first-century reality, I reflect on childhood and youth encounters with the noisy disturbers of nature, and on my solitude, remembering an ambience of the wood at Thad Hill. I recall that day when Gin ordered Charlie to remove the Atwater Kent from her presence. Her serene privacy had been temporarily interrupted before she soon entered an eternal silence. As things turned out, John Sprona's Philco interrupted my sensory journey for a longer period.

The Shinola commercial and the bass voice of the announcer blaring, "From WWL in the Roosevelt Hotel, downtown New Orleans," still rattle round my cranium. Life is full of unavoidable echoes.

Noise was never the first purpose of most inventions. It was the spin-off of market consideration. But, one is left to ponder that market. Who can put a value on a train whistle, the roar of an airplane jet, a Beethoven sonata, or a president's fireside chat, versus the bray of a donkey, the crow of a rooster, the wafting of wind through corn stalks on a hot August afternoon, or the lapping of ocean's waves against land's crags? When I think of my first reaction to the clatter of the Grand Ole Opry and the silly voice of Minnie Pearl, I cringe. Yet, I didn't turn the off knob, and I didn't walk away from the Philco. In fact, I began cozying up to the console. Beginning with the talking machine, new sounds became embedded in my brain; their deleterious effects were apparently discounted.

Over time I cut out unbearable offenses to my ear that were dispensed by all the noise boxes. As Keats wrote in his immortal poem "Ode on a Grecian Urn": "Heard melodies are sweet, but those unheard / Are sweeter . . ." Those lines raise the spiritual question in me as to the primacy of audition over vision. I wonder: Is the ear the organ of divine perception? I have used music to break the monotony of existence. My daughter Brenda recently gave me a disc of favorites from the rebellious 1960s. I immediately put it in my iMac and scrolled to Simon and Garfunkel's "Sounds of Silence." "Hello darkness, my old friend . . ."

The Avera I Knew

STATELY AND TACITURN HE STOOD THERE, whistle in hand, watching them. Facing the wood-frame Mutual Rights schoolhouse from the front, they formed two lines according to class, waiting to march in when he gave the signal. A young man, already gray, his face reflected not only worries of being principal but of being community leader, caretaker of his parents, and father of four. The Great Depression had set in, and the children of Avera's jobless mill workers bore down on his conscience. He felt an unusual responsibility to lead, to educate, and to give hope.

Sensitive to the cold, on this raw February day in 1932, he was appropriately dressed: union suit, wool shirt and trousers, sweater and appropriate jacket, and a tie. Underneath it all was a tar plaster, worn to ward off colds and the flu. Before appearing at school he had already milked the cow, slopped the hogs at the little barn across the road from the teacher's home, a hundred yards diagonally distant from the schoolhouse. Breakfast and coffee were routine before starting the day's work.

Standing there his thoughts must have flashed back to his own youth. Education was a rare commodity in Old Washington when he began school in the 1890s. Still a teenager, he was driving oxen and snaking logs from the Leaf River swamp when his father suddenly announced one day that his son must go to college. He hadn't been prepared for what apparently was a desultory decision. Resisting, he said that he preferred to remain at home, help on the farm, and continue in the timber business. Charles Hillman, not to be disputed, replied, "You're going to Clarke College at Newton. When you're finished, if you want to return here, you'll be a better ox driver." *What insight from an uneducated old man. That's the way I got into this business, and by the Lord's calling,* he thought to himself. Blame

Joseph Levi Hillman at age twenty-two.

it on the Lord. A thin smile crossed his face as he often related that story to us at home; and I, who was in the school line that morning, could read his mind by his countenance when he raised the whistle to his lips. This was my father, Joseph Levi Jefferson Hillman, "Mister Hillman," to the schoolchildren across Greene County.

His wife herded the children into class lines, cheerfully calling each by name with "Line up, line up." Still thin in her thirties, she was strong, energetic, and determined, and had that morning dressed three of her own children, fed and hustled them uphill to the schoolhouse, and directed them to the appropriate line.

She wore a self-made gingham dress, and a heavy wool sweater covered her broad shoulders before falling to her hips. The cold was no problem for her warm-natured physiology. Always the first out of bed at the teacher's home, she built fires in kitchen and fireplace, directed the dressing of the children, "got herself together" for the school day, ate breakfast, and then picked up from a side table school materials she had prepared the night before.

Barely twenty, she had received her teaching certificate at Georgia State Normal, and was enchanted by escaping the family's small peach farm, having heard her two brothers talk of Paris, where they spent time during the Great War. Responding to a job notice in a Mississippi teachers' magazine, she was surprised and delighted that she had landed the position. It was now more than a decade since she had met Mr. Hillman at Pineville.

I was seven years old when my parents moved to Avera, a village crossroads in northern Greene County. We occupied the teacher's home at Mutual Rights School where Father became principal in 1930. Avera had been a boomtown prior to and during World War I, but was fading fast from its glory days. The crash of 1929 accelerated its decline, sounding the town's death knell. Like many sawmill villages, Avera was on the way to becoming a ghost town.

In the early 1900s Mutual Rights, a grade school, was built on a hill near Avera Methodist church, south and east of the emerging village. The school quickly evolved to service the community, and buildings were constructed accordingly. This happened before the village got its present name. The school overlooked the gravel road to Leakesville and the Neely and McLain highway. Longleaf pine saplings dotted the low-rolling hills, and a few were scattered about the school. Avera cemetery bordered the school and the church on the south, but we never looked that way. I remember that Father offered us a quarter if we would pick it off one of the gravestones. We never dared take him up on it.

The teacher's home was a white two-story elegant construction from the beautiful timber sawed, planed, and kiln-dried locally. Between the school and teacher's home stood a massive water pump from which everyone drank. It was a gathering point for children during recess and lunch. Toilet facilities were on the other side, east of the school, outdoors to be sure. The occupants of the teacher's home, the Hillman family in this case, also depended on the pump as a source of water; we had no indoor running water or private toilet facilities. We kept a milk cow and some chickens in a little barn across the feeder road. In a small garden we grew the basic vegetables like collards, peas, and tomatoes, and on our occasional trips to Neely Mother gathered other vegetables from Grandpa's garden.

The school was the focal point and the pride of the town and its environs. Children of the rich and poor, from the mills and farms, first through the eighth grades, all gathered for lessons in that one building. High schoolers were bused to Sand Hill, midpoint between Avera and Piave, another mill town farther north. One of my prize possessions is a classic picture taken in 1931 of the entire school, all 108 pupils, and teachers Mr. J. L. and Mrs. Agnes Hillman, Mrs. O. B. Bowen, and Mrs. Edith Smith. Mr. O'Steen came all the way from Amory in northern Mississippi to take that photo. I can still match the faces of more than ninety of the children with their names. Even though I was only eight or nine, I was in love with all the eighth-grade girls. Pondering that picture today in my ninth decade, I wonder who might still be alive and where they are.

Alas! I vividly remember the stately structure of our school going up in smoke on a late afternoon in the fall of 1933. My little brother Elmer and I were playing when we noticed smoke coming from the new government soup kitchen on the second floor. I ran to the building, up the stairs, and was met by flames belching from a fire that had apparently ignited from ashes left in a cardboard box. Alarm spread rapidly, but it was too late. By nightfall the building was aflame, and all Avera was watching, wondering, "What shall we do now?" Like air escaping from a balloon, the burning schoolhouse seemed to deflate the hopes of a town already in deep despair.

I look at the picture of the schoolchildren and teachers of Mutual Rights and see reflected in their faces the families of those who made Avera the town it was. Sawmill technicians seeking their fortune or a good-paying job, marginal farm labor, and others looking for employment, excitement, and escape from drudgery—they all came to Avera to get in on the good times. Mrs. O. B. Bowen, first-grade teacher from Florida, wore an expensive coat with fur collar that really stood out among raggedy children. The coat gave a false impression that the Bowen family was wealthy.

Jimmye at Avera school, ca. 1931.

The Cragers owned a sawmill and were involved directly in timber. Echo Crager, daughter of "Old Tom" the boss man, was a bit hard of hearing. Lillie Mae and Frank Gunther were very smart; their father was the town's barber, who cut anyone's hair who could afford the fifteen cents. Joe Edgar Keys was a burly type and could have been a wrestler, but Charlie Frank, his brother, was just the opposite, quiet and reserved. You wouldn't think the two were brothers. Their folks were reclusive and the only people in Avera I never met. Eleanor McIlwain, whose mother worked as the town postmistress, was the most beautiful girl in school with her long brunette bangs. She was one of those eighth-grade girls I loved.

Avera at its zenith was a booming mill town. The bank, whose chairman was Mr. O. Buelo Bowen, thrived until the 1929 market crash, when it closed along with thousands of other financial institutions. Two garages maintained the town's small fleet of Model T Fords, later Model A's, and a few Chevrolets. Mr. Ed West was a popular car dealer, a fast-talker who wore his dark hair slicked under a straw katie; this was in a period when auto dealerships dotted every small town. Avera was home to half a dozen mercantile stores that sold dry goods and hardware imported from everywhere in the United States. A drugstore, railway station, hotel and boarding houses, several churches, and a variety of attendant service establishments once made it a center of economic activity. Much folklore exists about Avera's "rise and fall."

During its economic decline, school life and social activity continued, and recent visits jogged my memory and helped me pull things together. Recently I received an e-mail correspondence from a person unknown to me, Carla Vowell in Tennessee, who asked if I was related to the Hillman teachers in Avera. She had family connections with the Roberts and Byrd families with whom I went to school. Surprisingly, we quickly discovered that her mother, one of eight children who were left destitute by the death of their father, stayed in our home and helped Mother with household chores and baby care. It turns out that I have a picture of the industrious Sadie Rae Byrd, a rural princess, as she poses for the camera.

When I imagine Avera, I visualize looking from the front porch of the teacher's home and seeing smoke rising from Turner's timber mill. There, a rail line hauled virgin yellow pine logs and dumped them into the millpond, later to be sucked up into the mill and sawn into a lumber, famous the world over. Turner's mill was associated with Turner's pasture, a vast land reserve to the east along Highway 63, several miles away. The pasture was liberating for me because the parents of a playmate, Vernon Cox, lived in a modest cottage down there as caretakers, and I spent many weekends with the Coxes, roaming the woods, wading in the branches, hunting for Indian arrowheads.

Special things take place among growing boys. Vernon was approaching puberty, and one night when we were sleeping, he punched me saying, "Jimmye, wake up! I've got on a hard!" Little did he know that his dad was listening in a bed on the other side of

Mutual Rights School (at left) and teacher's home at Avera, ca. 1932.

the room. The next day, as we were sitting in the front porch swing, with his wry sense of humor and to my utter embarrassment, he asked, "Jimmye, what's a 'hard'?"

The pond alongside Turner's mill was a haven of sorts for me in off-school hours. I developed a friendship with several Negro boys who lived in the "quarters" near the pond. They were natural athletes. We raced and climbed trees, and I took them over to the Bowens' house where we boxed with real leather gloves belonging to the Bowen sons, Buelo and Bill. My nose often got bloodied. I had a close friendship with one of the boys, Edward Timms. On Saturdays and holidays we hunted birds with our slingshots and fished in the millpond. His dad did odd jobs for us, but neither ever entered the house. They waited as we ate, and Mother sometimes offered them our leftovers with cornbread, collards, and black-eyed peas. Times were tough for us but much worse for black people.

Turner's sawmill in Avera, ca. 1920.

The schoolhouse was never replaced after the fire. Pastor Kinsey and the board of the Methodist church gave permission to hold classes in the church, but there was no space to divide up all the classes. Byron West, Mr. Ed's younger brother, bused some children to Sand Hill, five miles away. Each morning about daylight the shrill sound from the school bus whistle awakened us, and the children congregating near the teacher's home boarded the homemade vehicle, a rickety crate of seats bolted to the back of a flatbed truck. Looking back on the hours and the inconveniences that accompanied that busing, I don't feel too sorry for children today who ride so luxuriously.

With his Irish Catholic wit, Al Smith, Democratic presidential candidate in 1928, mocked his "chicken in every pot" opponent, Herbert Hoover. Unfortunately, the Happy Warrior's humor didn't persuade the electorate, and the Republican was elected. Disaster struck seven months later with the market crash, and Hoover became Satan, horns and all. Avera, once the center of commerce in north central Greene County, disintegrated when the last sawmill shut down in 1932. The Great Depression was under way, and those families who had kin with farm or garden fled to the safety of food and shelter. The Brelands, Byrds, Dunhams, Roberts, Smiths, Turners, Walleys, Wests, Williamses, and many others were farmers, petite bourgeoisie, and laborers, who scattered to the four winds in search of regular employment, subsistence, and survival. Only a decade earlier the Bank of Avera had lent money on easy terms, and Fords and Buicks lined its dirt streets.

Fortunately, that spot of geography never lost its identity, as did many other villages in Greene County, especially the fifteen or more dotting the Gulf, Mobile & Ohio railroad spur between McLain and Piave. The barons of timber and turpentine in the early twentieth century escaped for brighter prospects. A few old houses of my childhood remain, but most of them are unrecognizable. Even octogenarians such as I can hardly say for certain where the icehouse sat, or where Ed West's automobile agency had its showroom, or where the beautiful Bowen house rose above the neighborhood. Just when did Alphaeus A. Batson's commissary finally disappear? The railroad no longer exists, and few know where the depot stood. A paved highway now passes over the soil where Mr. Rufus "Ruf" Smith and other merchants once did business.

Two visitors in downtown Avera in the 1920s.

Remembrance, like history and progress, while acting as a cleanser, is brutal to the psyches of old men. Recently, I drove with friends to the fenced spot once occupied by Mutual Rights School. Now overgrown, it was still redolent of the voices and feet of the children who frolicked on those lovely grounds. A plaque near the gate suggests that this is now a park. A new chapel has replaced the old church. Synthetic flowers, god-awful to me, cover the cemetery, and the ghosts that resided there during the nights of my childhood have evaporated. The large live oaks and longleaf saplings departed with age and modern chain saw.

I wandered alone over to where the teacher's home had been and looked north across an expanse of scrub bushes, visualizing the millpond, once filled with logs. Oblivious to the world, I heard the bell ringing from the schoolhouse, and listened intently as Father blew the whistle atop the steps at the front door: "Children, line up and march to your rooms." A hundred children marched in, primer to fourth in one line, fifth to eighth the other. Some stolid, some with alacrity, but each obedient, moving to home room and home seat.

Fewer than a dozen of us are still alive.

Avera class of 1932. Bud in center back wearing tie; Agnes in back row between women in fur coats; Jimmye in overalls, second row, eighth from right.

Thad Hill

IN 1935, MY PARENTS MOVED THE FAMILY from the teacher's home in Avera back to Neely, the geographical center of Greene County Hillman origins. Employment possibilities as teachers were bleak, but they decided to build a house. They started construction at a spot that overlooked Highway 24, the Neely-McLain highway, located at the southernmost border of the historic Thaddeus Green homestead. What faith.

The entire farm and our home were called the "Thad Place," using Thaddeus as a namesake. The family of "Tinner" Green, an Irish settler, had acquired the original property. Thaddeus, son of Tinner, born in 1843, was brother to my paternal grandmother, Virginia Green Hillman. The homestead had been proved up sometime after the Civil War, cleared and used as a place for Thaddeus to raise a family, most of whom migrated from the farm soon after the turn of the century. Mother dubbed the place "Thad Hill" when we first moved in, and the name stuck.

After we moved to Thad Hill, our lives became a flurry of activity, a new venture for the family. My parents for more than a decade had occupied teachers' homes, and houses owned by others, including Grandpa Charlie. Since marriage, Mother had never lived in her own house, and she hit the ground running, beginning life on the farm with vision and exceptional energy. She never stopped until forty years later a heart attack stilled her restless energy forever.

Aunt Lora, one of Father's sisters, once admonished Mother about always working so hard, being so fastidious, and so strict of etiquette: "Agnes, why do you work like you do? Why not relax and get Bud to hire you some help? Y'know, when you die, and when they lay you out there in the church, people will pass by yo coffin and say under their breath, 'There's ol Agnes. She wuz from Georgia and a hard workin old bitch'!"

Old Washington School (Neely), ca. 1880.

Thad Hill entered my consciousness almost at birth as a place-name for family cultural identity. It had been an important reference point in local lore ever since settlers swarmed the area after Mississippi statehood in 1817, and the homesteading that followed. It ultimately became part of the Charles Hillman estate, but in the years that followed our arrival from Avera it became the center of my lifelong sentiment.

It was little more than a rise in Earth's crust, but it was a *hill* to us. I liked the term "Thad Hill," and the association even more; it evoked space and location, as well as geomorphic relevance, and time. We knew about Saint Paul's sermon on Mars Hill, and I had read about Nob Hill in San Francisco and Boar's Hill in Oxford. Then, in our family vocabulary there were Bald Hill, Chinquapin Hill, and Hickory Hill that had been at sometime, somewhere located on one of Grandpa's properties. The Hillman Hills and the Geedee (god-damned) Hills were in Skull Fork, a finger of land bounded by Skull Creek and one of its tributary branches, part of the original Great-grandfather Pinckney George Hillman homestead he had settled in the 1840s.

Hills were an important feature in our family's lexicon of geography and sentiment. Possibly, we gave the idea of a hill disproportionate importance because male members of the Hillman clan liked to use prominent terra firma for expansive dreaming. Atop hills my male elders fantasized about their rural settings. They dismounted from automobile or pickup truck to summon hogs, to chew tobacco and spit, and to observe buzzards soaring high above the next ridge while circling carrion.

Ponderous in thought, my father and grandfather mumbled between themselves on Bald Hill what to me as a child were indistinct phrases about hogs and the land. On these various high spots, they gazed at the next horizon, studied the surrounding biosphere, and secretly wished that they owned the entire lot, or at least the "forty" bordering their own. Mountaintop experiences, indeed!

A hill also distinguished the important from the trivial when male dreaming turned to serious conversation in the porch swing on Sunday afternoons, after everyone had accommodated the fried-chicken-okra-collards-cornbread dinner. Earnest conversation about the land and its proprietorship gave dignity to those who could look down from an imagined summit, a high hill on a supposed family estate, share with those who were listening below, and infuse meaning and aspiration to them, those landless, and the masses of lesser social status.

The possession of land was one thing, a house up on a high spot away from the hoi polloi another. There was something sacred about it. Probably such thinking inspired Charles Gabriel to write that old hymn "Higher Ground":

> I'm pressing on the upward way
> New heights I'm gaining every day
> . . . .
> Lord lift me up and let me stand
> By faith, on heaven's tableland.

Land ownership appeared to inspire some sort of godliness, and higher ground, metaphorically, signified that one is yet holier. Thad Hill was an elevated, wooded spot of soil two miles south of Old Washington church and Neely School. Sloping upward from Cobb's Crossway, it appeared higher than it really was, perhaps because of the stately longleaf pines that dotted its crest. An acro-illusion. Southward in the opposite direction, the land was covered by scrub oak and eased gently down toward Widow Smith's place, a well-known local landmark even long after her death. Thad Hill also soon became a well-known location in the community. Our family honored and harbored local tradition, but from the beginning Thad Hill evolved into a beacon that cast light on ignorance and bias.

While the entire country lay at the bottom of the Great Depression, Father and Mother began building the house. Lumber was so cheap and the economy so dead that this construction material became a bartered commodity. When the mills closed or went bankrupt, laborers were paid in lumber and would then trade it for anything, including food. As a worried child, I drank in all the facts: heart pine, fourteen dollars per thousand running board feet; labor, twenty-five cents per hour.

Father contracted with Mr. Dewitt Davis, a nephew by marriage, to assist Mother in drawing up the plans, called architecture by some.

Rev. George Lemuel Nicholas, contemporary quarter-time minister at the local Methodist church, and master carpenter on the side, was employed to oversee the building and to finish the project.

Assisting Nicholas was his neighbor, Mr. Jesse Ekes, a docile gentleman with large Scandinavian skeleton, who lived across the road opposite the church. He handed Nicholas tools and helped lift the heavy timbers. Another helper, Felix Kim Daughdrill, Father's brother-in-law and would-be carpenter, was of questionable value because he was losing his eyesight. He lost more nails than he hammered, hitting his fingers more often than nails, which was sadistic fun for the Hillman children, who were always watching. I doubt if he was paid anything; he just wanted to be part of the excitement.

Father paid Brother Nicholas in kind with a beautiful Jersey milk cow. The minister wanted milk for his children; the agreed-upon price for the cow was thirty-five dollars, and she was worked out at twenty-five cents per hour. Father paid Jesse Ekes with garden produce and fresh pork.

The carpenters argued frequently, mainly about the quality of cutting and fitting of timbers, boards, and joints. Nicholas, a perfectionist, always checked everything with Mother and was adamant: no shortcuts, no shoddy work, and no nail heads showing. He would say, "I'm sorry, Mr. Daughdrill. Mrs. Hillman won't like that. Please check with me before sawing those planks. We must conserve, and must plane each board to fit. It's an angle of five-eighths, and corners must be beveled and smoothed." The Hillman children dubbed him "Nicholas the Beveler."

Uncle Kim, called "Kimmy" by my father, often mumbled under his breath, then went outside and exploded: "That damned preacher, what does he know about building a house?" Evidently, a lot. The houses that Kimmy had built have long since deteriorated. Shrub grows where they sat. But the house on Thad Hill still stands today.

I recently returned to Neely hoping for a sentimental remembrance and uplift from Thad Hill and its sacred groves. I traveled the Neely-McLain highway and looked at what was once one of the most beautiful homes and gardens in Greene County. Brother Nicholas's masterpiece was still standing, although unpainted and not much more than a weathered box beneath a galvanized tin roof. I quickly turned my head away, thinking: *Mother must be frowning in Heaven.*

Thad Hill, the center of the Hillman universe, ca. 1940.

When the house construction was completed, it came time to build a barn and an outhouse, and to drill for water. Father asked the ubiquitous family helper, Felder Breland, to assist in finding water. He was an expert in water witching. Distance was important, as all water had to be carried indoors from a well or pump. With a prong of a forked dogwood branch in each hand, Felder paced the grass a few yards behind the house. First, the witch dragged him toward the spring branch, where there was already water. Then it took him off toward the corncrib, where he abruptly turned back toward us, mumbling as he stumbled over pinecones and an occasional oak limb. Finally, the single shaft of the dogwood pointed to the ground right in front of us. "It's right under there, Mr. Bud," Felder exclaimed. "Are you sure, Felder?" my dad asked. At which point he replied, a little exasperated: "I ain't missed one in years." *How could he?* I thought to myself. *I've been finding water everywhere I dig a deep posthole.*

Drilling for water began at that specific spot. After connecting an auger to a twenty-foot section of steel pipe, Felder and my dad began twisting the pipe into the soft, sandy loam. Soon, at a depth of ten to fifteen feet, the drill struck the aquifer and a large sluice of water belched forth. The two continued drilling as their clothes soaked. I noticed that each time Felder bent over, Mother and Aunt Cannie cackled from the kitchen window. From my angle, I couldn't see what the commotion was about. But then Felder turned his back toward me and, as he bent over again, his "credentials" swung out into broad daylight through a large hole in his overalls.

This became known as the day the moon shone on Hillman water prospects.

Thad Hill became a very comfortable abode for our family, and the well still runs to this day. For our home, Father had mandated several specific features. Most important, it had to have a metal roof, galvanized sheet-metal strips, called a "tin roof" by my dad. We had already experienced the burning of four houses, one of which was ours.

After the Carr fire in Pineville, the Charles Hillman five-gabled house in Neely, built just after the turn of the century, went up in flames in 1929. Later, a house Father had bought on credit in the 1920s for eventual retirement in Neely, the so-called Ulmer place, suddenly caught fire on a spring day in 1932, producing more cinders and ashes. (Aunt Nora had already burned her first house in Bothwell.) No fire insurance on any of them.

Poor roofing and ill-fitted flues and chimneys were the main causes of fires. In our rural area, if a house caught fire that could not be quickly doused, it burned completely. Each family was its own fire department, and water from the rain tubs was the main fire prevention.

Davis and Nicholas built our new house high off the ground with a porch on three sides to create ventilation on hot Mississippi summer days. It sat on massive twelve-by-twelve joists that were supported by huge blocks from the heart of longleaf pine. Each bedroom had a fireplace, which in our case meant a log burner. In addition, there was the kitchen for our Home Comfort stove. All energy came from firewood. We used pine as a starter, and sustained the fire with the bountiful oak of every genus.

Our new house on Thad Hill stood a half-mile, but generations away in virtual time, from the old homestead, the spot of the original Thaddeus Green dwelling. Something remote and mysterious pervaded those ancient environs and its crumbled remains. Fields, or

Old kitchen stove.

more accurately, small patches of land, had not been tilled for years, and briars and vines grew over spots once occupied by house, barn, outhouse, and field fences. As with many such homesites, an old "dug well" invited disaster. As we prepared to renovate the farm, our first task was to discover the deep well, fill it in, pack the dirt tightly as we went, then apply topsoil.

Preparatory to the initial planting that spring, we removed all debris from the acreage surrounding the site, which became known as the "back field." Clusters of wild persimmon sprouts grew everywhere and were a nuisance to remove and to keep under control. A small parcel of land known as the "Mace Patch" joined the farm still farther away, uphill and along the road. It got its name from Benjamin Mace, who was a sharecropper in the early twentieth century and first cleared about five acres of new land while hiring out to Father.

From Thad Hill on a clear day you could see the enormous gate and posts of the original Thaddeus Green homestead, rising against a background of large red oak in the back field. The structure probably had been there since the first European settlement. Our own Great Gate of Kiev.

The official 160 acres had distinct boundaries and land markers. When settled, it lay on the Old Mobile Road, as it was called (Mobile, Alabama, to Natchez, Mississippi, via State Line in Greene County), which ran parallel to the homestead and the back field. Old Mobile Road's sole purpose since the construction of the new Highway 24 was for mule and wagon, occasional log-truck traffic, and Father's pickup trucks, used to feed hogs at the foot of Sand Ridge and at Big Branch Crossing.

The homestead was well watered. Spring Branch rose not more than a hundred yards from the back-field gate, ran west, and fed into Bear Branch, a large tributary of Atkinson Creek. To the south was Big Branch, with its source, or head, just behind what was now our new house on Thad Hill.

Highway 24 ran generally parallel to the east boundary, and a loamy extension of Sand Ridge was on the north, bordered the Mace Patch, and was part of the property of Dantzler Lumber Company or some other timber baron. Noname Branch, with its origin in the hollow a few hundred yards across from the back-field gate, flowed eastward, ran through a culvert at Cobb's Crossway, and joined Courthouse Creek five miles away.

Thad Hill, as the original settlers must have known, sat on a rise between two watersheds, a local "continental divide." To the west, all water flowed into Atkinson Creek, to the east, Courthouse Creek. By some strange natural force of geology, these two creeks meandered through the wooded countryside miles apart but ultimately joined

Leaf River not more than a quarter mile away from each other, a spot of historic importance in the development of Greene County. The first county courthouse was built after statehood in 1817 on Boise's Bluff overlooking the confluence of Courthouse Creek and the river.

The old Thad homestead required immediate attention. Clearing bushes, dense hedges, and trees from fencerows became a first order of business. Then we had to repair aging fences by replacing rotting fence posts and cutting new posts from weathered pine tops. These tops, called "liteard," a slurring of the word "lightwood," were filled with pitch. They were leftover waste from nineteenth-century timber exploitation in the area. Pine stumps dotted the greater farmstead and became highly valuable, particularly during World War II when they were used as an ingredient for naval stores and explosives.

We were confronted with the problem of procuring and managing livestock. Greene County had no stock law at the time, and animals were free to wander and graze over woods, fields, and farm. It was the responsibility of owners to keep intruding animals out of the planted fields. We needed urgently a barn, cow lots, pigpens, and special stalls for our two mules. Indeed, Mother demanded that her yard be enclosed with meshed fence and appropriate steel posts as protection from hogs and other animals, domestic and wild.

Years of rain and erosion and destructive tilling had guttered the fields. We were fortunate that the county agricultural agent, Mr. G. L. Beavers, was both engineer and surveyor. He agreed to lay out a system of contour terraces for the fields. Terracing, plus winter cover crops, resulted in the capture of moisture, improved soil tilth, and reduced runoff. Father was an early environmentalist and almost fanatic about the prevention of erosion. During heavy rains we walked the terraces to see that furrows weren't clogged and that at rows' end the water was flowing to an adequate ditch outlet.

Farm programs enacted during the administration of President Franklin D. Roosevelt worked miracles to assist subsistence farmers like Father to reclaim rundown homesteads that had been eroding since Reconstruction.

After a few years, Thad Hill became a small center of rural experimentation, conservation demonstration, and a community crossroads for elementary farm practices. Over time we cleared additional small acreages to supplement those in the original homestead.

After we settled into the community, our home became the center of local gossip and information and later an outpost of political activity. The family, following tradition, was active in church, school, and social affairs, but my parents were very careful about assuming official leadership—that is, until Father entered local political life years later. After retiring from teaching, he was elected to the Greene County Board of Supervisors. His leadership was widely recognized, and additional numbers of people traveled Highway 24 to Thad Hill for conversations with "Mr. Bud."

Our lives on Thad Hill continued to improve as we moved through the 1930s. We were not isolated from dramatic events such as the Spanish Civil War, labor unrest during the Depression, Franklin Roosevelt's fireside chats, and the emerging cloud of European fascism. Daily newspapers from New Orleans or Mobile always arrived a day late on our rural postal route, so most of our news came from our battery-operated Philco radio.

One day in May 1937, I was plowing in the front field a small distance from the house. Suddenly, there was a commotion from the public road. Hitching Old Mattie to a fence post, I hurried to find out what was going on. Mother had already come from the house, and as we neared the mailbox the mailman was loudly repeating, "Rockefeller's dead! Rockefeller's dead!"

Important news to be sure, but John Davison Rockefeller was not thought of as a friend to Mississippi small farmers, petite bourgeoisie, and working people. Good riddance, some thought. Financial, transportation, and commercial magnates like the Fords, Morgans, Carnegies, DuPonts, and Harrimans, along with Herbert Hoover, were the enemy. The electorate had resoundingly rejected them again in 1936.

My two brothers, sister, and I grew up at Thad Hill. Its fields, wild animals, extensive woods, ubiquitous streams, and pure air became part of daily life. There were few game animals and birds because economic depression had stimulated their hunting, almost to extinction. Isolation, though not appreciated at the time, gave me time to read

Hillman family outside Thad Hill, ca. 1940: Elmer, Bud, Agnes, Lora Jean.

and think and to dream—when I was not too tired from plowing, chopping cotton, picking cucumbers, sawing logs and pulpwood, dealing with mules, and the other farm tasks. Social life was minimal, other than church and school parties. If we did go to someone's house on Saturday night for fun, after returning (never later than nine) Father, in his corny sense of humor would ask, "What kind of party was it, Boy? Bread and water?" We never knew what he meant by this, but supposed he was joking about the half-pints of bootleg whiskey that occasionally appeared from some boy's bib overalls front pocket and were passed around in the backyard after dark. I was in my midteens before I had time to "fall in love," but unfortunately every other boy also was hooked on the same little blonde: Paula Clyde Wright. I never found out who won that competition.

Perhaps my most enjoyable hours were spent strolling down Sand Ridge to the spot where it slopes steeply and joins Spring Branch, then follows a parallel, almost imperceptible trail to Bear Branch. Along this short route in the late afternoons, I wandered under the oaks and watched squirrels, sapsuckers and yellow hammers, and an occasional skunk. Redbirds tweeted among the low branches while jorees explored the leaf litter with beak and feet. (These names are Mississippi for cardinal and rufous-sided towhee.) At Bear Branch, the trail widened, bent back south, and ran through thick brush into a larger path, which was shaded by black gum, poplar, and slash pine.

Several hundred yards along a broad path led to an old logging road that always seemed wet and boggy. Turning left, in an easterly direction, this road wound uphill to a junction with Old Mobile Road, a level spot where Father began baiting wild hogs soon after our arrival at Thad Hill. These hogs had escaped from farms and fields for miles around and wandered into the woods, scrounging food, living off acorns, roots, wild berries, worms, and insects, and becoming increasingly feral.

From here along the Old Mobile Road, it was a pleasant walk to the back gate. This part of Thad Hill was dear to me because of family sentiment. Completing this historic trek, my boyish mind wondered: *What pioneers had trod this road before Thaddeus Green settled here? Where were they going, what were they escaping, and what destiny awaited them?* My father used to say that the Old Mobile Road led to Three Chop Way, a mythical passage associated with thousands of westward-bound pioneers, which historian Jack D. Elliott Jr. claims never existed.

During the summer months there were days that I saw no other human being, except family. Few motor vehicles came along Highway 24, which Mr. Dan Ware graded each month with a pair of black mules and a Caterpillar road grader. People couldn't afford cars and didn't have money to buy gas, even at nineteen cents per gallon. Our family was fortunate to spend most Saturday evenings in McLain, the children ambling past the several stores on Main Street, doubling back past the artesian fountain in the middle of the street, making sure to pass Mr. Sam Green's merchandise to watch his black customers enjoy themselves with a box of soda crackers, a can of sardines, and a Coke.

The boarded-up stately building of the defunct McLain Bank was a reminder of hard times. Blacks seldom came to Main Street except to see Dr. Dan McLeod, whose office was in the rear of the drugstore. Mr. Joe McCoy's dry-cleaning establishment was a curiosity. But after just a few minutes of idle walk we were ready for the highlight of the evening, a five-cent cone of vanilla ice cream at Mr. Ben DeShazo's drugstore. My little brother Elmer preferred to spend an extra nickel on a box of Nabisco animal crackers, but I bought peppermint candy. Father gave us each a quarter as a weekly allowance and admonished us, "Bring me back what you don't spend."

Posey's was a catfish hangout run by a black woman, and a favorite dining spot. Rumor had it that blacks and whites mixed there. Sounded exciting; why couldn't we eat at Posey's, I often thought, knowing that half-pints of moonshine were passed around under the counter.

Father's week wasn't complete without a visit to his sisters. We hated it. Their homes were across from each other on the road entering McLain, but they seldom spoke because of ancient sibling jealousies. My father became a bridge in the tenuous family rivalry with its typical small-town feuding. Visiting kin meant small talk, boring gossip to us children, and after ten minutes we were yawning and squirming, anxious to leave. Suddenly it was back to Thad Hill to prepare for Sunday school and church the next day.

Such was the routine. Summer activity changed radically with the beginning of school. The days grew shorter, and the pace of my life seemed to quicken. Summer to summer, year to year; soon September was here again.

Memory does not break, however; it bends and binds the real self to the soil and the culture through which a person passes his formative years. Laden with hard work, deprivation, and isolation in these years, my thoughts were singed but not branded by the fires of ignorance and bias. The time had been spent with family, predominantly in quiet peaceful environs that were friendly to the accumulation of wisdom. Though I didn't recognize it then, I had lived a lifetime since coming from Avera. Thad Hill laid the foundation of my biological, social, and spiritual structures, and for my character.

Trains

OVER THE DOG'S WHINE, the voice of the nightly freight train spoke forlornly. Its message through the moist evening air above Thad Hill wafted as clearly as that sent by the odor of creosote from the paper mill upriver from the town. Sound plus smell. But the whistle evoked a unique sensation that transported my other senses to worlds other than that of possums, dogs, and the daily drudgery of a Mississippi subsistence farm. Its long, drawn-out mechanical bleat pierced the ether and resonated across the woods as the train approached the main highway in McLain. It sounded a warning not only to people, but to porcine, bovine, equine, or other animal intruders on its tracks, a warning that trailed off as distance and foliage softened the high-pitched mournful wail, issuing from the throat of its aperture.

Trains became part of my life rather early when my mother took me with her to her family home in the red hills of northern Georgia. Many freight trains in the rural South during the early twentieth century maintained a passenger car or two to transport people from town to town. Engines had "cowcatchers" out front to prevent large animals from derailing the train. This was before the major growth in the automobile industry and the public road system. Trains that carried only passengers operated between major cities. On local runs the passenger car was attached to the last freight vehicle, just ahead of the caboose. We called these vehicles "doodlebugs." Many such passenger cars were hand-me-downs from streamlined railroad companies, and were often of a less-than-comfortable accommodation. In early years, the cabin was constructed of wood, as were the seats. By the time of my first ride, the interior had improved, although most riders still brought along a blanket or pillow to sit on. Food also had to be packed, as there were few eating establishments associated with the train depot. Two daily arrivals in McLain, including the "night

train," on north-south runs were important events in the life of
the community.

So it was in May 1925 that my mother, with meticulous care given
only to a first-born child, dressed me in a starched shirt, knee pants,
little skullcap, and bow tie—very appropriate for traveling by train.
She and I then boarded a car on the Rebel in McLain, heading for
Mobile, Alabama, sixty miles away, and ultimately for Atlanta after a
night's ride. We arrived in rural northeastern Georgia by local spur
coach, where she showed me off to Benjamin and Mary Butler. I was
their first grandchild. It was a long trip, but the excitement of it all
left an impression, even at two. No doubt, it was the trains that did it.

We repeated this routine for the next few years, until a little
brother and sister came along, making the price of tickets prohibi-
tive. I remember those trips vividly, until they ceased in my sixth
year with the economic crash of 1929. "We won't be going to see
Georgia-mamma this year," Mother said.

For those journeys, the train route was the same: McLain, Mobile,
Atlanta, Elberton via Athens, with appropriate stops between. In
addition to the awe with which I beheld the giant engine, steam
issuing from its frame, two things stand out in my memory as we
boarded. Lots of noise and activity, and lots of room on the car to run
and romp up and down the aisles—just what a little boy needed. We
were soon moving fast; newfound diversions tired me, and Mother
as well. There were the long waits at the stations. Our bodies and
clothes always got dirty from the soot and grime of the engine that
burned wood, coal, or oil. My immaculate dress was pretty soiled by
the time we reached Atlanta next morning, well spent.

The firemen, engineers, and conductors, the men who wore duck-
bill caps with a variety of insignia, bib overalls with watch chain and
fob across their chests, were fascinating to me. But my heroes were
the men in the blue suits and French Foreign Legion-looking caps,
who yelled "board!" just before the train pulled away from a stop.
That's what I wanted to be when I grew up. I might have thought
differently if I had known then that during Reconstruction—about
the time the railroad first came through the mountains of northern
Georgia—some local Confederate veterans mistook the blue-suited
conductors for Union soldiers and proceeded to extract retribution

for their war crimes. The story goes that the conductors disappeared into the mountains and were never seen again.

My romantic notion of the smoke-billowing Iron Horse shifted with the economic downturn. Because high freight rates robbed Southern farmers, we saw the railroad barons as the enemy, an oppressor. Their size and inflexibility as an economic force made them an unequal bargaining agent with small farmers. We hated them, along with the banks and cotton merchants, fallout from Yankee capitalism. Jesse James was a hero because, in addition to banks, he robbed trains.

Yet, the train itself remained as a savior, a transport vehicle for escape from a life of deprivation and hardship on the farm and in rural slums. It was escape from the sweltering sun and cotton fields to freedom and luxury, imagined as we read travel ads in the Sunday *Mobile Register* and *New Orleans Times Picayune* and listened to and viewed stories about California and Texas on the new media of radio and talking movies. Trains had a mystique of longed-for "far away places with strange sounding names."

Into this world of dreams came the voice and personality of Jimmie Rodgers, the tubercular brakeman's son from Meridian, Mississippi, who enchanted young and old alike with colorful ballads and haunting blues music, much of which was about railroads and rounders. All across the South, indeed the entire country, people were caught up in his songs that focused on trains and railroad life. It wasn't called country music then, but Rodgers was later christened the "father of country music." Writing this memoir all these years later, I recall instantly every word of Rodgers's "Waiting for a Train":

> All around the water tank, waiting for a train,
> A thousand miles away from home, sleeping in the rain.
>
> I walked up to a brakeman to give him a line of talk.
> He said, "If you've got money, I'll see that you don't walk."
> I haven't got a nickel, not a penny can I show.
> He said, "Get off you railroad bum," and he slammed the
>   boxcar door.
> [Yodel]

He put me off in Texas, a place I dearly* love,
Wide open spaces 'round me, the moon and stars above.

Nobody seems to want me, or lend me a helping hand.
I'm on my way from Frisco, goin' back to Dixieland.
My pocket book is empty, my heart is full of pain.
I'm a thousand miles away from home, just a waiting for a train.
[Yodel]

*The official version from Guitar Tabs Archive (which has it wrong) uses "surely."

These train songs and blue yodels were part of the entertainment repertoire for many boys in our region. Dreams and imagination were put to action with hoboing. Hitching a ride west on a freight train was one way of realizing a poor young man's aspirations. "I'm going to California where they sleep out every night" was a line from one of Rodgers's songs. He also wrote "Hobo Bill's Last Ride" to accommodate those bitten by the bug of wanderlust and longing. If the bitter scene created by the words, "The smile still lingered on his face, but Hobo Bill was dead . . . ," was supposed to discourage his audience from roaming, they didn't. I was too young and too circumscribed by a nuclear family life to enter the hobo's arena, but seeds of the process of moving on were solidly planted in my boyhood fancy. They bore fruit a hundredfold later in life as I traveled the world—seventy countries and four continents. Toward the end, I was going *first class*, even on trains.

After high school graduation, some older boys began actively hitching freights, despite the dangers associated with it and the rough and tumble existence on the road. Every whistle stop in Greene County was a venue for grabbing a boxcar for places unknown. Generally, the hobo at the train stations in his travel strategy followed a routine: walk the track to a location outside the town or city; then as the train was still moving slowly but gathering speed toward its appointed destination, the freeloader would run alongside a boxcar, grab a rung of the ladder on the end of the car, and hoist himself upward. Aboard, he would try to find an empty, dry, and warm space inside to rest or sleep. Often, however, he was relegated to riding atop one of the cars, suffering the boys who would run along the railroad and throw bottles at him. And there was always the weather, hot and cold, sun and sleet. Police and railroad officials were numerous around most depots, so a similar debarking process had to be followed when the train approached each station.

Unfortunately, this itinerant mode of travel was not always safe. One of the Walley boys, a friend from Sand Hill, missed his footing as a train was gathering speed outside Houston one night in June 1934. His mangled body was found later, steel wheels having crushed it against the rails.

Despite the monopolistic elements in the transportation industry, we understood the contribution of trains to our society. Music, song, and myth were instruments of expressing the exploits of Casey Jones and a great number like him, romance and desire as well as that of economy. That most famous railroader had it sung of him:

> Casey said just before he died
> There was one more train he wanted to ride,
> The fireman asked, "What can it be?" . . .
> "The Atchison, Topeka and the Santa Fe!"

Heroes and bums alike were equal participants in an expansion of the American frontier. "I've been working on the railroad . . ." became a folk-song line, traditional fare for sing-alongs. My own favorite was a creation called "Lost John," played only on the harmonica, at its best when performed by one who put his entire soul into the action.

I once saw such a rendition by a local boy. When asked if he knew "Lost John," he said nothing, but pulled out his harmonica from a back pocket in his overalls and launched into this memorable musical saga. We were rapt, accompanying a mythical train engineer in his daily routine through the harmonics of the instrument paralleling the train's struggle, low notes droning out the engine noise, high scales and cadenzas spoken by the train whistle and blare from the smokestack, the train negotiating obstacles, highway crossings, curves, valleys, and hills, until one night John got lost on the slope of a formidable mountain. Poignantly, the harmonica registered cacophonous confusion on its lower scale, the struggle "Lost John" was experiencing, the grinding sound of wheels against rails, the slow, arrhythmic stroke of the giant pistons, puffing for a destination, an unknown place to the ordinary engineer, a respite from this world of common toil. Suddenly, and finally, the summit appeared. He was above the clouds in a haven of locomotive ecstasy.

Trains were central to one reality—the transportation of heavy burdens and commercial necessities that man and beast couldn't easily handle. In the early 1930s, the last stands of longleaf pine were being cut in Greene County. Timber of all sorts, and turpentine, were the chief sources of cash income, even more important than cotton, and cheap transport was necessary to move it from producer to consumer. The Leaf and Pascagoula Rivers, eight-wheel ox-drawn wagons, mule-drawn skids, had all given way to train and rail.

In earlier times, timber mills were located on the Gulf Coast at places like Moss Point at the mouth of the Pascagoula, and eventually at Pascagoula village itself. Enormous knot-free logs were beautifully sawn, the timber kiln-dried, then sent to market by ocean transport to the East Coast and as far away as England. Later, the mills came to the timber source. It was the trains that moved the logs and other materials related to this industry. New tracks, and spurs, had to be laid to accommodate the trains, locomotives, dummies, and this massive haulage. The term "railroad track" became part of local reference and lore. I remember the lines and the tune but have no idea of the title of the following:

> I'm lookin down that lonesome railroad track
> And wonderin if my mamma's ever comin back!

Remembered also are the times we would mount the rails barefoot and vie as to how far we could walk without falling off. One such challenge was to walk from Bob McKay's Camp, or even from Denco another mile distant, to the Leaf River Bridge, which spanned the river to McLain. A long trestle preceded the bridge and we had to be absolutely certain of our footing—and the train schedule—when walking the rails atop it.

Nothing could compare, however, with my first trip from McLain to Piave, on the "Mud Line" of the GM&O, mounting that lone passenger car behind all those freight cars and log wagons, arriving

Leaf River Bridge as it looks today.

twenty-five miles and an hour and a half later, sooty and excited. My father had business in Piave and just this once took me along. Among other minor stops on our trip were Denco, Neely, Avent, Wilson, Garner, Byrd, Reba, Colgreen (we called it "Carl Green"), Herringburg, Avera, Bothwell, and Grafton, most now deserted spots among scattered cinders. Father seemed to have a story that related to each of these communities. Having grown up in this county, he

had observed their rise and fall with the timber and turpentine industries. He also had kin in many hamlets, and there was a twist in his
tales about relatives, such as the one about Uncle Benjamin. Known
as "Bear Ben," he lived at Byrd and got the nickname from a neighbor during a fight when the neighbor said, "Take him off me, he's
worse than a bear." As we neared Avera, Father began naming folks
and families in an affectionate way. Little surprise that a year later the
trustees of the school there asked him to serve as its principal. Soon
we were in Piave, the north end of the Mud Line. How insightful for
the village fathers to give an ugly mill town such a beautiful Italian
name. In the *Greene County Herald*, James T. Dunnam writes of this
boom-time train era, which terminated with the exhaustion of the
timber. These giant masses of iron with their gear-driven locomotives
provided the power for moving the forests of conifers. Their owners
and lumber company proprietors were seemingly oblivious to the
rape of the sandy hills of the Gulf Coastal Plain. The lumber magnates
bought large tracts of pristine timber, cut and removed it rapidly, and
hauled it to the mills on these crude wagon cars. In our local case,
the Tatum Company dominated timber operations, hauling timber
to Hattiesburg forty miles away for milling. It was a process hardly
less deleterious for man and land than what is now known as "slash
and burn." In the end, all that was left of the cutover piney woods
was firewood and naval stores made from the stumps.

It was obvious—even to a youngster like me—that with all this
exploitation, quick jobs, and easy money, something was awry.
Indeed, it was the admired goliath of steel, with its cohorts, that was
again the "enemy." After the removal of this almost-nonrenewable
resource, a groundcover that nature had taken millennia to evolve,
the community was left holding the bag. It was an irresponsible act
when the companies packed up for the next episode of cutting, leaving much of the land to revert to state ownership for overdue taxes.
The putative power and glory of trains had clouded my innocent
mind about this disastrous action. Love and hate soon again characterized my imagery of the railroad and its legacy.

During the 1920s my father supplemented his schoolteacher's pay by
sawing fuel wood to feed the monster engines that pulled the logs to
mill. Fuel wood derived principally from oak that grew bountifully

Gear-driven locomotives provided the power for removing whole forests of timber.

on Hillman property. A Shay locomotive, which consumed a lot of fuel, often pulled as many as twenty-five cars, piled high with logs. I became involved at an early age, and was an expert with crosscut saw and axe. Our job was to cut and deliver the wood to the rail ramp in McLain at a price of two dollars per cord. A cord of wood is 4' × 4' × 8', or 128 cubic feet, a large pile of wood. Firemen were kept busy all day tossing chunky pieces into the furnace behind the engine. There was little romance in these hot tasks of energy production and consumption. In reality, I didn't care to be associated with this type of train life . . . too mundane, brutal, and sweaty. It all disappeared suddenly during the early 1930s, as the timber stands gave out, the pervasive Depression ensued, and the mills shut down. The railroad tracks disappeared soon thereafter and the engines fell silent.

In September 1938 Mother and Father deposited their fifteen-year-old eldest son and a steamer trunk on the passenger platform at State Line, an old railroad town across the county on the border with Alabama. My destination was State College, Mississippi. The station was abuzz with other parents and college-bound youngsters.

My initial reaction was one of amazement, but soon I could think of little else save poor Mother and Father who had made such sacrifice to assure my initiation into higher learning. The engine of the passenger line, the GM&O, was fired up, belching steam and ready to depart. It guaranteed my safe travel north to regions of the state I had never known and had only read about. Suddenly, I felt lonely. Then the conductor yelled, "Board!"

It was my first real ride on a passenger train since those Georgia trips of childhood. We said appropriate good-byes, and although both my parents were in tears, I managed to remain dry-eyed until the train rolled away. I neither looked back nor waved, but that parting scene was to be imprinted on my mind forever. The noise of the train and all the bustle of departure could not suppress a most important feeling, some mystical force of approval and support.

My experience was not unlike that of many men who grew up as farm boys in rural America. I looked on as certain villages emerged into transportation centers. There were many of these railroad towns in Mississippi. The shops, depots, warehouses, round tables for turning engines, and other paraphernalia were placed in strategic locations. Railroads provided employment, and the old families and "running men" lingered long in these towns after the decline set in. Railroad influence diminished, but the old enchanting memories and tales remained.

Recently I tried to no avail to locate the old rail track that was once at Avent near Neely. In desperation, I went to the site where Denco once flourished, a former haven for all those working locomotives. The mill town and its surroundings were the center for timber exploitation and wealth creation a century ago. Nothing! I looked for the old dummy line, but could find no trace of rails, ties, or even cinders among the thick saplings, planted like corn by machine, a genus of a conifer far different from its ancient stately cousin *Pinus palustris*, the original longleaf pine forest. Of the trains and their once lively universe, there now remain but stories, a series of old photos in the hands of collectors, and a few aging memories such as mine.

Depots have become museums, restaurants, and other places of art and commerce. Tracks have been removed and automobile roadbeds superimposed. Gone, or vastly changed, are the Illinois Central, Gulf, Mobile & Ohio, and the Southern, whose lines crisscrossed the state of Mississippi. Comparatively little economic and political influence remains of the vast railroad empires built between the Civil War and World War I. Yet, not until the old families disappear, or their grandchildren scatter to the four winds, will the Iron Horse be forgotten. Even then the ghosts of the railroad men, brakemen, firemen, yardmaster, switchmen, and numerous other workmen will haunt many towns. And on long winter nights, or at summer's eve, that mournful sound of the train whistle will still be creating wistful sensations among those who abide and give ear.

Widow Smith's Blue Boar

If there are no listeners, stories will not be told.
—*An old Algonquin Indian saying*

THE OLD MAN TOOK A DEEP BREATH in contemplation. A late-vintage Model T Ford jerked its way forward over ruts, made principally by mule and wagon. Balloon tires had not yet been perfected, and the ride was rough. As we neared the crest of Bald Hill, he became increasingly anxious and spat tobacco through a busted hole in the celluloid windowpane. Heavy brows arched over a pair of deep-set and sad eyes. His gray mustache was brown and gummy from the tobacco.

As the car slowed to a stop, he focused on the horizon to the south. He unlatched the door, pushed it aside with one hand, then reached for the cud of tobacco with the other and in one motion flung it well into the brush. Then he turned in his seat, placed both feet on the running board, and bellowed that weird sound that began in his belly and issued from the throat like a vocal cornucopia: "GooOOOOBH! GoooOOOOOOBH! GoooOOOOOOOOOOBH!" with each utterance increasing in volume. For miles around, any hog familiar with that sound would hesitate, perk up its ears, and head toward it, often responding with its own weird porcine noise. This is one of my earliest memories of Charles Hillman, my grandfather.

Once I asked him, "Grandpa, what does 'GooOOOOBH' mean?" He gave me a condescending look and grunted, which I knew meant: *What did a child know about the mind of a hog, and about the relationship between hogs and men?* For to us, "hog," not "pig," was the generic term, and hogs were serious business. Along with the corn they ate, they made up a large part of the typical family subsistence.

Hogs and people understood each other, and a certain cultural mystique was built around that relationship in our rural world.

Later I began to comprehend all this, and over the years knowledge about the man-hog interdependence provided me with a key to understanding Charles Hillman. And it was not news to me when I read recently that physicians and psychologists have concluded that the pig is more akin to *Homo sapiens* than any other farm animal.

Woods hogs, rakestraws, or piney-woods rooters, as they were called in southern Mississippi, tended to be ubiquitous because there was no livestock law, the countryside being the Commons in an English sense. These animals were not of a domesticated variety. Neither were they totally feral in nature, like what Australians call "Captain Cookers." They were *woods hogs*, and they knew their place. If people wanted their property protected from these hogs, they had to fence it.

The Hillman clan ran deep and wide in Greene County, dating to the origins of Mississippi statehood in 1817. My grandfather, with astute management, had acquired bits and pieces of land in several locations about the western part of the county. He liked to keep hogs, which ranged over his land as well as that of others. The estates of land barons, who had acquired the original public domain for timber, were particularly inviting. Such acreage surrounded Bald Hill, and my grandfather saw no reason why a few sows couldn't forage there, especially since he owned a "forty" nearby.

One could stand on Bald Hill and see all the way to Progress in another county. In an opposite direction lay Denco and a forest wasteland. The Hill, that highest local protuberance of earth, was a well-known landmark to those infrequent travelers of the late 1920s and early 1930s who took the primitive dirt road from Neely to Merrill at the forks of the Pascagoula River. Its prominence had been accentuated by the removal of the virgin forest of giant longleaf pine, which once graced all the Gulf Coastal Plain from the Carolinas to Texas. Now the scrub oak, gallberry bushes, and occasional pine sapling presented no obstacle to an extended vision in every direction. Thus, there was little to obstruct Charles Hillman's resonant hog call. People said you could hear the "GooOOOOBH" for miles around.

Progress hamlet, which also occupied high ground to the south and west, was more of an idea than a place. It once had been an agricultural boarding school, a product of the Smith-Hughes Act, early-twentieth-century federal legislation designed to assist in the education of rural Americans. We know it today as vocational agricultural education, or VocAg. As the crow flies, it was not a long distance from Bald Hill, but in the minds of those who had traveled little, Progress was a dream place. Despite the timber removal, when the eye was lifted to the western horizon, the canopies of vast forests of hardwood in Leaf River swamp and still-uncut pine between the two locations gave the impression of an unknown and unexplored domain. The very idea of Progress invited a fantasy for people and children like me, who imagined another world beyond Bald Hill. But a world without hogs was a place beyond dreaming.

Denco, on the other hand, lay in the wasteland of the exploitative timber operations. Once an active mill town, in the 1930s it was without inhabitants except hogs. You couldn't even call it a ghost town; there were no buildings. What remained was the post-digestive stage of timber cutting. It was noted principally for the artesian well that flowed on what was once its principal street. Hunters, farmers, and stray cows or hogs used the well as a communal watering hole. The land, clear-cut and of little value, had reverted to a primitive state. Local and state governments had long since assumed ownership of much of the acreage for unpaid taxes.

The road forked at the foot of Bald Hill, and an overgrown trail wound over the top, through blackjack oak and other scrub, then downhill to an old homestead a mile or so away. These isolated acres, known as the Old Turner Place, are where we began the traditional hog hunt. We entered the tougher bush along the narrowing road to the river swamp via Bob McKay's Camp, which lay on the railroad. We crossed the tracks there. The camp was always the rest stop for those going to and from the marshy bottomland and the Hillman Dead River, which characterized the *real* swamp. Rumors had it that Widow Smith's Blue Boar had been seen near the camp, but everybody knew this was well beyond the limits of his normal range.

Charles Hillman owned not only the Turner Place but also almost a thousand acres of the swamp itself, including part of a dead river. Everyone knew of the Hillman Dead River, an oxbow lake that had resulted from a rechanneling of the Leaf River after one of its massive floods. It normally was the terminus of the Hillman hog hunting, and a paradise for hogs. But the dense foliage was not for the Blue Boar. He preferred the rolling expanses of branches and piney woods.

On a gray and windy October Saturday in 1935, not even Charles Hillman, whose bones now lay in Old Washington cemetery, could have guessed the outcome. There is the possibility that fortune played a hand in what occurred. Nor was divine ordination out of the question for some who sought an explanation. In their minds, such an episode could not be explained other than by God's intervention. Or, perhaps it was simply the fact that one ubiquitous hog was attempting to survive in an environment that was closing in on him. These are foreign notions, however, when passions are high, as was the case with my dad, his brother Bo (Uncle Bo to us children), and me, riding with our dogs that afternoon in the stripped-down Model A Ford.

Suddenly Father yelled, "God a'mighty knows!" which was the extent of his cursing. "Yonder he goes. He's headin for that branch." The only thing he could be *that* excited about, we knew, was Widow Smith's Blue Boar. It was as if he had seen the legendary Bigfoot.

Father stopped the car quickly, first by gearing to low, then using the more inefficient mechanical brakes. "Bo, take Jim and the dogs and try to head'im toward that head, else he'll get to the main branch and we'll never stop'im til he gets to Courthouse Creek where the dogs will lose the trail. I'll run to the house and get Trim because we'll probably need'em all to tire'im, stop'im, and have a chance to catch'im." Off he sped to our house about five miles away. The Blue Boar had survived many attempts at capture, men with traps and snares, dogs, and other devices. Shooting such an animal for sport was frowned upon, and besides, the meat of an old boar was inedible without the necessary castration and fattening. Once, two men on horseback spotted him on a ridge near Denco and, ignorant of a wild hog's maneuvers, tried to run him down. Their story of failure joined those of many. His elusive nature and ability to escape capture had given the hog a reputation of mythical proportions.

I had seen him several years ago at a distance with a bunch of sows and pigs we had been feeding near Denco. Now hurrying and excited, I pictured his size, shape, and markings. Imagination can bring strong emotion, and, when reinforced with the many stories about him, the hog quickly became reality more than phantom.

I obeyed Father's command, trying to follow the path of the chase by the movement of brush and tall grass. The "branch" was almost a mile away, a tributary of Courthouse Creek, which emptied into Leaf River north and west of the Turner Place. It offered a labyrinth of safety for hogs, but it was the creek that was the Blue Boar's home. The "head" referred to by my father was a little overgrown, marshy thicket around a spring that eventually emptied into the branch.

I followed Bill-dog, whose mother was a bird dog, with the rest of his genealogy split between mixed pit bull and just "dog." He had proven himself year in and out at stopping hogs, but his age of six or seven years had slowed his pace. His reflexes were not what they had been even a year ago, but the bird-dog alertness, the determination, and the bulldog grit remained undiminished. He was white, with large brown spots over his body and a brown left leg and right ear. He wasn't large, but pound for pound he was just what every man needed who hunted woods hogs. In hot pursuit of prey, he shrieked rather than barked, an *eek, eek, eek*, which grew in intensity as he closed the distance between dog and hog.

Behind Bill-dog came Frank, an aging dog well beyond his prime. He was almost half bulldog, with the rest of his bloodline deriving from some type of hound. He was slow, but with an immeasurable obstinacy. With a cold nose, he had an advantage over most other hog-hunting dogs, and when paired with a faster, bigger, and more alert companion he was formidable. Nothing could throw him off a trail. Brown with cropped ears, he had an abbreviated body and short legs. He always started barking and looking around for scent at the command, "Go, Frank!" There was little intensity in his bark, only a cacophonous monotony. He barked the same whether he was far away or close to his quarry, an unrelenting *waownh, waownh, waownh*. We always knew where he was, and so did the hog.

Frank was Uncle Bo's dog. We called him "Bo" because he hated his given name, Bobby Gene. He was the youngest of nine children, and the only other male besides my father in the Charles Hillman clan. Spoiled from birth, he always induced someone's assistance when in trouble, or when in need of money. He had an elfin cleverness and legendary ability in dealing with hogs. My father once said, "Bo even thinks like a hog!" He needed all this and more today to deal with Widow Smith's Blue Boar.

The hog was not exactly blue. He had been born a gray-black pig to a litter of a woods sow owned by Mrs. Smith, who lived a mile west of us on the Neely-McLain road. All his siblings, as well as his mother, had gone the way of most hogs: to the smokehouse or to the lard can. In the 1930s, it was said, "We ate everything but the squeal." But somehow, the Blue Boar had escaped the ravages of men, hunger, and boscage violence, and seemingly the fetters of time itself.

In adulthood, he had grown abnormally large tusks for a wild boar. Thick shields of cartilage covered his shoulders, and his hair had grayed to near white. At a distance, he appeared to have a bluish sheen, hence the appellation "blue boar." Few in the community were aware of his presence, but the hog-loving Hillmans had stalked him for years. My dad had gotten permission from Mrs. Smith to hunt him and had bargained with her for his head.

I had heard about this hog all my young life. I was thus fully indoctrinated with hog lore and psychology. We often repeated the adventure of the No-yer'd Bar in the Cypress Log and the Suddy Sow of Bear Branch, and over and over my grandfather had told me stories of Widow Smith's Blue Boar. I had already shouldered one end of a hog pole, bearing a hog-tied animal upside down out of the Leaf River swamp. At twelve years of age, I was not only assisting Uncle Bo in an exciting chase, but proving my hog-hunting prowess and adding my name to local legend. Yet, the Blue Boar was a different load without Grandpa.

Eek, eek, eek, waownh, waownh, waownh, yelped the dogs as they gave chase. Uncle Bo and I followed them with whistles, yells, and hollering. The wind assured us that they would keep to the scent. Bill-dog and Frank broke toward the hog, which had dashed to a lead of a hundred yards or so. We knew where he wanted to go: the branch. So we angled sharply toward it to bluff him back to the head with its clump of trees and surrounding brush. The wind was blowing toward the branch, suggesting that Bo and I should run that way with the dogs in order to keep the scent hot for them. All the while we continued to make loud noises to let the hog know our positions.

Soon, we entered the deep scrub. We couldn't see, but we could hear the sonorous sounds of Frank. "Go thataway, Jim," yelled Bo. "But if he comes toward you make lots of noise and get out of his way!" Bill-dog's barks indicated that he was not coming my way and that he was gaining on the boar. This was a relief because I was limping and bleeding after stubbing a toe on a protruding root. It hadn't been cold enough to wear shoes. Nothing could faze me, however. My adrenaline was flowing. My mind was in the primitive, conscienceless state of the hunt.

Bo had run on and was now between the branch and the head. If the boar were still intent on getting to the branch, he had to breach the gap between us and backtrack toward the dogs. To our apparent good fortune, he decided to try his luck at the head. Did he know what he was doing? Something we didn't? Had he survived all these years only to miscalculate at one critical moment? *Eek, waownh, waownh, eek, waownh, eek, eek, eek.* The dogs were getting closer. I was slowing because of my foot, but from a small rise I could see Bo dashing with the dogs a hundred yards out front and plunging pell-mell into the thicket at the head. Soon the boar would be at bay. I screamed at my lungs' capacity, "We've cornered him! We've cornered him!"

Perhaps he thought he had chosen the least unpalatable of the alternatives open to him. Most hog men know that hogs are as susceptible as man to existential conclusions, and they don't have to read Sartre and Heidegger. The Blue Boar raced straight to the densest part of the head, a few yards from where the spring bubbled from the earth, and whirled around to face the dogs. He had made it before to Courthouse Creek, and had always prevailed, but we had cut him off. Scars all over his body, from his hocks arrears to his dewlap and both ears in front, gave evidence of these encounters. Not a few dogs were sorry that they had challenged him.

He was once again at bay, however, and it was the pleasure of a man, a boy, and two aging dogs to deal with him. *What is the mind of a hog?* I wondered. Grandpa Charles Hillman had died that past summer, and I reflected back on his stare that day on Bald Hill. What could Widow Smith's Blue Boar be thinking at *this* moment when his whole world had suddenly been reduced and threatened with obliteration?

Mouth agape and foaming, tusks flashing, hot breath puffing, he stood his ground. His head swung wildly at the dogs, which were nabbing at his heels and jowls. He faced us, his protagonists, and the world. I was transfixed by his seeming audacity, his apparent defiance. I studied him carefully, there in the mud, and invoking the spirit of Charles Hillman, considered what must be going on in the mind of this hog:

> *Oh for my wallow, my place in the mossy loam, my comfort low in the spongy soil, so wet and warm; oh to return to my wallow; yet, I must once again prove to lesser quadrupeds, and to these latter-day monkeys who use only two legs for running, that a hog has his rights. My subsistence I have rooted from the ground, pine roots, grubs, carrion, all save that which falls from heavenly trees. My freedom has never come free; it had a price in blood, some of it my own. My welfare and contentment converge in a singular objective, survival; my body, even to my skin, appears to be the carnivorous, sensual design of my enemies. No surprise that my hair is graying.*
>
> *Oh for the days when acorn, beech mast, and pine sapling roots were plentiful in my land; and when I didn't have to compete with so many possums and buzzards for road kill.*
>
> *That sound! That ringing in my ears, is it a squealing pig? Or the echo of a memory drenched in blood? Oh for my wallow . . . my wallow . . . for some peace of mind in my wallow. For years I survived alone in this, my habitat, trusting no other species, even my own, for my security and well-being. This moment of my wallow I dream. Such a place of comfort, my wallow. The thousands of times that I frequented and enjoyed it. Oh, to return again!*

The boar, buoyed by instinct and experience, charged the dogs. Bill-dog and Frank retreated with barks and frantic yelps. The boar used every weapon in his arsenal, particularly the tusks. The longest were four to six inches, one for each side of the jowl, curving ferociously forward, upward then outward. Efficient at grubbing the soil for food, they were formidable defense tools as well, slashing and ripping to threads everything in their path. In the wild, these protrusions had become fully functional for fighting and bloody close-in combat.

More ferocious by the moment, the boar lunged forward and sideward toward Bo, the dogs, and me, uttering a deep guttural snort that brought on my first moment of apprehension and fright. The dogs became more and more impatient. Urged on by Bo and me, they attacked, nipping at the boar's rear, Bill-dog at one side, Frank the other. *Eek, eek, eek; waownh, waownh, waownh!* The boar was tiring, but so were the dogs. Then, disaster. Bill-dog, intent on keeping the boar from escaping, struck for a rear leg. The dog was too slow, and the boar swung his tusks on him, ripping open the dog's left flank and exposing his insides. Blood spurted everywhere. As Bill-dog retreated, I dashed to him, gathered him in my arms, and ran to the safety of dry ground a few yards away. I stuffed my T-shirt into the gash, but it was obviously too late to save him.

We left Uncle Bo and Frank with the boar. Surprisingly, Frank, with all the noise of his bark, plus a wariness resulting from years of hog chasing, kept him at bay. Bo was in a frenzied state, being tested as never before to come up with a game plan to capture this famous hog.

Help came with the sound of the Model A approaching. My father pulled the car off on a knoll near the hill and soon located where we held the boar at bay. He and Trim, the young brindled son of Bill-dog, barely out of puppyhood, headed toward us, with Trim streaking out front and barking in his own wild voice. In less than five minutes, Trim took his place alongside Frank, energetically and recklessly testing the boar's stance.

Father arrived a few minutes after Trim, assessed the situation, and immediately made a decision. Though the boar was tired, at two hundred pounds plus, he was stronger than any man, and very dangerous. By this time, Trim had already received a slight cut on his right leg from a tusk. Frank had been reduced to little more than a bark. Bo was tired and frustrated. I was nursing a dying Bill-dog. My father had brought along two other people, but they were of little help. Kimmy, my father's aging brother-in-law, had in the excitement run from the car toward the head and lost his shoes in the process. My nine-year-old brother, Elmer, was told to stay away from the action. We could not rush the boar and capture him because this was too dangerous. Father's plan was one he had used many times before. "Elmer, run to the car and bring that rope in the back seat," he yelled.

Although Hillmans were slipping nooses over the heads of hogs long before Prokofiev and his music were ever heard of, we reenacted the story of Peter and the Wolf, Mississippi style.

My little brother raced back with a hemp rope, as my father finished cutting a reed cane. He wrapped the rope three times around its small end and constructed a loop sufficiently large to go over the boar's head and tusks. The rest of the rope he brought back along the pole eight or ten feet and wound it around to prevent it from dragging. He then cut a second stick with a small fork at the end, which could be used to slide the noose off the pole onto the boar's head at the right moment.

By now the boar was ferocious, wildly foaming at the mouth. Bo had roped many hogs, so was again elected to the challenge. To mask Bo's movement, and to distract the boar, we moved in on him at the same time, urging on Frank and Trim. I had given Bill-dog to Elmer, and he watched from a safe vantage point on the knoll. Bo, with the roping gear, circled widely to the rear, keeping out of sight. When he got to a spot directly behind the animal, he approached it cautiously. Thick brush prevented quick movement, but it also shielded him from the hog's vision.

A young boy nursed a dying dog on dry ground overlooking the action, well away from any danger. A diminutive, shoeless old man sat on the ground nearby, fuming, spitting, and talking to himself about God knows what, certainly wondering with regret why he had gotten caught up in this chase. My father, now in the marshy part of the head, was assessing the situation, directing every activity of man and dog as was his custom, with an occasional "God a'mighty knows!" most of which was for no apparent reason and directed at no one in particular. I stood in the marsh near my father, now emboldened by the success of our quest thus far and, oblivious to the pain of my bloody toe, moved restlessly and with courage, but scared as hell, staring with mixed emotion at the tiring boar. Uncle Bo, directly opposite me, well behind the animal and hidden by the brush, was cagily calculating his options.

Fortuitously, unseen by any of us up to now, a fallen bay tree measuring about a foot in diameter lay hidden in the brush behind the boar at a small angle to the ground. After Father discovered it, he passed the good news to his brother. I thought, *The tree's the thing wherein we'll catch* . . . This approach to the boar was more than an analogy to Shakespeare's *Hamlet*. It was a godsend.

Bo fixed the roping gear, mounted the log near its trunk, a distance of about twenty-five feet from the hog and dogs. The density of the brush, while providing a blind between him and the animals, made it necessary to proceed slowly and carefully so as not to arouse the boar's suspicion. At the same time the rest of us continued to make noise and to sic the dogs on the boar to keep him distracted and in place.

"Running a log" is not easy, even without poles and ropes in your hands. A wet, mossy bay log and slick shoes put Bo at a distinct risk, not only of botching the job but also of falling ten feet, head first, into the bramble. But Bo was experienced at walking railroad tracks, which concentrated the mind. His toes pointed in opposite directions, and the arches of his feet hugged the curve of the log.

He inched along the log as the rest of us watched his shadow through the brush and held our breath. Suddenly all was quiet save for the occasional bark. The boar was thinking. He uttered a noise that sounded more like a snort than a grunt. Bo was thinking, too, but maintained absolute silence. As Bo neared the boar, he cleared his mind of all else; the hog's thoughts became his thoughts.

He laid down the forked stick on top of the brush alongside and moved to a position almost directly above where the boar reclined on his haunches in the mud. With the dexterity of a surgeon, Bo lowered the noose over his enormous head and tusks. Taking up the forked stick, he nudged the rope off the cane, back over the ears and jowls, then slowly began to tighten the rope around the animal's neck, casting aside both sticks. The boar was in the noose but by no means bagged.

"Daddy, let's get him!" I shouted impulsively. My father, taken by surprise, yelled, "God a'mighty knows! Come back, boy, come back!" But it was too late. Looking up at Bo, I yelled, "Tighten the rope," and simultaneously incited the dogs. "Sic'im, Frank. Sic'im Trim. Sic'im, sic'im! I plunged toward the boar with my father close behind. Fortunately for both of us, the rope had served its purpose by cutting off the boar's oxygen. We had to push the dogs away to prevent further injury to him. Each of us grabbed a rear leg and held on, with the hog still trying to escape. Bo climbed down from his perch and joined us, and the boar made one final attempt at freedom.

Feeling the slack in the rope, he lunged forward, jerking his legs from our hands. The dogs immediately attacked. Bo jerked the rope tight, causing the hog to crash into the muck and lie still.

Widow Smith's Blue Boar was finally at our mercy. We dragged him to dry ground and hog-tied him, a condition that exceeds all other states of impotence. With a grimace of resignation, tusks manifest, eyes following our every move, the Blue Boar heaved regularly, punctuated by grunts and heavy breathing.

We cut a pole to slip between his tied legs and belly and hoisted him onto our shoulders. We carried him several hundred yards, loaded him onto a wagon, and hauled him back to our farm, stopping along the way to douse his hot body with water and to display our prize to all passersby in celebrated victory.

Soon after dark we arrived home. In addition to the immediate family, several neighbors had heard of the catch and joined in the excitement. Even Kimmy, who had found his shoes, wandered among the crowd muttering to himself. I thought I heard the name Charles Hillman uttered more than once. "Yes," someone spoke from out the crowd, "it's a shame that Uncle Charlie isn't here to enjoy all this."

Piney-woods rooter, hog-tied and ready for the hog pen.

Bill-dog died that night. It was Elmer's and my duty early the next morning to bury him. We placed his stiff, scarred body in an old croker sack. Father had chosen an appropriate spot for his grave behind the barn in the pasture, just off the lane that we used every day to go to the fields. Trim looked on quizzingly, but Frank was nowhere to be seen, too old and depleted to care. It was a sad ceremony, and as we covered the hole, I meditated: *Bill-dog paid the ultimate price of a hog-hunting dog.*

We deposited Widow Smith's Blue Boar in a maximum-security hog pen behind the barn. The next week, Father summarily castrated him. His slaughter at the hog kill several months later was rather anticlimactic.

For me, the Blue Boar's capture was a milestone. Charles Hillman had said, "What does a child know about the mind of a hog?" *Survival,* in fact, is what I learned to be first in the mind of a hog. The instinct for existence permeates everything, all things. But, I deduced, in moments of trial the luxury of time for thought and action is human invention, and most illusory. Survival is a lottery.

The earthly departures of Charles Hillman and the legendary Blue Boar began a period of desolation for Bald Hill. Ghosts and memories are its only inhabitants today.

Charles Hillman

"WHO WAS PINCKNEY GEORGE?" my granddaughter Louisa asked. "I can barely read his name on the headstone. It says, 'Born 1829.' Lots of Hillmans in this graveyard."

We had been wandering through Old Washington cemetery on the first leg of a trip to my boyhood stomping grounds in Neely. We had rendezvoused at New Orleans International Airport, she coming from Connecticut and I from Arizona, and after a three-hour drive we were now in another world.

I told her, "He was among the pioneers in Greene County, Mississippi, father of Charles Hillman, a local Carolus Magnus, who rests underneath the slab where I'm standing; grandfather of Joseph Levi, my father, whose tomb is over there in the corner." I pointed to a massive granite structure some distance away. "There must be at least a hundred of us in here. Some with other names, but Hillmans, nevertheless. Ninety percent of the bones in this place are probably DNA-related. You are Pinckney's great-great-great-granddaughter, six generations counting your mother."

"Wow," she said. "Almost two hundred years of history right here beneath us. Shades of Allen Tate's 'Ode to the Confederate Dead.'"

"Yes," I said. "Lots of sentiment. Pink was with Waltham's Mississippi Brigade in the War, injured at Chickamauga, which was the last battle the Confederates won decisively. Grandpa Charlie was born in 1861 while his father was away. Another of your great-great-great-granddaddies lies over there with the Greens. James Samuel 'Tinner' Green, born in England in 1819, came up here from Mobile in the 1830s and married one of the Moody girls, Priscilla. Our Moody family had a Choctaw chief in its lineage, which is a reason for all those high cheekbones you see in some Hillmans. Tinner fought Grant at Vicksburg and almost died in the siege."

Pinckney George Hillman clan: Pinckney (with pipe), wife Sally (behind),
Charles and Virginia, children Lora and Bo.

Her eyes wandered over the several acres of tombstones marking
the remains of settlers and villagers dating from the late 1700s. "What
did you mean a while ago by 'other names, Hillmans nevertheless'?"

I mustered courage and replied, "Grass widows, grass colts, lots of
em in here, right alongside their half-brothers and half-sisters. People
think those rural folks were more monogamous and less human than
they really were. There was lots of hanky-panky and monkey business
in these quiet woods. The men folks didn't have to be off at war for
the odd amorous encounter to take place."

"Oh, I get it . . ." Lulu said.

We returned to the gate in a leisurely way, and I suggested we visit the little Baptist church beside the cemetery, the doors of which are open most daylight hours. Except for the surrounding foliage, a slightly expanded sanctuary, and a new roof, little had changed from what I knew eighty years ago. Inside, the smell of pine tar and mold transported me to my days of Sunday school in the corner behind the pulpit.

"There has been some type of tabernacle for worship on this spot for at least a hundred and fifty years," I said. "Hillmans were normally the backbone of the congregation. Pinckney led the way. He was a lay preacher in the latter part of his life, but it was Charles's support that always saw the church through tough times. He gave the land for both the building and cemetery, and he always supported the preacher. There was no formal church budget. He also gave the land to build the first high school, which you see over there."

"Lay preacher? What's that?" she asked. "There seems to have been lots of religion with the Hillmans."

"Yeah, but no priests and rabbis out here. Pink, who was before my time, would substitute when the regular preacher didn't show up. He always had a limited repertory of sermons. My mother said his favorite text was a takeoff on Saint Matthew 24:42, in which Jesus warns His disciples to be constantly vigilant. About every two minutes he reminded the congregation to, 'Watch. The devil might be lurking in the shadows. Watch!' Repetition was a large part of the sermons of such preachers. Anyway, as the saying goes, if only these walls could speak."

The sun was setting through the oaks. I noticed that Louisa was tiring, and I suggested that we move along to visit my siblings, cousins, and friends. "We have lots of time to talk about your kinfolk. You'll probably get sick and tired of Hillman-related stuff before next Tuesday. Since Charles Hillman was the hub around which the so-called dynasty was built, I suggest we begin with him. He was the 'majordomo' of western Greene County during the late nineteenth and early twentieth centuries."

We got into the rental car and Louisa turned on her tape recorder. My memory of Charles Hillman and bits of our relationship began to unfold.

"Let me tell you briefly about how and when he died. It was at Old House after a few months of illness, during which his insides rotted out, probably from colon cancer. He chewed tobacco all his life, ate a high-fat diet, and had all the other bad eating habits."

"I've never been to a funeral," she said.

"Too bad," I said. "Death is part of living. When I was a child here, we were always burying somebody: old, young, all ages, but especially babies and young mammas. Bacteria and filth were everywhere, lots of disease, poor health care, few doctors. There always seemed to be a wake going on. But Grandpa's departure was something special, a big event. People came from all over because he was well known and respected. I still have the obituary notice that appeared in the *Greene County Herald* on July 23, 1935."

I continued to describe the wake. "It was held the evening of the day he died because people were buried immediately in those days, some without embalming. On the evening of the first full day after his death, friends and relatives arrived, eating and drinking foods that Aunt Nora had arranged. We didn't call it a wake; it was, *Who's gonna sit up with Uncle Charlie?* Grandpa's old buddies, nephews, and cousins, men of Irish or Scottish ancestry, assured that the wake went on all night under the stars. It was an evening of telling tales, chewing tobacco and spitting, and speculating about which of the family might be favored with Uncle Charlie's dwindling property bundle. They wove stories about his hog-hunting prowess, raising them to epic proportions. A half-pint bottle might have appeared and a few would take one swig.

"Next day Brother Dan Moulder, a lifelong friend of Grandpa's, preached, using as text all of Saint Peter's First Epistle. Not a dry eye in the house after an hour-long oration. Then someone read Psalm 37, his favorite Bible passage: 'Fret not thyself because of evil doers.' The congregation sang, 'In the Sweet By and By,' 'The Unclouded Day,' and 'It Is Well with My Soul.' When the church service was over, some men bore the plain wooden coffin outside to the grave pit, dug by Brother Rile Dixon and other friends, the place where you just saw his tombstone. Then after a prayer by Preacher Moulder, Charles Hillman was lowered by six men into the sandy loam of his beloved Old Washington hamlet. The grave was shoveled full of dirt.

Charles Hillman with Aunts Lora and Nora at Big House, ca. 1925.

Then Moulder's ancient, resonant, and gravelly voice commended
Grandpa to Heaven."

Before Charles Hillman came Pink. Pinckney George Hillman, my
great-grandfather, was the son of Charles Lewis Hillman, who was
part of the so-called Broad River migration from South Carolina and
Georgia into the Black Belt of Alabama. Pinckney was born in 1829
at Cahawba. Old Cahawba, as it is still called, was the first capital of
the state of Alabama (1820–26) and a thriving antebellum rivertown.
Pinckney George and a brother, James Alex Hillman, departed Alabama in the early 1850s for greener pastures, homesteading in the
rich pine forests of southern Mississippi. Their tribe increased rapidly,
particularly after the Civil War.

The name Pinckney was appropriated from the famous brothers
Charles and Thomas Pinckney, South Carolina statesmen and early
leaders in the Revolutionary War. Pink, as he was called, full of wanderlust like his ancestors, crossed the Tombigbee and Chickasawhay
Rivers and wound up in Greene County. He finally put down stakes
in the village of Skull Fork before the Civil War, marrying Elizabeth Harvison in 1855, a seventeen-year-old daughter of farmers.
His new family did not preclude him from joining the Confederate
army. Injured at Shiloh, and carrying a bullet from Chickamauga, he
returned with the Twenty-fourth Mississippi Volunteers after General
Lee's surrender at Appomattox Court House.

One of General Grant's significant acts in the traumatic aftermath
of the war was permitting Confederate soldiers to immediately go
home to plant and to farm. Memories of Confederate defeat passed
grudgingly but inevitably, as Pink returned to Skull Fork and picked
up where he left off.

James, who had migrated with Pinckney from Alabama, settled
in the southeastern part of the county. Eventually, Hillmans were
everywhere, as Pink had nine children by Elizabeth, who died at age
thirty-three, and five more by his second wife, Sarah Jane Williams.
James also had a large family, and even had a village named after him
(Hillman, Mississippi) because of his commissary and its post office.
The name is still on the Rand McNally map, but now Sweetwater
Baptist Church has replaced the post office.

In 1861, the fourth child of Pink and Elizabeth was born at Skull Fork. His name was Charles Hillman, and he was my grandfather. His birthplace is no longer on the map. Patches of oak and a scattering of loblolly pine dot the horizon where the old village once lay. A rutted Skull Fork Road of dirt and sand winds its way to several modest houses dispersed among the trees.

Charlie was one of the more plucky and progressive of the flock, and early on his abilities for hard work and leadership became apparent. Even though economic development and growth were slow in Greene County during Reconstruction, timber activity accelerated toward the end of the nineteenth century and continued in the first two decades of the twentieth. And Charles knew the lumber business.

Charles Hillman became "Uncle Charlie" to everybody in the community life of Old Washington, later to become Neely. Yet, he never traveled beyond a fifty-mile radius from Skull Fork. Even now his bones lie only a few miles from his birthplace. This was his choice, like many other rural people, not to wander far from what was a cultural backwater for a century or more ahead.

His marriage in 1884 to Virginia Green, daughter of a successful Irish immigrant, furthered his entrepreneurial success that came without benefit of higher education. All of their nine children were born at what we called "Old House," a traditional Southern structure. Charlie and his siblings, Dave, Jim, and Levi, completed Old House from a frame house begun by his father, Pink. Charlie used yellow pine and common sense, raising a simple home with a running front porch and central, open hallway dividing the bedrooms, two on each side. A fireplace split each pair of bedrooms; another in the kitchen was later adapted for the famous Home Comfort stove. I recall a pantry-smokehouse that rose in what was designated the backyard. The toilet, always a prerequisite, stood about fifty yards toward the branch, alee from the well. For more than half a century, Old House was the navel of the Charles Hillman clan.

Charles and Virginia had seven daughters, and people considered these girls with long dark hair, dark eyes, and high cheekbones "prize catches." All wed before reaching their nineteenth year. Miranda, the oldest daughter, married a farmer who religiously planted corn on February 14 for the earliest bootleg whiskey harvest.

Charles Hillman clan at Old House, ca. 1910.

Charles Hillman family: Charles and Virginia with children, including youngest, Lora (with doll) and Bo, ca. 1912.

The *Greene County Herald* announced their wedding on Friday, May 17, 1901:

Matrimony

May, the month of beautiful flowers, was ushered into nineteen hundred and one's history by an event, which made Washington's little settlement all astir. It was the uniting together in wedlock of Miss Mariannie [*sic*] Lavinia Hillman and Mr. Wilson Cochran. The wedding took place at the home of the bride's parents. The most impressive event of the wedding was the approach of the groom and party. Being about fifty in number, they came on horses at full gallop, making known their onward approach by constant yells of "Hurrah!"

Charley and Virginia also had two sons. Bobby Gene, the baby, known to all simply as "Bo," never ventured more than an hour's drive from Neely. Joseph Levi became Charles Hillman's lodestar; my grandfather wouldn't make a decision without consulting him. His sisters believed my dad to be Jesus come again, and I know for a fact that his feet never touched the ground before he turned five.

Charles Hillman also had the savvy to make local business alliances with other farmers, stockmen, timber dealers, and even peddlers. A particularly important relationship was built with brother-in-law Jefferson Davis Byrd, who married Charles's older sister, Lavena, Aunt Veen to everyone. Timber was the gold of the Gulf Coastal Plains, and its by-product turpentine provided the principal cash income of Greene County. He and Jeff Byrd rapidly built a strategic partnership recognized as vital to the community. Everybody in southern Mississippi honored checks drawn on the Bank of McLain in their names, a rather unique phenomenon in those days.

Their timber enterprise revolved around cutting virgin pine and rafting it down Leaf River to the Gulf Coast where it was transported to the East Coast or exported to foreign markets. In 1973, I visited an English colleague and friend, John Ashton (later "Sir John"), in his luxurious nineteenth-century Victorian house in Newcastle upon Tyne. Knowing my origins, he couldn't wait to lead me up his beautiful spiral staircase and show me the polished four-by-eight-inch rafters in his salon, saying, "Dixie longleaf pine of the last century."

"And probably cut by my grandfather, Charles Hillman," I said. It was a warm connection in a distant land.

Grandfather wasn't only interested in timber, though. With his profits, he bought inexpensive homesteads and small properties around Neely. The cutover acres in the piney woods and the low-lying lands in the branches and creeks were a bargain. The Leaf River swampland was especially cheap.

One could agree with an expression of the time, "He's land rich but cash poor." Even so, Charles Hillman's modest empire survived the market crash of 1929 and the Depression because he was an efficient hands-on manager of his subsistence plots. He rented these places to needy but trustworthy tenants, mostly taking payment in kind. At his death in 1935, the remnant properties passed to selected individuals in the family, but none of these remain today.

I was not his first grandchild, but I was the son of his first son and "that Georgia woman," as my grandfather called her. If he had any intentions of coddling me, he obviously didn't know the mind of my mother. She allowed no coddling and no preferences among her brood, even from Charles Hillman.

Years later, Mother told me that the day I was born, Grandpa was an emotional wreck. He was visibly nervous, though friend and enemy alike would tell you that Charles Hillman had never shown fear, that neither man nor beast frightened him, that he had nerves of steel. But that day he paced the floor, he harrumphed, looked out toward the enormous cluster of tall oaks up the lane at Old House, cleared his throat, and spat tobacco juice off the porch onto the clumps of hydrangeas along the drip line.

My father was worried about his wife's condition, and Grandpa was worried just as much about his son's condition. "Bud," he said to my father. "I'm gonna take Jim and get McLeod, cause by the time we get back she'll be ready to drop it." Dr. McLeod was five miles away in McLain, the only medical doctor in these parts. Grandpa jumped into his Model T, his brother Jim cranked it, and off they sped up the lane and onto the Neely-McLain road.

When Dr. McLeod arrived, Grandma had the water boiling. My father disappeared to the porch with Grandpa and Uncle Jim. But no sooner had the male trio retreated than a squawk emerged from the house with McLeod yelling, "Com'ere, Bud, you and Agnes have a boy." Thus, on a beautiful Friday morning on the first day of March 1923, I was "dropped" in the Carr Place at Neely, Greene County, Mississippi.

Charles Hillman, who was apt to make grandiose pronouncements at the birth of his grandsons, took one look at me and exclaimed, "I think I'll give'im Old Dick!" Old Dick was his prize bull, and his gesture of Southern beneficence became my first birthday present. Mother and Father didn't react, but Dr. McLeod and Uncle Jim chuckled. Grandpa muttered, "My God, what a long head." Perhaps this was the origin of my first nickname, "Long Head," or just "Long" during my early years. It was local Southern custom to attach a singular, oddball nickname to a young boy. My mother's endearing "Baby-Doll" gave way to "Long," followed by "Dick" and several other unappealing appellations in my first decade.

A similar ritual came with the birth of my brother, Elmer, three years later. Grandpa's pronouncement was, "He's the ugliest un I ever seed. Take away the Belt from Jack-Darlin; he's held it long enough. Give it to this un." Jack "Darlin" Cochran was another grandson and about my age. His doting sisters hung "Darlin" on him in childhood, and the name became his for life. No one would have recognized him by his given name, Henry Wilson Cochran Jr. Neither he nor Elmer received a benefaction from Grandfather like Old Dick.

No one seemed to have thought about what to call me, not even my parents. Uncle Jim was the only nonimmediate family member present when I was born. "Yaller Jim," as he was known everywhere, was visiting with Grandpa about a logging deal. Wealthy from a fortune made in timber and naval stores, he had taken an instant liking to my mother because of her reputation as a strict disciplinarian. Where the name Yaller Jim came from is conjecture. Father thought it derived from his association with yellow pine timber, but I heard a convincing rumor that it came from Jim's escape from service in the Civil War by being suspect of having sympathies with Abe Lincoln's crowd; hence, he had a yellow streak.

Maybe that affinity toward my mother is another explanation of his presence. His spontaneous reaction to my birth was, "Agnes, if you'll name that boy for me I'll take care of him when he grows up," meaning I would inherit some of the fortune of one of the richest men in Greene County. Though my mother was cautious of the propensity for Hillmans to make grandiose promises, she believed him. "All right, Uncle Jim," she answered without hesitation. "Let's call him Jimmy, or Little Jim, but let's do it different and add an 'e' and make it Jimmye." Uncle Jim agreed.

Uncle Jim died shortly after my birth, but my promised fortune never arrived. Nobody in his family, including Charles Hillman, seemed to have heard of his deal with that Georgia woman.

Thus, I entered the world with two crosses to bear: "a lost fortune" and an oddly spelled name. My name has raised questions for eight decades. I have never come across another "Jimmye." One of my wife's relations, upon hearing that Helen had married a man called "Jimmye," sneered and said, "Even English butlers are called James."

I was to pay a price for Grandpa's giving me Old Dick *and* his name. I became the diversion when we visited Old House. That massive Red Devon ruled over everything in the pasture. "Jim, here's how ya gonna whip'im," said Grandpa when I once came to visit at the age of three. Sitting in his personal rocking chair by the fireplace, he lifted me to his knee and outlined the stratagem.

It was an icy winter evening. Charles Hillman's muscular arms encircled my tiny waist as we faced the fire. I stayed as far away as I could from his substantial, untended moustache, recoiling from his strong chewing-tobacco breath. His shaggy and grizzled hands moved in loops in front of us, closing slowly and gently. Clinching into fists, they came to a halt about eighteen inches apart. "Here's you," he said, indicating his right fist with a strong centrifugal motion. I looked on approvingly. "And, here's Old Dick," he countered, maneuvering the left fist menacingly up and down, to and fro.

I felt a bit uneasy. Dick looked invincible even as a sunburned fist. I fixed my eyes on one fist, then the other, but I didn't flinch. Even as Charles Hillman enjoyed this moment of play, I knew that everything would be all right.

Then came the drama, and the arena, and my imagination took over. Old Dick was pawing and snorting before me. Grandpa began advising as to how I should conduct the fight. Waving the right fist, he growled in his deep graveled voice, "Git down on your hands and knees. Look'im in the eyes, and charge! Your head's much harder'n his." Then he slammed his fists together and mauled his gross knuckles right against left, describing with glee the fight in the pasture as if he were ringside.

I watched Grandpa's throat and brown mustache, and those tremendous fists. It was pure fantasy mixed with virtual reality. The battle between fists must have gone on for only a few minutes, but to me it seemed interminable. "You're gettin'im, Jim. Butt'im. Butt'im. Butt. Dodge! Watch his horns, don't let'im hook ya. You're gettin'im. Look'im in the eyes. Beller at'im. Beller. Beller! Now lock horns with'im."

At the height of the fray, he let out a blood-curdling yell that brought Grandma running in to admonish, "Calm down, Charlie! Calm down!" At which point Grandpa assessed my condition and said, "Boy, Old Dick's getting tired; let'im rest a bit."

But the contest had to be resolved. "You're gettin'im. There, you got'im going. Butt'im again. Go after'im. I think he's got abait o you, boy." Then, after jamming his fists together, he knocked the left fist completely out of position. My victory was declared when his left hand dropped limply, palm upward, toward the floor. "Ya got'im. Jim," Grandpa would yell, tightening his right fist and shooting it forward. "You whipped Old Dick. Atta boy."

Initially, I was terrified by these encounters, and had I not been a favorite grandchild, who was treated with deference by the Hillman grandparents on our frequent visits, I might not have played the game. Father had already introduced me to Old Dick during our walks in the pasture. I had witnessed his domination of the herd and his demonstrative prowess. Besides, he was blood red and ferocious, even while lying down and placidly chewing his cud.

"Wanna fight Old Dick?" Grandfather asked me each time we visited from the Gulf Coast. With fear and trembling I always replied, "Yeah, Grandpa," then cloaked my fear with a smile.

Fighting Old Dick became a game between Grandpa and me, and to impress him I brought up my own fight plan. Each experience not only reduced my fear of Old Dick and other scary notions on the farm, but also gradually translated what at first memory had been a fearful image of my grandfather into a pleasant, respectful relationship, which soon became a strong bond. Charles Hillman, the tough, gruff, farmer-timber man of Old Washington, a respected churchgoer, citizen, and public benefactor, thus became a victim of a plot by his young grandson.

"Who stoled my seed watermelons that I had marked 'C. H.'?" Grandpa roared early one Sunday morning in July. I knew who had done it and who had done it last year. I was terrified, but Father had overheard the ruckus and stepped in to say, "Pa, must've been Robert Brown; I told him to get a dozen or so when he went to Hattiesburg last week. They're selling for fifty cents up there. I'll buy new seed next spring; you need that new variety, Cuban Queen, anyway. They're much sweeter, and easier to grow and carry."

"But I had *my name* on it!" Grandpa replied

Charles Hillman's legacy was the collective trust that the community placed in the Hillman name. His name was as good as cash at the bank or the grocery store, and if he shook your hand after a business deal, you could count on it. No contract or lawyer was needed. If his name was on a watermelon, you better not touch it.

His legacy was his name and his support of his community. I couldn't help but think of Grandpa every time I drove past the Neely gymnasium. Grandpa was a rabid fan of our local basketball team and helped finance the gym. (He had given land for the Neely School building and was always interested in who was "running the school," as he put it.) I loved going to high school basketball games with him on Friday nights. "Rotten referee," he mumbled one time as we left the new building. The Neely boys had just lost the game to Raleigh on that November night, but according to my grandfather, "Danned rotten referee stole that game." In his mind, the referee was always rotten if Neely lost, especially if his adopted grandson, Charlie Thompson, was playing. "I'm gonna tell Coach to see to it that that bastid ain't round to call the next game," Charles Hillman growled as he reached for his cut of Blood Hound chewing tobacco. We were walking away from the gym as he continued: "Our boys shoulda froze it when they had the lead." Nevertheless, justice was his overriding concern, and by the time we were back at Old House he had cooled off and was mumbling, "Who do we play next?"

Basketball took second place to church, however. Charles Hillman practiced religion without being "religious," a characteristic inherited by my father and one that I admired as a child. "Most o them holy-rollers are hypocrites," he would say. "Shout on Sunday, and steal hogs on Monday!" He didn't believe in taking God's name in vain. No work on Sunday—the fourth commandment was sacrosanct. Other sins might be negotiable, but he was the judge as to what was permissible and who was guilty. His motto seemed to follow the admonition of Saint Paul to the Roman Church: If you can't settle a dispute with your brother privately, take it to the congregation and let them have at it with transparency. He was passionate about justice. His was an Old Testament ethic, tempered by the Christian Gospels and his hardscrabble life. But most Sundays you could find him in the porch swing, finding comfort from the Psalms, many of which he quoted extensively. I often wondered if he compared his internal wars with those of King David. He deferred to others to care for church organization, activity, and policy; but he watched closely the collection plate, and made sure the preacher was paid.

I once heard him tell Homer Breland with a chuckle, "Don't criticize m'preacher unless you've put in yo money." His use of the possessive about mules and preachers I understood as reflective of his caring for things he could do something about. He also checked on the deacons, seeing to it that they fulfilled their obligation to widows and orphans. He was particularly concerned about Lou Ladner and "Froggie" Vanderman, two widows whose husbands had died young and left them with many children. I heard him say to my father, "Bud, check with them widows. If they need cornmeal and grits, we'll take em some Saturday after we grind at Callie Creel's."

No one dared question Charles Hillman's integrity. Once I was with him and my father in McLain when Isom Moody, a man of boulderlike shoulders whom no one messed with, confronted him about a minor transaction that involved paper wood. A small crowd had gathered. "Charles Hillman, that's a lie, you owe me three dollars!" Grandpa's right fist splayed Moody flat on his back. The following day, fully recovered, Moody came by Old House and apologized to

Uncle Charlie for his indiscretion. He offered that he had misinterpreted the figures.

Grandpa's personal integrity was all about fulfilling roles. He paid little attention to household chores, such as yard work, flowers, and gardening, which he perceived as beneath his place. He dug the wells, bought the pump, or fenced off the spring from animals. But he was above carrying water to the back porch water buckets or to the kitchen stove. He fenced, planted, cultivated, tilled, fertilized, and put up the scarecrow, but he never picked the tomatoes or baked the cornbread. Cooking, caring for children, washing, and ironing were all women's work.

Grandpa hated to get stove wood, and for him the task of delivering stove wood from the woodpile to the wood box next to the Home Comfort in the kitchen was the most contentious. He often refused to lift a finger until Grandma Ginny threatened. He would saw, chop, and split the wood, but it was Grandma's job to bring it in. I loved Grandma dearly and often felt that Grandpa lacked understanding of the work she had to do to run the house. "Charlie, won't ya bring in some wood so I can cook your dinner?" was always Grandma's plaintive plea.

Grandpa led a simple lifestyle, which was all work and little play, unless you think of hog hunting and shooting squirrels as diversion. He tolerated me quite well, but when other children were in the house we had to be very quiet and careful. He was particularly crabbed about children jumping on his bed. "Dad-dannit! Git off my bed!" he would say. In fact, we were seldom permitted in his bedroom. I always wondered what Grandpa and Grandma slept in. In the winter, men usually wore union suits and women a heavy gown. But given the hot, humid Mississippi summers with no electricity, and poor ventilation, the fewer body covers the better. Yet, I could never visualize Charles Hillman au naturel.

I feel the presence of Charles Hillman each time I return to Old Washington. In a rather imponderable, perhaps mystical way, my grandfather showed me how to come to terms with a brutal world by squarely facing it. He was born in a period of national civil strife, was buffeted by poverty, war, and uncertainty, and he overcame many hardships. He survived, even prospered, among village stupidity, bias, and opposition.

As I grew up, I learned from him that if you can deal with mules and an occasional hog you can easily deal with men. These experiences with Grandpa on the farm gave me the wedge with which I could split the big timber facing a young man. I learned more common sense in those years than I have in the following seven decades. And when common sense failed, there was always the basic assurance Grandpa reminded me of from Psalm 37: "Fret not thyself over evildoers . . . verily thou shalt be fed . . . the Lord shall bring it to pass . . ."

In his last year, his family and friends often gathered on his front porch at Old House. I remember sitting with him in the swing when someone asked, "Uncle Charlie, what do you want on your tombstone?" He reflected for a moment, looked at Grandma, and laughed. "Gin'll take care o that. She'll probably put on it: 'Done gittin stove wood.'"

The Old Turner Place

"GRANDPA, OF ALL YOUR PROPERTIES, what's your favorite?" I asked, risking another of his condescending grunts, as he and I were walking toward the barn. Only seven, I was sufficiently adroit to know that he himself had never asked the question. I should have known that all his properties were equal—as long as they had hogs on them. At the same time I did know that the place we stood at that moment had a special niche in Charles Hillman's soul. That spot, in a field clearing, was just a few hundred yards south and east of the confluence of Courthouse Creek and Leaf River.

He stopped, removed his crumpled felt hat to swat the ever-present gnats, and wiped the sweat from his forehead. He knew I was fudging to get in my own bias, so I blurted it out: "The Turner Place is my favorite spot in the world!"

He struck at the gnats again, and slowly turned 360 degrees to look at the dense woods surrounding us. Then, glancing up at a clear blue autumn sky, he replaced his hat, and began walking and mumbling, "Yer dan'd right, boy; good hog country, cept for them bootleggers down there." He pointed toward the river under the swampy bluff. We were in a fallow field at one of the most sentimental places of my childhood. It was a paradise of wild birds and butterflies, bees and honey, and earthy solitude.

From the earliest days, an old homestead occupied ground a short piece from the bluff. In my childhood, the frame house sat beside the little dirt road on equally high ground that led from Bald Hill. Denco was to the east, and Bob McKay's Camp to the west. The property was on the edge of the river swamp and near the McLain-Piave spur track. A few yards farther up the river from the bluff flowed Atkinson Creek, draining the west side of Greene County.

A typical front porch of an old house in Mississippi.

Tradition has it that William and Mary Turner came to Greene County from South Carolina. Their son, James Turner, worked at the courthouse at the time of Mississippi statehood in 1817 and possibly owned the property.

The history of this homestead is vague, but the Turners probably first laid claim to it when other European settlers were coming inland up Leaf River from the Gulf of Mexico. The Turner Place and its small fenced plots lay adjacent to the wild hills bounding the river. Well known as a hog paradise, the swamp was one of three places my grandfather cut timber.

During Prohibition (1920–33), the Turner Place guaranteed a hideout for bootleggers. Sour mash whiskey and the sacks of corn for its production came and went across the river. McLain was the local hub for bootleg liquor distribution, with connections south to the Gulf Coast and north to cities as far away as Chicago. On a busy day, you could see the smoke from shinny stills, though they were meticulously hidden in the bramble under the steep bluff. On a windy day, you couldn't see the smoke, but you could still smell what was going on. The distillation apparatus could be purchased in Hattiesburg and easily assembled by the average handyman with

A typical front porch with chairs.

wrenches, screwdrivers, and pliers. Buckets, tubs, and barrels lay about the still. The odor of yeast wafted for miles.

Every time we visited the Turner Place, Father or Grandpa repeated the warning, "Don't go behind the fence at that steep bluff!" Their initial message seemed to imply that we might fall off and get lost in the dense thicket below. But the word soon got out that a nefarious process was going on down there: "demon corn." Years later, I discovered that a deacon in the McLain Baptist church, along with taking up collections, was mashing and fermenting.

A few strategic preachers, along with the distiller and the county sheriff, made a strange coalition in the bootlegger culture. The bootlegger paid off the sheriff as the moonshine dripped slowly but quietly in the swamp's stillness. At the same time, to assuage community suspicion and to rectify his evil deed and sin, he would drop coins into the church coffers. Mississippi law forbade sheriffs from succeeding themselves in office, so the consortium had to work rapidly. The sheriff had only four years to get rich, and the bootlegger had to bribe every new one. One such notable lawman was simply known as "Whiskey Jim."

I once heard about a politician who was in the mortuary business and got caught transporting moonshine. He hulled out the inside of several hearses, placed large tanks inside them, filled them with corn liquor, and headed for Chicago. A Tennessee patrolman became suspicious when he noticed a hearse bearing Mississippi license plates laden with an overweight corpse. The patrolman made the driver open a spigot, and both watched as the ninety-proof corn mash watered the soil of the Volunteer State.

Large, level pieces of tillable land within the Turner homestead were few, but over the decades tenants had cleared small plots, and in the 1930s about fifteen acres were under cultivation by man and mule. The property was never more than an isolated subsistence farm. I have often wondered if any of Grandpa's tenants grew corn for its liquefaction under the hill.

Recently, while visiting my old home at Thad Hill, I said to my cousin Sean Hillman, "Let's take your four-wheeler and go to the Turner Place." He cautioned, "Are you sure? After fifty years it ain't the same place, Jim. I was in there last winter shootin turkeys, and it's mighty rough."

In a thicket, back of one of the fields, not more than a hundred yards from Boise's Bluff, overlooking the river, Sean and I came upon several graves, all of their headstones long since worn smooth. Except one:

In Sacred Memory
RACHAEL MOODY
(unreadable date) 1776 October 29 1849

She was born during the American Revolution, and died before the Civil War. She was born Rachael Schuler in the Orangeburg

A modern photo of the grave of Rachael Moody in a family cemetery deep in the woods.

District, South Carolina. John Harger, Rachael's first husband, and Martin Moody, her second, occupy two of the unmarked stones. Nancy E. Draughn, first wife of James Turner, occupies the third. No doubt, the Old Turner Place got its name from that connection.

With every visit to the Turner Place, a decision had to be made on how far to take the car as we approached Bald Hill. Sometimes we parked the Model A Ford, "Jitney," there and walked the rest of the way, depending on the weather. Riding was rough, and there was always the possibility of a flat tire. Rain turned the clay roads into impassable mud ruts. The branch road from the Hill to the Turner Place was primitive, but by foot it was pleasant, even enjoyable.

Grandpa always took account of his hogs. On foot, we might encounter and catch a hog from his stock of animals that wandered wild. Many were unmarked and were game for any man with a dog.

If we were lucky, we would find a chinquapin tree with its small, sweet nuts, or a bullace vine full of dark clusters of fruit. Chinquapin, a dwarf chestnut, grew widely in the Gulf Coastal Plain woods during my childhood, but now has been virtually destroyed by the chestnut blight and other diseases. Bullaces were also abundant. A wild version of the muscadine family, they flourished in the woods around the Turner Place. Hogs foraged on these in the fall. Growing boys ate them, too.

The isolation and infrequency of visitors often left the Turner Place tenants suspended in time. I smile when I remember a visit Father and I made one Sunday afternoon to collect the rent from Fred Beech. Beech was swatting horseflies and wrestling with his Oliver Goober behind his mule as we approached. My father said, "Freddie, don't you know the Devil will get you for plowing on Sunday?" Fred appeared shocked and responded, "Mist Bud, it don't be a Sunday, do it?"

Fred reversed the mule and plow in midrow, headed the mule toward the barn, and unharnessed it. He could not afford to have the story get out that he was plowing on the Lord's Day. "Mist Bud, you won't tell nobody? An' yer boy won't neither?"

"Don't worry, Fred, all of us lose a sense of time once in a while," my father said as we walked toward the old Turner house.

The last time I remember visiting the Turner Place with my grandfather was during a local flood on the Leaf River in the early thirties. We had driven our cows out of the swamp to high ground and the barn, hog pens, and paddocks. As we were alone on that occasion, I asked Grandpa, "What do you like doing most down here, rounding up cows, huntin hogs, robbing bees, or huntin squirrels?" It was another of my questions where I thought I knew his answer and hoped his answer matched mine, which was robbing bees.

Grandpa had carefully built and cared for an apiary, which seemed to be a part of every Southern homestead. He kept thirteen beehives in the clearing of a thicket near the spring. The annual honey extraction was a highlight of my childhood with him. There were massive quantities of wild honey, dark in color and strong in taste, which came from swamp flowers, and I became hooked on its molasses-like texture.

My question drew a long silence from Grandpa. "Hmm." More silence, and finally, "Dan'd if I know. Why do you ask these dan'd-fool questions, Jim?"

"Because I wanna like what you like, Grandpa. I love you and Grandma." That drew even a longer silence from him.

I felt big on those days when we had walked all the way from Bald Hill into the swamp. I learned to tie a hog in these woods, and to carry

Leaf River Bluff as it looks today.

it out of the swamp on my shoulders with a hog pole, one man forward, another arrear, with the hog in between wiggling and swinging.

Finally, Grandpa looked at me in a way he never had and said
what I knew he would. "Boy, someday you gonna find out how
important a hog is to livin. Bees 'n' squirrels 'n' cattle are good, but
ain't nothin like hogs."

On that recent visit with Cousin Sean, I proposed that we leave the
four-wheel drive behind and walk to the old Turner house through
the pines that had now grown up in the small fields. I pointed to the
edge of the pines where the bluff plunges toward the river and said,
"When I was a boy, Grandpa and my daddy never permitted us to go
near there. They didn't tell me, but I learned later that shinny-makin
was the reason."

Sean said, "Jim, turn round and point yo nose toward McLain and
the River. Close yo mouth and take two or three deep breaths. Tell
me what you smell." The wind was blowing softly in my face as I
followed his instructions. After the second breath I guffawed loudly
in an imitation of Grandpa's voice, "Dan'd if they ain't still at it!"

The No-yer'd Bar

In the end we all come to be cured of our sentiments. Those whom
life does not cure death will. The world is quite ruthless in selecting
between the dream and the reality . . . Between the wish and the
thing the world lies waiting.
—*Cormac McCarthy, All the Pretty Horses*

THE ANCIENT PRE-HELLENIC GREEK PRACTICE of making sacred the
slaughter and consumption of a domestic animal was far from a
miraculous process, but it contained an element of induced nobility
on the part of the animal, and perhaps was cathartic for those *Homo
sapiens* whose blood was not spilt. Our hog-killing ritual was a festival
for the Hillman family. It was not Dionysian, but we marked the
practice with special theater: washing, dressing in clean garments,
and adorning aprons, gloves, and ear muffs. Animals were chosen,
sprinkled with "holy water," which is to say their slaughter had been
accepted and blessed, and by some strange interpretive action, such
as a look in their eyes or a nodding of their head, I believed they had
assented to their own sacrifice.

Before the discovery of agriculture, it appears that man practiced
the ritual of the sacrificial meal, which focused on the hunting of big
game as a source of food. Killing to eat, as Walter Burkert describes
in his book *Greek Religion*, was an unalterable commandment, yet
the bloody act was not without danger and fear. The evolution of
animal sacrifice and slaughter for consumption continued in Near
East and Semitic cultures, culminating with the famous command
from God to Simon Peter on the rooftop of the house of the Roman
centurion Cornelius: "Rise, kill, and eat." Nothing blessed by God,
and sacred, was to be considered "unclean." Thus it was that through
the centuries animal slaughter for food became a sanctioned part of

Christendom, and Western tradition. And so it was that decades of Hillman family practice took very seriously the slaughter of animals as a necessity for our survival and well-being.

Our custom of winter hog killing had become a ritual, but not one with ulterior intent. It was not pagan in the sense of the ancient Greek ceremony. Perhaps there was some unspoken feeling between man and animal, because, after all, both had eaten the same corn, potatoes, and herbs. But there was nothing more than a momentary reflective pause on the part of the man whose job it was to stun the hog's brain and bleed the gullet: no killer regret, nor remorse for his actions. The process was an act of senseless reflection. Sacrifice in this sense was not a word in our vocabulary. And most assuredly, the animal showed no sign of tacit or feigned understanding of the oncoming act. In our culture, there was ritual but no suggestion of religious motif in the killing of hogs.

Yet as a farm lad on these occasions, I sensed a mystery. We were taking one animal's life so that another might endure, replacing temporal with immortal. Over time, "kill and eat" became more disturbing to me, although I never became a vegetarian. Only decades later did I discover what the Greek word *koinonia* really means: Community must sacrifice flesh and blood in order to renew humankind's journey toward Being.

Hogs were ubiquitous and played a quintessential role in the early-nineteenth-century development of Greene County. By the 1920s and 1930s, all human routine of the extended family of Charles Hillman was focused on subsistence living. Hogs were central to every activity. While not revered in a religious sense, they were respected for their role. We never mistreated them. Although Mississippi custom did not equate hog and man, one local sage had it: "Even a hog's got his rights."

The Crash of 1929 deepened the already depressed economic conditions in Greene County, causing both man and hog to suffer. These economic disruptions had hastened the flight of the destitute in the cities to their families and friends in the rural countryside. We grew subsistence crops, but since cotton and timber were the foci of commercial activity, acreage was always devoted to them, as they were the only source for cash. Hogs supplemented our marginal living, and pork dominated all meat consumption.

Aunt Gin, my grandmother, was one of the few who were not afraid to confront Grandpa Charlie. Perhaps it was her Celtic spunk. Virginia Green, second-generation daughter of immigrant Irishman James Matthew "Tinner" Green, the forerunner of all Greens in Greene County at the time, commanded attention and got results, even from her man before whom other men trembled. With some urgency in a high-pitched voice, she would say to him, "Charlie, all you do is to plant corn to feed mules and hogs, to plant more corn to feed more mules and hogs to plant more corn. When and where will it ever end?" She was quick-minded and compassionate, but yoked to the Hillman legacy, she never understood the single-minded involvement of her husband with hogs. Charles Hillman's response was simply, "Mules for plowing, hogs for meat!"

Pork accounted for at least three-quarters of the Hillman family's meat consumption, and for almost all the cooking fat or lard until the perfection and acceptance of oleomargarine. Beef was too expensive, and Father considered chicken to be inferior to red meats. We occasionally ate mutton, venison, wild turkey, and squirrel in season. Quail and rabbit were more infrequent. Pork, however, was standard fare. Moreover, before electricity and refrigeration came to Greene County, we slaughtered a small animal about every two weeks—my father used the term, "kill a pork." By "pork," he meant a young hog that we ate within a short period of time. We shared it with neighbors, and kept the remainder in an icebox on the back porch. The iceman came on Saturdays, and a quarter's worth usually lasted all week.

In mid-January 1936, there had been a hard freeze, and it was as cold as it was likely to get that winter. Even the ground was frozen, the day blustery, and it was one of those stand-close-to-the-fire-to-keep-warm days. It was unusual weather for southern Mississippi, but ideal for killing hogs. It was daybreak on a Saturday, and my father had already made the decision the night before to kill our meat hogs. Meat hogs were those animals of considerable size, the carcasses of which in large part were salted down, smoked, and preserved for use throughout the year. Hickory smoke cured and flavored the hams and sides, now called "pork bellies" on the US commodity exchanges.

There was an element of tradition about our process of hog killing, so the basic preparations had been made already. Father had sharpened the knives, and Mother brought out the appropriate pots and pans. The boys had stacked next to the smokehouse a small wagonload of hickory wood for curing, and a kind of yucca we called bear grass that has long, thin, strong leaves, which we used like twine for hanging the large cuts. Down in the hog pen waited the Suddy Sow, Widow Smith's Blue Boar, and one other, the No-yer'd Bar.

Before he died the previous summer, my grandfather spoke of a mysterious hog without ears, calling it the "No-eared Barrow" (pronounced "No-yer'd Bar"). I remember him once musing, "Wonder whatever happened to that No-yer'd Bar?" And I thought, *How did he lose his ears?* We regularly castrated pigs, making a "barrow" out of a boar, and turned them loose in the woods. They were seldom seen again. Grandpa knew that the hog ranged widely around the Hillman Dead River. Today, he would meet his destiny.

Down in the pasture the water was heating in two giant iron pots. On the ground next to the pots sat two metal barrels to receive the water and the hogs. The best water temperature for scalding hogs is just before it boils. We didn't want to cook them—yet. We dug into the ground and set the barrels at a forty-five-degree angle so that the hog torsos could be thrown in headfirst and rotated repeatedly. The hot water loosened the hair and tendered the hide so that the animal could be more easily scraped and cleaned before being "dressed out," or gutted. We threw into the hot water pieces of hardened pine tar and green pine needles. These served as a catalyst to facilitate hair removal. My father or Uncle Bo would dip a forefinger into the water, then rub it against the thumb to test the hogs' final bath.

When the water was ready, Father and Bo went to the hog pen, stunned one animal with an axe head, stuck a butcher knife into its aorta, and lifted its hind legs until the unconscious hog bled out. The two men then dragged it to the scalding barrel and threw it in headfirst and rotated it several times. Father tested for hair slippage, and when it was ready, he pulled the hog out onto an old door or wood platform. Immediately, everyone present, my two brothers, Bill and Elmer, and neighbor Felder Breland and I, descended onto the hog and began scraping off its hair with sticks or knives or our bare hands. Once Father had checked the hide and was satisfied, he gave the hog a final rinse with a ten-quart bucket of hot water and hung it from an oak limb for gutting.

I was excited with anticipation. One of my distinct recollections is of that moment when my father removed the liver, handed it to me, and said, "Here boy, run to the house and tell yo mama to fix it for dinner." Now, at twelve years, I could "gut a hog" by myself, being careful to not puncture the entrails, spoiling the meat, and to remove the edible organs and to sever the head right at the exact vertebral juncture.

Of course, the hogs remaining in the pens nearby were unaware of all these preparations. One of those probably wouldn't have heard it anyway—the fabled No-yer'd Bar, another of those mythical hogs in the Hillman lexicon. "Woods hogs," as we called them, feral in nature, eat predominantly an herbaceous diet of roots, young plants, acorns, and seeds. Their meat is more flavorful than grain-fed hogs, and their fat never gels or hardens in cold weather. Perhaps it is more healthful because of that, not containing as much cholesterol.

How we captured the No-yer'd Bar was one of the greatest adventures of my childhood. It began with my dad parking the Model A Ford at Bald Hill on a cold Saturday in November 1935. Cutting a plug of tobacco and sharing it with Uncle Dave, Father had to restrain himself from calling his sows and shoats. Bill and I took the dogs and moved leeward to avoid the tobacco spit. Bo sauntered around the car, rolling a cigarette from a Prince Albert tin. The plan was for us to walk the rest of the way, even to the Dead River, which in every sense was another world to us but home to certain hogs. The ride had been rough, slowed by flat tires, and the rainy weather meant getting bogged down in a muddy ditch. Father always made the decision as to how far to take the car. But being afoot worked to our advantage because we might encounter a stray, unmarked hog. Many were unidentified as to the owner and were "up for grabs." We always brought along a pair of dogs on every trip into hog country.

Distance was relative, and time more so for such a fall Saturday hunt. The mile from Bald Hill to the Turner Place seemed brief compared to the additional mile to Bob McKay's Camp, where we crossed the railroad tracks and entered the Leaf River swamp. Trek-king from the camp to the Dead River, also a mile, was another matter, as the path narrowed and the brush grew thicker. Beyond a certain point the path disappeared altogether, and navigating the swamp tested our ingenuity.

At Bald Hill we had plunged into the center of hog cosmos. The branch road to the Turner Place was primitive, but by foot it was pleasant travel, especially in October. In a good year, post oak, red oak, even blackjack oak might hang with acorn, their leaves bleeding from yellow to orange to cinnamon and brown. Sweet gum and black gum clustered in low wet spots, surrounded by tall wafting pine.

The Turner Place was an ancient homestead that my grandfather was leasing to sharecroppers. It wasn't much more than raw unim-proved land, but during the Depression millions of people were set-tling on such places in rural America. Grandpa had no expectation of receiving rent money. The place remains vivid in my memory because of a large apiary that my grandfather had so carefully built and cared for. The annual "robbing of the bees" was a highlight of my early years with my grandfather. That wild honey, which got its character from swamp pollen, was as strong in taste as it was dark in color.

In a thicket, back of one of the fields near the Turner Place, we came near the grave of Rachael Moody, one of my great-great-grandmothers. My father often spoke of his "Moody connections," and every time I passed this place I wondered if he meant Rachael.

From the Turner Place, we headed directly into the Leaf River swamp. The final possible stop was Bob McKay's Camp, which at one time had been a temporary structure on the railroad from McLain to Piave to the north and east in Greene County. I never learned just who Bob McKay was and what his claim to fame was; I might have asked him but he was never home. His camp was more of an idea than actual geography. Bordering the edge of the swamp on the north side, the railroad to the west soon entered the swamp itself. We followed the tracks to a point just before a trestle bridged the swamp and the river.

I was never allowed to walk on the trestle without an adult, and always entered the swamp with a sense of awe and wonderment. Though some of the virgin pine and cypress had been cut and rafted downriver to Moss Point on the Gulf Coast, enormous stands of hardwood and pine towered above us. In the 1930s there was little market for any of it. My father told us stories about turn-of-the-century rafting: logs were cut, tediously bound and bolted together, and pulled to the edge of the river, there to wait for seasonal rains. I always wanted to ride one of those rafts for the two weeks it took to get from McLain to Moss Point. But the log trucks had already replaced the river.

Magnolia and giant water oak (*Quercus nigra*) formed a massive and tall canopy that, along with heavy undergrowth—even on sunny days in the swamp—suggested obscurity as well as uncertainty. Spanish moss hung in gray masses from the limbs of trees. A mossy-musty aroma permeated an ambience of a dank nature. Mayhaw fruit floated in the many ponds that dotted the swamp. These, with the mushrooms, berries, roots, and worms, made the Leaf River swamp a hog paradise.

To get to the Hillman Dead River, we took the route that passed Moody Lake, a small body of water named for Rachael's family. We came here regularly, not only to protect it from poachers but to harvest its resources—timber, squirrels, turkeys, and mayhaws. The Hillman Dead River was the limit of our hog hunting.

As we walked along the railroad tracks our conversations were whispered. A dialogue between Uncle Dave and me focused on the hunt and a puzzling conjecture about the social activity of hogs. The conversation between Father and Uncle Bo was more of a monologue from Bo on women, which ended abruptly when my father admonished his thirty-year-old brother to "Shut up, and wash yo mouth out when you git back to th'house!" My brother Bill had fallen behind, but ran to catch up as we turned toward the Dead River.

To me, the No-yer'd Bar was enigmatic and mythical. There were many things unknown about him and, until this day, some remain unexplained. One fact was clearly certain: he was earless. We didn't know his exact color or his size, just that he had no ears. The Barrow was a non-entity outside the Hillman hogsmen circle. And even among the family, few had seen the hog. A sylvan ghost, if he was ever discussed, the stories about him were without substance.

To everyone else he seemed to be just another hog. But this little-mentioned apparition had a way of gnawing away at my curiosity and imagination. I was dismayed to have a hint of his story, only to be told, "Maybe someday . . ." Such off-putting was tantalizing, and made me want to risk everything to learn more. Besides, if the rumors were true, his wagon-sized carcass in our smokehouse would be the envy of the county.

No one knew who the Barrow really belonged to, and it was entirely possible that he could have wandered miles afar from his origins. Many people had hogs ranging across the land. Hence, identification was often a problem, especially if there was a mingling of animals in the woods without appropriate marking. Most owners of livestock recorded "earmarks" with the county and state authorities. (I'm sure Southern politicians borrowed the term for their legerdemain spending as part of their "pork barrel politics.")

The process involved slitting, notching, or cropping the ear of the animal in such fashion that it could be readily identified. Combinations of these markings were almost endless, but any responsible farmer or stockman knew the marks of his neighbors. My father knew dozens. He could read a mark at a hundred yards. "That's Louis Breland's sow." Or, "That's old man Alex Ball's bull," he would say, when I could barely see the ear itself. To this day I remember my father's mark: "split and over-bit" in the right ear, "under-square and split" in the left. Grandfather's was "split and over-bit" in both ears; Uncle Joe Byrd's, "swallow-fork" in both ears. A swallow-fork took the form of a large V, and most, when using the knife, cut the mark too large and obliterated the tip of the ear, leaving two dangling-flapping pieces on each side of the animal's temple. Marking, like castration and branding, were normally performed when the animal was young.

How did our hog with no ears get that way? Was the Barrow as a piglet the victim of an overzealous ear-marker like the former Senator Stevens of Alaska? Were the ears frozen off during one of our severe cold snaps? Were they chewed off by another hog? Or, could it be the screwworm infestation in the mid-1930s? In any event, my father was sure that neither he nor my grandfather was responsible.

Uncle Dave became noticeably quiet as we walked along. David A. Hillman was grandfather's oldest brother. The two had married women who were sisters, never lived more than five miles from each other, but had few common interests except for hogs.

Tall and thin, Uncle Dave had a broad and graying moustache that drew attention to his otherwise scrawny face and protruding nose. He always wore an ancient and musty felt hat, old overalls with holes at the knees, and gallowses twisted in the rear and latched wrongly in the front. He didn't care for underclothes, but an old sweater covered his blue denim shirt and overalls. His brogans were full of holes from his endless walking on gravel roads.

Each week for decades, with a sack of corn swung over his wiry six-foot frame, Uncle Dave trekked from his house above Neely to grandfather's property in the Leaf River swamp, a distance of nine miles one way. Often he appeared at our house at five in the morning, sat on the back doorsteps until Mother stirred, at which point he muttered loudly, "Ag, when will coffee be ready?" My mother hated to be called "Ag."

His purpose apparently was to keep on the move and to feed itinerant hogs, because I don't remember his ever killing any of the animals for his own personal use. He lived past his ninety-sixth birthday and died of pneumonia, not of old age. His tombstone, a few yards from Grandfather's in Old Washington cemetery, reads: "Born September 1, 1857. Died September 26, 1953."

Part of the reason we were now slogging through the Leaf River swamp relates to a Sunday afternoon visit to Uncle Dave's home. After church, it seemed my parents figured God wouldn't mind children listening while the male adults sat around, chewed tobacco, and exchanged wild hog stories. Truth never appeared to be the objective, and there were not a few mild expletives woven into the conversation as the voices grew louder and louder.

"Uncle Dave," my father asked, "do you know anything about a weird-looking hog without ears down in the swamp? Have you ever seen him when you feed hogs down there? Some say it's a barrow. Bo swore he saw him last spring with a sow and pigs and some shoats just below Bob McKay's Camp." No one had ever asked Uncle Dave about this animal, and he appeared to have been waiting for just such an occasion.

"I seed that No-yer'd Bar down there last week when I was feedin my pigs." He sped through the opening my father had provided and began a one-sided conversation that went on for more than an hour. "I've been baitin'im fer a while. Yeah, I've knowed'im since he was a pig. I cut'im four or five years back, and cropped his yers fer no real reason exceptin that I could compare him to other pigs in the litter as I went down there from time to time. No one had ever did that before, and he was such a healthy pig at that. Since growin up, like all old bars, he's always with sows an' pigs and other hogs, never by hisself. Seldom crosses the railroad anymore. Feed's been so good 'n the swamp. But don't know where he's been a holin up o late. Last time I seed'im was about Easter. He's Charlie's hog, anyway. Come from that old listed sow's litter back then. Shore is funny lookin now."

On and on went the banter, with my father finally saying, "We gotta get'im this fall as we're short o meat hogs at my place."

From that summer afternoon of hog banter until the day we pulled him, rear end first, from that giant cypress log, my father was focused intently on a strategy to catch the No-yer'd Bar. Uncle Dave had given him the key and was his counselor, Bo was his henchman, my brother Bill was a spectator, and I an excited twelve-year-old hoping for a piece of the action.

It was cold and had begun to drizzle in the swamp—not the best way to spend a Saturday hunting hogs, I thought to myself. Even the dogs were shivering and uncomfortable. But my father had a mindset that was surpassed only by that of his late father. We must bring in the No-yer'd Bar. Father wouldn't even accept luck to do so.

Did we need luck to catch a hog? I had never believed in luck. Fortune, maybe; miracle is better. Hope and faith are preferred words for philosophical imponderables. But the No-yer'd Bar was real, not virtual. Uncle Dave, who for me was just like my grandfather, raised all my expectations of catching the hog. So while betting on fortune, I was drawing heavily on hope at this moment, a "substance of things not seen."

We walked rapidly along a path where Uncle Dave had last sighted the Barrow. It was an opportune route—the dogs were already fidgety. Where we descended the bushy railroad grade, the dogs began to go crazy. They had whiffed the fresh scent of hog. Bo unleashed them with commands, "Go, Frank!" "Sic'em Trim!" Both bolted forward, barking in their individual voices, Frank following the younger but less experienced Trim. They dashed quickly through dense brush and out of view, a cacophony of sound filling the misty swamp air. I missed Bill-dog, Trim's sire, with his eeking bark, which had been silenced by a tusk of Widow Smith's Blue Boar.

Bill and I followed Bo as fast as the brush permitted, and the path soon played out. We couldn't run at top speed in this type of swamp terrain. Not only did we have to watch for low-hanging tree branches and cypress knees, and contend with prickly shrubs, including a thorny vine we called "bamboo" (*Smilax laurifolia*), there were sinkholes and quicksand in which the unwary might disappear altogether. But we had been navigating such swampy places all our young lives. From behind we could hear Father yelling, "Stay with'em! Stay with'em!"

Suddenly the urgent bark of the dogs changed to baying. Then it stopped altogether, except for an occasional yelp. We were no more than a quarter mile behind and in a few minutes within sight of the dogs. When we appeared, they started to bay just out of sight. Rather than rushing closer, Bo shouted, "Jim! Bill! Let's wait till Bud and Uncle Dave get here."

Father's first words were, "Whatcha got there? Where are they?" Bo replied, "Don't know, they're over behind that clump o bushes." Uncle Dave, well into his seventies, wasn't even breathing deeply and seemed rejuvenated by the chase and excitement. "Let's go and see," he said.

In unison we all moved toward the dogs, whose baying was now less energetic and more irregular. Old Frank was persistent, however, with his coarse *waonh, waonh, waonh!* Pushing the shrubs aside before him, and stomping bushes underfoot, Bo waded through the clump as the rest of us followed closely. Approaching a gentle incline, he stopped suddenly, moved his head from right to left and back repeatedly. "My God!" he exclaimed.

We moved abreast him and immediately understood. The dogs, yo-yoing behind the trunk of a giant log, were whining and barking and looking at a hole in the butt of a fallen cypress.

The log was at least seven feet in diameter at the base, tapering to four feet near the end of its fifty-foot length. It appeared to have been in place for a long time. Green mosses and beards of gray lichen covered its length, and the tall grasses grew alongside. Everyone fell silent, gazing at the log. Finally, Father ventured quizzically, "Wonder what's in there?" With authority and without hesitation, Uncle Dave spoke up, "A sow an' pigs are in there with a boar."

We took turns looking into the hole and listening. At first, my sagacity as a fledgling hog hunter couldn't corroborate Uncle Dave's assertion. He had experience, but I had a child's discriminating sense of smell. The scent of hogs permeated the log. Intensified after a rapid chase, the smell was earthy, fusty, and almost fetid. Males, particularly old boars, have distinct and strong odors, even among hogs. My nose told me there was no boar in the log, but something close akin—a castrated boar.

Putting one ear, then the other, at the opening, I recognized the moderate breathing of one hog. The sow? Then I heard the heavier breathing of another, and the soft panting of several smaller animals. Moving away from the log, I announced, "Uncle Dave's half right. Must be a sow and pigs. But there's no boar; maybe the No-yer'd Bar!"

Father dispatched Bo and me to the Turner Place to get a crosscut saw, axes, wedges, kerosene, and large pieces of pasteboard, while the others guarded the log. Cypress is a soft wood, but very durable. We began by sawing through the log in several places well above where we thought the animals might be. Then, we used an axe to chop through to the cavity. With little effort we reamed out a hole large enough to start a fire. We used the pasteboard, brushy limbs, even our hats to fan the smoke into the hollow. Bo, Bill, and I took up positions at the entrance, while Father and Uncle Dave continued fanning, simultaneously yelling and beating the log with sticks. At our end we waited for movement. Everyone was aware of Father's strategy: take only the Barrow if, indeed, he was there. Leave the rest for another day.

Suddenly, here they came. One by one, small, supple, and grimy, they rapidly backed out, turned, and dashed into the swamp. The old sow emerged rear-end first and joined her pigs. Immediately behind her, the rear of a sizeable hog appeared through the smoke, backing slowly out of the log, scraping rotting wood on all sides. Dried mud covered his entire backside and hind legs; we could tell it was not female.

The Barrow, indeed. He uttered a strange gruntlike noise that I freely interpreted as, *What in hell is going on here? I'm smothering!*

Bo, who was now at the mouth of the cavity, grabbed one of his legs in each hand and shouted, "Help me, Jim! Help me, Bill!" Taking care to avoid the dangerous protruding tusks, we rushed in and each took hold of a leg with both hands. Father hurried toward us yelling, "God a'mighty knows! God a'mighty knows!" His famous curse words. "That's him! That's him. Uncle Dave, com'ere quick, we got'im!" Uncle Dave spat, grinned, and pronounced the obvious, "That's him alright." He went to the log, stuck in his head, ragged felt hat and all, and announced: "Guess there ain't no more in there."

We were hard put to hang onto the No-yer'd Bar. Bo adjured Father, "Bud, quick, get a rope around his head!" Father took a small rope from his pocket, gave it to Uncle Dave, who formed a noose and lassoed him. The noose went tight around his trachea and within minutes we had forced him broadside to the ground where Father could hog-tie him. As a final indignity to the Barrow, Bo cut a strong, straight pole and slipped it between his belly and legs, and we carried him out from his beloved habitat to a destiny beyond his animal imagination.

Feeling the weight of the Barrow on my shoulder, a mixture of courage and regret swept over me. Proud that I was becoming a man, almost equal to Uncle Bo and the Hillman men in the handling of hogs, I also lamented the state of the No-yer'd Bar. Who was I to express such self-defined and lordly command?

I read the Barrow's thinking as surely as the Ancient Mariner shot the albatross.

> *I have no ears but I can hear that my number is being called.*
>
> *As he stands over me here today, gloating, making pronouncements in a garbled, aging voice, so he appeared that day when I was young and in the same state of helpless captivity. This is he who performed the dastardly act.*
>
> *He sat on a log near here and removed a sharp instrument from his tattered overalls, placed me rear-outward, belly-upward between his knees and proceeded to relieve me of my testicles, my reproductive organs, my potential for paternity. It was the accepted*

operation for piglets, but it wasn't finished for me. He grabbed first
my right ear and with one swipe of his weapon removed it from my
head; then the left ear. A guttural laugh burst through his gray,
tobacco-stained moustache as he let my bloody little body drop to
the ground. Such is the gratuitous cruelty of Man.

Removing the No-yer'd Bar from the swamp took the rest of that day. First, to the railroad cutoff, then to Bob McKay's Camp, finally to the Turner Place, with each of us taking turns under the hog pole. Father went to Bald Hill and brought the car, in which his prize catch got the first ride home. My father's basic food objective had once again been met: to have hog meat available year-round. An additional trip was necessary to transport us of lesser importance.

Thus it was that the No-yer'd Bar entered Hillman hog lore. Indeed, the Barrow's "number" was called on that cold Saturday in January along with Widow Smith's Blue Boar. Uncle Dave took center stage and ultimately did him in while the ghost of Charles Hillman looked on.

Greene County Dictionary

Greene County, Mississippi, Select Dictionary of Words and Aphorisms

I HAVE JUST READ TWO SMALL, DELIGHTFUL BOOKS: Simon Winchester's *The Meaning of Everything*, the story of the evolution of the *Oxford English Dictionary*, which is the culmination of a half-million-word effort to capture every word in the English vernacular; also to trace their origins, to define them, and to suggest a proper usage. The other book, *Eats, Shoots & Leaves*, by Lynne Truss, is an attempt to make English words and symbols more meaningful through appropriate punctuation. Neither volume ventures into the history of language, the primordial, sensuous grunts and groans of our ancient ancestors; nor do they treat the unwritten, unspoken, unsung communicative devices of an evolving mankind.

Like a Scotch-Irish village, Old Washington was bathed in a steady stream of aphorisms and witticisms, some innocent and representative, others cutting and vulgar. There were new word creations. I have recorded those unique words and brief sayings that I deem to be my personal or family creations and/or unique to Old Washington, those which I have heard and used in my lifetime. Not all of them are original in spelling and meaning, and the pronunciation of many is certainly the result of bad dentition.

I offer them here for your information and entertainment.

Greene County Courthouse, ca. 1920.

abait. A sufficiency; enough. "He ate that watermelon fast," Grandpa would say. "He's got abait of it pretty quick."

Adam's off ox. A lack of ability to distinguish another. My mother used the expression to indicate her lack of knowledge about another. "I don't know him from Adam's off ox."

Agnes's heart. A personal reference to my mother's relationship to me. One of my aunts said, "Jimmye is not only Agnes's heart, he's her liver, lights, and all the rest!"

anothergin. Baby talk for "again." "Do it anothergin, Daddy, anothergin, please!"

avoirdupois. (Colloquial) One's rear end. "Throw the rascal out on his avoirdupois," my mother would say.

bassackards. The reverse of a story or proposition. "Yo facts are right, but you got it bassackards. Ya gotta tell it straight!"

bellywash. A generic word for any type of soda water. "Mr. Bud, we don't have nothin to drink cept coffee and bellywash."

biscuit hound. A stray dog that eats anything thrown to it. We liked to sing a little ditty that went: "I don't care if he's a hound / You gotta quit kickin my dog around / even though he's just a biscuit hound."

bixcuse. Defecation. A compression of "to be excused," which as a verb usually meant going to the toilet. It was used as a noun for the defecation itself. "Careful! Don't step in that bixcuse!"

Blaylock's bull. Mean, tenacious, even dangerous, referring to a bull belonging to Grandpa's friend, Mr. Blaylock. "Don't cross him! He's like Blaylock's bull."

Blue Dog Democrat (aka "Boll Weevil"). A Democratic member of the US Congress who before voting the party line will threaten to vote Republican to get what he (she) wants.

blue john. Cow's milk that hasn't been pasteurized or homogenized, and which has had the cream skimmed off, resulting in a bluish liquid. "I prefer clabber to blue john."

boocoodles. Lots and lots. "She had boocoodles of charm." Possibly an adaptation of the French word "beaucoup."

booie. An unusually ugly person. "Look at that buck-toothed, jug-eared booie."

boozakums-woozakums. Baby talk by an adult, usually accompanied with a tickle under the baby's chin.

boozie. State of drunkenness. "Come Sad'day nite, I'm gwinna McLain and git on a big boozie."

Bosepheus and Bohunkus. Twin brothers of my childhood mythical kingdom.

bo-shine. Word additive to emphasize the importance of a point to be made. "Man, he was a singing bo-shine!"

boy howdy. An exclamation for a pleasant outcome. "Boy howdy! Did we ever beat'em bad."

bread and water party. A party at which no alcoholic beverages are served. A dull party.

breadkind. A generic term used by my grandfather, Charles Hillman, for any type of bread. "Gin, whatcha got for breadkind in the house?"

bring to taw. An act of forcing someone to keep a promise.

bullrat. A student who transfers from junior college to a four-year college. Specific to Mississippi State College in the 1930s and 1940s.

bully fellow. An amiable, likeable, pleasant, and positive male personality. One of my father's favorite sayings was, "That new man on the mail route seems to be a bully fellow."

bumble bee cotton. An inferior cotton, like buzzfuzz, but of a shorter stalk.

buskull. A drinking binge, usually with hard liquor.

buttcut. A short person. "His roommate in college was Ol Buttcut Amory."

buzzfuzz. An inferior cotton, of low fiber quality and short staple length. "They don't grow nothin up around Amarillo except buzzfuzz."

by grabs. Like "by golly," a substitute for "by God," which was taking God's name in vain and a violation of the third commandment.

calf rope. A cry of surrender among boys who are wrestling. If one pinned another, before he would let him loose the victor would demand: "Say calf rope!" After obtaining "calf rope," the victor might require further acknowledgment of his superiority by demanding, "Say bull rope, too!"

chill bumps. A warm feeling, evoked by a memory of a daring experience or by an exciting adventure story. A cousin of "goose bumps."

chinkypin hunting. A tryst, implying a sexual encounter in the woods. "Have you seen Leo?" "Nope, him and Annie went towards McLain, probably out there huntin chinkypins."

choker. Peanut butter, before its complete hydrogenization and the addition of extra oil. "What's in your sandwich, Son?" "Choker 'n' jelly."

clabbercodded. Vulgar slang, referring to the scrotum.

clabberhead. A really dumb person.

Clark's dog. A smartass. "He's not just smart; he's like (Old Man) Clark's dog–too damned smart!"

closet redneck. A person who seems public-spirited, liberal, and objective, but is actually tight-fisted, mean, and racist.

cocker. Any special type of gourmet food. "Boy, that banana pudding is good cocker."

cold coffee. Harassment of a male by a female, usually by a female spouse. "She gave me cold coffee after I came in so late."

cold nose. Ability of a dog to pick up any old scent.

coon's age. A long time; normally implies more than a year.

cooter shell. Same as "turtle shell" in automobile terminology. The convertible rear part of a 1930s Model A Ford coupe.

cornholing. Sodomy, or anal sex, between two men.

cotton to him. Affinity. Often, to take a liking to, even to "butter up."

cotton-top. A youngster who has white, usually kinky, hair. An affectionate nickname.

crawfish. To backpedal in order to avoid confronting facts or the truth. "Don't trust him. He'll crawfish on you."

cush. Crumbled cornbread dipped in pot likker. Eaten usually by amassing with one's fingers and sopping in the liquid. Also used in a pejorative sense: for example, "I'm gonna knock the confounded cush out of you!"

dadgummit. A substitute for "goddamn it." Same as "doggonit," "dadblameit," "daddangit," "dadratit," and a number of other three-syllable creations, which in our Puritanical culture were not considered curse words or taking the Lord's name in vain.

dan, dang, darn, darned, darndest. Alterations of "damn" so as to be acceptable. "Jim, bring me that dan'd axe." Or, "You young'uns, git off my dan'd bed," my grandfather would say.

dinner. Always the midday meal. My mother would say, "You might as well eat this at dinner, because you'll get it for supper if you don't."

dog kin. Remote kinfolk or associates. "We're dog kin: his great-granddaddy's dog ran across my great-granddaddy's watermelon patch!"

drooze. The unanticipated enjoyment fallout of any sensuous-producing phenomenon. For example: "He was in a great state of drooze after that encounter (a meal, sports event, sex)." "He was droozy and woozy from that boozie!"

dry cattle. A boring social group. A "bread and water party." "Nothin went on last night. We were out with the dry cattle."

dry drizzle. A weather oxymoron. A minimal amount of rain. More than a mist but less than a shower. "Did it rain over at your house?" "Just a dry drizzle."

feist-dog. A contentious mongrel. A combative mutt. Seldom used unless hyphenated. "He was mad as a feist-dog."

fixinto. Preparing to perform an act or to make a decision. "She's fixinto tell'im that she ain't gonna marry'im."

flea bill. Alludes to the flea's propensity to crawl on your skin before biting: "It isn't their board bill I mind; it's the flea bill that drives me nuts!"

flivver. Synonymous with "jitney" or "jalopy." "My flivver is a handy vehicle to run around town in."

fumblefisted. Awkward, inept, all thumbs.

geehaw. To get along well together. From the combination of "gee," to steer right, and "haw," to steer left. "They just didn't geehaw, so they had to get a divorce."

goodum. Pronounced "goo-dum." Any tarry and gooey mixture. Mainly used in a construction context. "You need some more goo-dum between them bricks."

grass colt. A child whose father is unknown or absent. The offspring of a "grass widow."

grass widow. A poor woman with a child born out of wedlock.

greal. Muffled sound mixture of a hog's grunt and squeal. "The boar let out a loud greal when we cut'im."

gum it. To chew without teeth. "Uncle Alf had all his teeth pulled, and you should see him sit down to dinner and gum it."

gwinna or gwin. Going to. "I'm gwinna McLain."

haint. (1) A slurring of "haven't." "I haint seen him today." (2) A specter or ghost. "There's a haint in the old Raz Moody place!"

headknocker. The person in charge. A boss. Sometimes used affectionately. "Who's the headknocker in that outfit?" And, "He's a headknocker, alright; I like him."

heebie-jeebies. A state of nervous apprehension. "His weird looks give me the heebie-jeebies."

high cotton. An elevated state of personal fortune; a rich state of affairs. Can refer to a mental state or economic wealth. "He's living in high cotton."

Himmuns. Mispronounced nasal sound for "Hillmans." "Them Himmuns ain't lazy—Bud's family is smart; must be their mother!"

hind foot. A rebuttal in response to an assertion by another person. "The Governor's gonna come see us." "Aw, my hind foot, he is!"

hog-tied. Tied up to prevent physical, or even mental, activity; helpless. "We were hog-tied, couldn't get out from under her influence."

hold yo tater. Wait. An abbreviation for the expression, "Hold yo tater till the grease gets hot."

honeyfuggling. Sweet talk, flattery; leading on the opposite sex without intention of physical intimacy. "She just honeyfuggling old Bill; she ain't never gonna put out."

humpty-dumpty music. Any music and rhythmic beat that competes with or is substituted for traditional hymns and folk tunes. One of my mother's favorite expressions concerned New Gospel music such as "I'll Fly Away." "That's just humpy-dumpty stuff."

hyerd. A slurring of "heard." "I ain't hyerd frum'im in munts."

I Gad. A substitute for "by God," in deference to God's third commandment.

imagod'lins. By God! A form of blackguard cursing. Used predominantly by Albert Harvison, a Neely grocer.

Jake Rubenstein. An excellent bargain or price in the marketplace. Refers to a mythical peddler who always got it for you "wholesale." "I wouldn't have bought that car but old Mac gave me a Jake Rubenstein price on it."

jawlpee. A question, asking if you had gone to the bathroom.

jaybird. A blabbermouth with skinny legs.

jeet. A question, asking if you had eaten.

jeetyet. A question, asking if you had eaten yet.

Job's turkey. A condition indicating poverty. "He's as poor as Job's turkey."

joog (also "jeug"). To lightly poke or jab. "Give him a joog. That'll get his attention!"

joree. A mispronunciation of "towhee," a common bird. "We saw lots of mockers, jaybirds, thrashers, and jorees late yesterday afternoon."

kharn. A mispronunciation of "carrion." Commonly and often used to describe bad smells. We had a ditty that went: "You're a yarn / ya breath smells like kharn."

kiss m'foot. Polite substitute for "kiss my ass."

lay it by. The last plowing of the season. Throwing furrows of soil upon the crop with a mule and moldboard turn plow. John Lee Gibson would tell my father: "Mr. Bud, I'm fed up with that field of corn. I'm gonna lay it by, throw two furs on it, and let'er go to hell!"

liteard. Lightwood. Kindling from fat pine so filled with resin that it burns rapidly. "Mr. Bud, kin I git a bit o liteard frum behind yo field, that Mace Patch, so's I kin start me fires in the fireplace this winter?"

lowrate. To disparage; to denigrate or run down anybody or anything. "Don't go around lowratin yo neighbor," my father would say. "Old Joe lowrated everything in Mobile, and nobody believed him."

mare-in-goo. Meringue, mispronounced by Maggie Ware of Neely. "Agnes, that's wonderful mare-in-goo. Can I have your resype (recipe)?"

me-go-Stud. Strong determination; having it your way. A phrase we used that was derived from a story about my cousin Flick-Ella Green, who always insisted on tagging along, even if we took the car and she had to ride the family horse named Stud. "Me-go. Me-go-Stud, me go!" Anyone who was strong-willed, we called a "Me-Studder."

moddimacking. To build false expectation. To conjure up a state of unfillable hope. "He's just moddimacking ya; he ain't gonna pay ya."

mooneymod. One's private parts, female or male.

mo'rain–mo'rest. An expression of my father indicating rain meant a day of rest, which was never true because there were always chores in the barn, woodshed, or sweet potato patch. (Sweet potato draws were often planted in the rain.)

muleyheaded. A person who won't listen, namely one who won't take advice.

mummux. A foul mixture; a mess of things. "He got hissef into a whoppin mummux!"

munt. Slurring of "month." "I hyerd frum Joe; he's comin next munt."

muttonhead. A dolt. A nonthinking person. "What a muttonhead he is!"

nut-cuttin. The essence of a process. "Quit foolin around, Jim. Let's git down to the nut-cuttin."

one-butt kitchen. A very small place to cook. "She had a one-butt kitchen and insisted on occupying it."

out-Jesused. A political expression, usually made by a losing candidate, admitting his opponent had beaten him by siding with religious groups. "He out-Jesused me! But the bastard better watch out in November; I'm gonna go to prayer meetin in every church in Greene County, at least once, tween now and then."

ox is in the ditch. An excuse to be working on the Sabbath, which was a violation of the fourth commandment. "I cain't be at church Sunday; the ox is in the ditch and I've gotta go to Mobile."

panic gravy. A cheap form of dressing for biscuits and cornbread in hard times. General recipe: Melt some lard or pork grease, stir in some flour, and cook until it browns. Add water and continue heating. Salt to taste.

peach pickin. Local expression meaning preference. "Uncle Doak, stop peach pickin." "I ain't pickin your peaches, Aunt Nora; I'm takin'em just as I come to'em."

pickup. A shot of morphine. "I'm going to see Dr. McLeod; he'll give me a pickup."

piney-woods rooter. A feral hog that roams cutover forest and feeds on pine sapling roots. See *rakestraw*.

pissypuser. An indecisive person; indifferent as to outcome. "He's been sittin on the fence far too long; like his dad, just a pissypuser."

podunker. An extremely awkward country rube.

pot likker. Liquid from which collard greens and hog trimmings, particularly hog jowl, have been removed after cooking.

prickteaser. A young female who encourages sexual thoughts among males, but who has no intention of fulfilling them.

pustlegutted. Fat. Also a term to denigrate a fat unfriendly person. As my dad used to say, "That pustlegutted bastid is lying to ya!"

rakestraw. Analogous to a piney-woods rooter or a razorback. Has no bloodline and is a feral hog that fends for itself.

resype. Mispronunciation of "recipe" by Maggie Ware of Neely. "Agnes, can I have your resype for that delicious chocolate cake?"

sapsucker. A cultural term often used half in derision and half in admiration. "He's a good-lookin sapsucker, isn't he?" or "That high-bred sapsucker's up to no good!"

saucered and blowed. Everything's ready. Typically in reference to coffee, as in "Here's yo cawfy, Uncle Buddy, all saucered and blowed." But also refers to anything in a state of readiness.

savin up coupons. Expecting a baby. An expression derived from a line in a folk song: "I don't know who told her but somehow she knows, I'm a savin up coupons to get one o those."

scanal-on-earth. A moral disaster. Normally, a personal pronouncement. "When they cut them mules' tails off at the Methodist Church," Aunt Nora said, "it's a scanal-on-earth."

scriddle. To fornicate. My dad would say, "Boys, if ya gonna scriddle, don't be like hogs and dogs, at least get in th'bushes!"

scroodles. A quantity: oodles and oodles.

semollian. One dollar, or one greenback. Variation of "simoleon." "That shirt cost me a whole semollian."

she-ro. Feminine hero. "Miz Agnes, Leo asked if I'm the hero, who's gonna be the she-ro?"

shinaree. A mispronunciation of the French word "charivari." Lots of noise usually made at the place newlyweds are spending their first wedding night. "We giv'em a big shinaree last night, a real blowout!"

shinny still. The production apparatus for bootleg whiskey.

shonuf. Slurred for "sure enough." Used mostly as a response to a declarative statement by another person; sometimes even in a question form. "Mary, I'm gonna bring you some candy from McLain." "Shonuf? Sho'll be good!" This slurred, combined form is also used for verbs, for example, "Shodo," "Shocan," "Shois," etc.

silent sow gets the slop. An expression meaning he who doesn't talk so much winds up with the money, prize, or reward.

simmon-eatin possum. From persimmon-eating. A person whose smile is possumlike, a cover-up expression; superficial. "Did you see ol George comin out of the bank looking like a simmon-eatin possum?"

slop jar. Repository for human refuse. Usually kept in the bedroom of adults.

slue-footed. A person with large ungainly feet. Observation usually made of one who is bare-footed. "He was slue-footed, knock-kneed, and ugly to boot!"

smile like a wave on a slopbucket. An expression describing an excessive grin. Similar to "simmon-eatin possum."

softsoaping. Giving another the runaround, avoiding a direct answer. Also: "softsoaper."

SOL. Soldiered outta luck. Greene County substitute for those who didn't use the four-letter word.

sootrake. A tool for removing ashes and refuse from the fireplace. We liked to call the school principal, O. U. Sullivan, "Old Sootrake."

Southern hypocracacy. My mother's expression for anyone using excessive flattery or emotive language. "Don't 'Darlin, honey-pie' me. That's just Southern hypocracacy."

spads. Loose bowels, used particularly by my dad in reference to animals. "Watch it! Don't get next to that heifer; she's been eatin green corn leaves and got the spads."

spizzerinctum. Energy-cum-imagination. Energized by an idea and having the will to see it through. "Seems Joe has the spizzerinctum to run for governor. Can't imagine why."

splendificence. A state or condition beyond either, or both, splendor and magnificence. "Their wedding was out of this world, full of splendificence!"

spondoula. Generic and aggregate term for money. Moolah. "Sorry I can't join you; I just don't have the spondoula."

spuke. Spew plus puke. Verb form: "Spuke it up! Spuke it up before it poisons you!"

stand hitched. Dependable in a tough situation. Originating from mule-driving. "She'll stand hitched, won't buckle."

stemwinding. Characteristic of being exciting. "After dinner the Senator gave a stemwinding speech, and everybody applauded and stomped."

still hunting. Hunting game with your senses and without the use of a dog or voice.

stove up. Aching condition due to a mild accident or overwork. "Mr. Bud, I cain't hep ya today. I'm all stove up."

strolope. To hang around without purpose. Strolopper: a lazy person. One of my mother's descriptive terms. "Just look at him, that good-for-nothing strolopper."

Studebaker-Lincoln. A drunk uncle's description of his dream car. "I'm goin to Hattiesburg and buy me a Studebaker-Lincoln."

stumpjumper. A person who is always just one step ahead of the law.

suck-egg dog. A slinking, cowardly person who attacks in the dark or from behind. "He's lower down than a suck-egg dog."

suckerbill. A person of jovial nature who is always on the margin of circumstance. Usage usually positive. "He's a lucky suckerbill."

sucking hind titty. An expression describing an unfortunate person. "When we all got in line for tickets, he was left sucking hind titty."

suitcase community. A village where people work but usually live somewhere else.

summers. An affectation for "somewhere." "Bye, Ann, see ya summers soon!"

surveyin and inhalin. Plowing a mule while breathing in the animal's farts. "Old Dan ain't got a job yet; jest surveyin and inhalin at the moment."

swallowed a watermelon seed. An expression for pregnancy. Also: "Mamma has gas on her stomach." And: "That gal done gone and drunk too much Big Creek water!"

sweetsoapin. Making another feel better for no good reason. Flattery. "He don't have nothin to tell ya. He's just sweetsoapin ya."

swunk up. Shrunken. Usually due to lack of food or because of an illness.

ten-quart-water-bucket-full. An unspecified liquid measure of a large amount. "That knife must've hit a big vein; he bled a ten-quart-water-bucket-full!"

towhead. A person, usually a youngster, with stringy long and white hair.

treacle. Sugar talk; overly sentimental gossip; "sweetsoap."

trettle. A special trigger mechanism for trapping wild animals and birds.

unlax. Loosen up, plus relax. Take it easy!

uptore. State of disquietude, disorientation. "Mr. Bud, I'm all uptore, nothin ain't goin right!"

wagon greasin. A lateral distance equal to the point from one greasing of an ox wagon to the next before the wagon stops due to friction. "He lives about three wagon greasin's behind the railroad from McLain on the road to Janice."

walkin the dog. An expression meaning a person who thinks of himself as being in a state of *haut éminence*. "He's walking the dog since he heard he was chosen for chairman."

wawsts'nez. Wasp's nest. Conflagration. "He sure stirred up a wawsts'nez when he mentioned Bilbo's name!"

wet weather spring. A sluice of water appearing in unexpected places after prolonged rains. My dad would say, "Did he have a cold? His nose was runnin like a wet weather spring."

whore's bath. Powder and perfume only; no water.

willies. A state of nervousness. Piss-willies: a state of exceptional nervousness. "Don't bother him just now, he's got the willies."

woods hogs. Feral hogs; wild hogs.

yellow dog Democrat. A registered Democrat voter who votes a straight party ticket under any circumstances; having a choice between a Republican and a yellow dog, he opts to cast his vote for the yellow dog.

Yellow Rabbit to Vinegar Bend. An entire, but unspecified, geographic distance. "We drove everywhere—from Yellow Rabbit to Vinegar Bend—looking for that dog."

zerned. Tally Harvison always said his dog was the most "zerned" of any he ever owned. No one knew what he meant.

zerves. Preserves. Any berry, fruit, or vegetable that is preserved in cans or jars.

Life on the Farm

One Mississippi Christmas, 1931

LAST NIGHT, I WENT TO MIDNIGHT MASS at St. Michael and All Angels Episcopal Church, with its Santa Fe architecture and southern Arizona desert setting conducive to memory of ancient Palestine. Its liturgy is a far cry from that which we celebrated in 1931 at First Baptist Church in Avera. This morning I arose and played "A Child's Christmas in Wales," read by Dylan Thomas, on an old 33 rpm disc through our aging Fisher stereo, which with almost technical perfection delivers that penetrating, mellifluous Welsh voice. On the Fisher, in long family tradition, I listened to Berlioz's haunting *L'Enfance du Christ*. My wife Helen and I celebrated quietly with a single guest. Then I rested, my newly inserted pacemaker beating to the rhythm of "Jingle Bells."

In 1931, the sawmills in Avera were shutting down, people were scrambling, anticipating another of America's fabled "panics." The name Hoover was already anathema, even for children. We didn't know how good 1931 was, however, until 1932, '33, '34, and '35 rolled around. But Christmas was still something to get excited about, to celebrate, the biggest holiday in the year for many rural Mississippians outside the birthday of Robert E. Lee.

On December 23 we had already celebrated my father's birthday. For a typical American household, birthdays were a day of festivity. But for Father the customary celebration was always lackluster, because of his arrival two days before that other Man. History had upstaged the first-born male of Charles and Virginia Hillman with a more important event: Baby Jesus. Advent. Christmas. That was *the* birthday for us. This year there wasn't even time to bake a cake for poor Father. As was tradition, we headed out on Christmas Eve to spend the holiday with Grandpa and Grandma at Old House.

We loaded the Model A Ford with presents, then climbed aboard Jitney and positioned ourselves for the ride, burrowing our warm bodies in its rear compartment to prepare for the bumpy ride over corduroy roads to Neely.

Under a tarpaulin lay homemade quilts from Aunt Cannie, and under the quilts on the bed of the vehicle was an amalgam of hay, corn shucks, and newspaper, anything to cushion us against the bumps. Three excited children, little sister Jean, Elmer, and me, squeezed our bodies between the quilts and the tarpaulin. Innocent and tickled at the thought of Christmas, we were oblivious to the odor from the motor exhaust and the occasional flatulation or "poots" in our makeshift shroud.

Our Model A was adapted with a "cooter shell" for a rear trunk, or boot, the door lid of which could be raised from the rear, outside, the space inside equivalent to the third tier in a modern station wagon. There was no barrier between front seat and the adapted rumble seat where we crouched, with a view out the back windows. In front, my oldest brother Bill rode between my mother and father. It was one enclosed space, capable of carrying small animals like pigs and chickens and dogs, farm cargo such as stove wood and corn, or squirming children anticipating fruitcake.

This Christmas Eve the twilight air was brisk, and we had already donned our union suits in preparation for bed. "Are y'all ready back there?" Father yelled as he took out the car crank to start the motor. Over the noise of the motor we heard, "Remember, I don't want no fightin back there, y'heah me?" his voice rising with each intonation. "We'll be there in less'n an hour," he said, settling behind the steering wheel.

Off we motored at a speed exceeding horse and buggy, but less than that of light, on the washboard roadbed. First, we passed the Methodist church and community cemetery, the last sign of life (or nonlife) for a few miles. Downhill, reaching a speed of at least twenty-five mile per hour, Jitney bore us across the branch headwaters of Bear Creek. Then past the Smith enclave, family homesteads spaced about every quarter mile, with their simple frame houses and marginal sandy soils. There was Rufus "Ruf" and "Whiskey Kim"; Henry and "Cabbage Head" John; and "Ida's John" or "John-Windy," as he was dubbed because of his big frame and garrulous nature. Farther along lived Arthur Smith, with his bunch of troublesome boys. Finally, "Miss" Meedy Smith, a widow whose "patch" lay outside Mutual Rights School District, and whose nickname no one ever seemed able to explain. It was all Smiths for several miles, and the woods are still full of them.

I remember that two of the Smith brothers later went hunting deer and only one returned. We always wondered what really happened. The surviving brother claimed he thought he'd shot a deer, but everyone knew there was no love lost between the two.

The railroad crossing at Byrd brought groans and a spontaneous cry of "Daddy, drive slower!" from beneath the cover. Residences were more frequent now: Will Breland's, then James Wright's, whose little blonde-headed Paula Clyde I was in love with at eight, but at a distance. She attended Neely School. We passed the side road, called Tung-oil Road, to Tom Harvey Byrd's house, where the annual sheepshearing took place. Tom's adopted sons, Lee and "Skin" Dunnam, were my schoolmates later at Neely and at Mississippi State College.

Then past Aunt Cynt Bradley's, which always reminded me of sugarcane syrup. She had the only mill and in October started juicing the fat stalks of the blue-ribbon cane and reducing it to molasses. At Uncle Dave Hillman's, there was a cluster of buildings including the homes of his sons Loke on the north and "Crazy" Mack on the south. We always checked out "Rance" Morris's place for all his girls, but it was too dark to see any. I identified with Rile Dixon's house because he helped Grandpa with mules and plowing. He had a funny-looking son, Arthur-Mack, who always wore a wide-brim straw hat, even on the coldest winter day. Behind his back we mocked the way he spoke, calling him "Buck-tooth Awshy-mac." Soon, we came to Bradley Crossway, a pond and spillway where the headwaters of Little Brushy Creek often flowed across the road in flood season.

At last! We crossed the railroad at Avent, which was just a mile from our destination. During this entire trip, we met not a single automobile. As we arrived, the last shafts of daylight passed through the big oaks around Old House and our grandparents came out to greet us. Merry Christmas! And there were hugs around. Grandmother, or

Aunt Gin, super mother hen that she always was to family and friends, threw a light wrap around each of us children and admonished, "Run into the house, Darlin, before you catch cold!"

After a light supper of leftovers, our Christmas began. We inspected the tree that stood in the windowless corner near the fireplace. My grandparents had cut a small holly from the vast population in the woods below the pasture and sprinkled it with "snow" consisting of bits of raw lint cotton and white rags, and with red berries from pyracantha and holly. No lights; electricity in rural Greene County was ten years away.

Christmas for us came in two manifestations. First, on the eve, we opened the presents that Santa had preordained: necessities like a pair of socks, a shirt, underwear, even a pair of shoes . . . nothing trivial. There was little ceremony.

At eight years, I had just begun to correlate the identity of the Santa, who saw my need for shoes and socks, with that of the North Pole Phantom who placed items in my stocking and on the fireplace edge with my name attached to them. Yet, still filled with wonder, although tainted by a bit of suspicion, I began to drowse. The day had been long. Soon we rushed from the fire, jumped into back-room featherbeds. No church to spoil the next day. No church on Christmas Day unless the feast day fell on Sunday. No feast days for Baptists, no pagan rites at Christmas. No Midnight Mass within a hundred miles of Neely.

Then, as darkness hovered over Old House, we waited in our beds with patience and near-reverence, expecting the surprises, specials, and the "excesses" that Santa's second coming would deposit in our enormous stockings. We had hung them on the face of the massive fireplace in the parlor.

The roosters always crowed at daylight at Old House, a curse and blessing of farm life. Grandma already had the fireplace ablaze, and one by one we came, union suit–clad, and warmed our bottoms. Our spirits were wide awake. It took awhile to awaken the body, pull on overalls, and to accommodate bodily functions at the "two-holer" in the backyard.

It took another hour to eat a breakfast of bacon, scrambled eggs, grits, "red-eye" gravy, biscuit, and sugarcane syrup, chased by cocoa. Eating in Grandma's commodious kitchen with its table made from resin-filled aged yellow pine—no tablecloth—a Home Comfort, the Cadillac of kitchen stoves, with all the smells from pepper and hot pork fat, saturated the senses. Even so, we children were getting anxious. The family soon retired to the parlor and its warm fireplace where Father announced Santa's unloading.

My brothers and I and our little redheaded sister had already garnered our stockings. Each contained an apple, an orange, about a cupful of mixed nuts-in-the-shell, and a cluster of seeded raisins from a wooden box of the Sun Maid brand. For my little brother Elmer there were two packages of No. 1 firecrackers, for me one package of No. 1s and one of No. 3s, and for Bill, the oldest, two packages of No. 5s, the big banger. All of the boys received a Roman candle and a package of sparklers. Little sister Lora Jean got beads and a matching bracelet in her stocking. Heavy gifts from Santa included a convoy of toy trucks, autos, and motor vehicles for Elmer, a fancy knife for me, and an air gun for Bill, one that made noise but launched no missile. Jean got a glistening little fake wristwatch, "Made in Japan." Everyone seemed pleased, a must, as Father countenanced no major gripes and dissatisfaction at Santa's beneficence.

I thought: In these hard times we must be especially thankful. I gleefully put my stocking away, thanked Father and Mother for the present, and congratulated myself on my luck and the bone-handled pocketknife, then declaimed a ditty making the rounds on the school grounds those days: "Buffalo handle, Barlow blade, best old knife that's ever been made." Barlow, after all, was the famous Sheffield, England, steel family. (The phrase describes the most famous knife of all, A. G. Russell's Texas Stockman.) Today, as I reflect on that Christmas, I am reminded of the poignant words attributed to a Mississippi statesman long ago: "The happiest Christmas I ever had was an apple, an orange, and a dime."

Afterward came the time for play, popping firecrackers, and for general romping about. Local custom was to set off fireworks at Christmas. Fireworks that announced the birth of Jesus seemed natural. I thought the planners had it all wrong to bring them out and make such a fuss on July 4th, which we didn't much celebrate, that being a Union holiday.

We boys escaped to that part of the yard that adjoined the pasture on one side and the main road on the other, the lee of Old House. About that time Uncle Till Hathorn, dressed as Santa Claus and shouting "HO-HO-HO," appeared up the road from Callie Creel's store on a heap of hay in a wagon drawn by a team of mules.

Flailing his arms vigorously, he jumped out and made his way toward Elmer, muttering, "Com'ere, li'l boy. Santa's got sumpin fer ya!" Elmer, having never encountered such an apparition, let out a scream and bolted toward the house. Uncle Till, with Santa's head in his hand, followed, pleading, "I ain't gonna hurt ya, l'il boy. I ain't gonna hurt ya!" Bawling yet louder, Elmer dashed toward Mother, who had come to investigate.

Bill and I commenced the fireworks, he with his No. 5s with their heavy load of powder, I with less noise and the No. 1s and 3s. To add more excitement and be more spectacular, he began placing the firecracker in the flap of his slingshot. I then lit the fuse and ran, at which time he launched the cargo into the heavens, some hundred feet or more. Alas! One of the firecracker fuses was very short, and he had barely released it when it exploded a few feet from his right ear. Swearing me to secrecy, he told me later that his hearing had been dulled for months.

Always served at noon at Old House, Christmas dinner meant young turnip sprouts as well as collards from Grandpa's garden, accompanied by fresh pork roast and baked sweet potatoes. Grandma's chow-chow was my favorite relish, a hodgepodge of diced green tomatoes, pickles, mustard, sugar, vinegar, and ginger. No turkey or deer—they had already been pretty well hunted out. No oysters from the Gulf Coast, so no oyster dressing that year. Black-eyed peas for sure, a Christmas and New Year's regular.

Before we sat, I watched Grandpa clear his throat and fake a cough, then open the cupboard door, reach to the top shelf, and remove two small flat bottles from behind the jars of fig and pear preserves. The words "Four Roses" and "Old Granddad" were written across the bottles, with pictures accordingly. Grandma surveyed the situation and quietly admonished, "Charlie!" Father and Mother

Charles and Virginia Hillman, ca. 1900.

giggled, and we children wondered. After pouring a small amount into his water glass, he took a deep quaff, swished it around in his mouth, and pretended to gargle. "The best cough medicine there is. Dr. McLeod uses it himself," he said. With a smirk that revealed vacancies in his upper incisors through a moist moustache, he added, "Ah! Better already."

Charles Hillman had little difficulty with being a bit of a rogue as counterpart to being the village of Neely's benevolent nabob and church leader. If Santa Claus hadn't already existed, "Uncle Charlie" could have played the role. Looking back on that family Christmas dinner scene, I laugh at Grandpa's throat-gargling "sin." If he wanted to finesse his saintly helpmeet with bourbon whiskey, or to embarrass his oldest son and his wife in front of their children, or even if he wanted to try to deceive his grandchildren with "cough medicine," then, good on him!

There were few naps at Christmas, but lots of visitors. My brothers and I played again that afternoon while the men sat on the front porch, chewed tobacco, spat, and told stories in the mode of their Irish and Scottish ancestors. Many of these conversations wound up on a Civil War theme. Grandpa speculated, "What if Stonewall

Jackson had lived?" After cleaning the kitchen, Mother and Grandma entertained the women. My mother was always a bit ill at ease within this social setting. Having come from Georgia, she would always be the outsider in Neely.

For the next week, the principal deviation from our daily routine at Old House was the Saturday visit to the Old Turner Place where Grandpa owned some woods hogs. They were mostly sows and shoats, and their eerie guttural evocations carried through the brush. Corn was their reward when Grandpa called, and I learned which part of a hog's grunt meant "Thank you!" We were baiting them for future pork roasts on a Christmas table.

After spending Christmas with Grandma and Grandpa, we drove back to Avera. In my innocence, I was certain that if there were a Santa Claus—just if—he would not forget me and, just maybe, our family lot would improve before next December.

One evening in the teacher's home at Mutual Rights, I pulled down our big Sears-Roebuck catalog, Memphis edition, and began paging through it. For several of the annual issues, there had been the same bucketful of candy, advertised in color. This year it was on page 269 with its usual temptation of sweet varieties, all for $1.79. (Let some doubter check this eighty-five-year-old memory.) Mother, who had been closely observing my wistful demeanor, reverted to her first name for me and said, "Baby Doll, Christmas will be even better next year."

Hestle

SHE CAME TO US IN 1931, MOSTLY ON HER TERMS. At the beginning of the Great Depression, my father and mother were teaching at Avera and we lived at the teacher's home. She had come to replace Iola Pipkins, our white helper who had to return home because of a family emergency. Like many other unmarried women, black or white, she needed a job. We could hire almost any woman to work for food and shelter, medical care, and five dollars a month. There were no other benefits.

Mother was particular as to whom she could trust, but was desperate, however, with four children and working as a full-time teacher with more than thirty students. Sadie Rae Byrd, a young girl in great need, had filled in for a few months but departed to finish high school. Father learned through the local "negro grapevine"—that was the term used at the time—about a mature, experienced woman from Shuqualak (everybody pronounced it "Sugarlock") in Noxubee County, the east-central Mississippi farm area of chalk, cotton, and, at one time, slaves.

Father and I made a special trip to Shuqualak to pick her up with her meager belongings. He had borrowed a pickup truck for the trip, and as we drove north through the rural hills of the Chickashawhay River watershed I was filled with anticipation. Passing through Kemper County I wondered out loud, "Daddy, whatever happened to cousin Leroy?" Leroy had gone berserk, holing up in the smokehouse with a double-barrel shotgun, axes, and picks, daring people to come get him. He ended up in the asylum at Meridian. My father responded with an unintelligible reply, and we drove on through the county, arriving at Shuqualak in time to drive back to Avera before dark.

So it was that Mary A. Hestle joined the Hillman family. She was an immediate hit with parents and children, and she would live with us until World War II.

She was the daughter of a slave. Her father had been freed after the Civil War with enough dignity to be employed as a blacksmith on a farm near Shuqualak. From her home she brought a double bed with a high, solid poplar headboard, decorated with figurines, two quilts made of old clothes and overalls, quilt clamps, a homemade iron cobbler shoe last, two smoothing irons, a blue enamel coffeepot, and two oversize dark green cane-bottom chairs made by her father. Today, all of this would be classified as antiques. Her trunk looked like it may have belonged to some Confederate general who lugged it from Manassas to Appomattox during the War.

We called her "Hestle" from the beginning. No other person ever gave me such insights into the culture, history, economics, religion, and everyday life of black people. She let us know that she, too, had taught school. And we took it for granted because she wrote well, read even better, and was assertive about being her own person. If someone made a derogatory comment about her or her relation to our family, she said to us, "Don't giv'em no attention. They ain't got no manners, noway!"

She couldn't be bought, not by our bribes, nor by our flattery. No one threatened her, though admittedly "Mr. Bud," as she called my father, was the boss. She taught us that discipline should be meted out uniformly and democratically, that fairness has one standard, and the scales between black and white weigh the same.

The only serious infraction of the rules was when she took it upon herself to discipline my little freckled-faced, redheaded sister, Lora Jean, whom she quickly dubbed "Redhead." The nickname stuck and soon everyone used it. Hestle's job included babysitting, and once baby Lora Jean sobbingly lied to my mother about being spanked. This almost caused my parents to fire Hestle. Being the baby, a girl at that, in a Southern household, Redhead could do no wrong. Perhaps my parents never really understood the totality of Hestle's assistance with their responsibilities, and her influence on our character.

Redhead is now in her ninth decade. She has been a great help with reminding me of Hestle's personal bearing. She was tall and erect. She let her hair grow, which she parted in the middle, braided, and gathered into two balls that she moved about on each side of her head from time to time. Her brown eyes always sparkled. A gold tooth shone in the front of her mouth. A dime on each ankle hung from finely woven chains wrapped in twine, attached loosely but not awkwardly. The dimes had worn thin over the years and the twine had soiled, but it all added to her mystery. When asked why she wore the dimes, she said they kept away sickness and spirits. A silver ring with a cheap amethyst setting graced her left ring finger.

Hestle was quite aware of the racial boundaries and the cultural ethos of her new surroundings. Also, what our behavior as white children should be. She could turn on the charm when necessary, such as when the preacher and his family were at the Hillmans' for Sunday dinner. In her mind, she had already joined the raceless, colorless throng beyond Olympus; she had been to the "Mountain" before Martin Luther King Jr. was born.

My brothers and I adjusted well to Hestle's care. She always made me feel special, and I from the first seemed to be her favorite. Maybe this was because I was older and reacted more positively to her. Our relationship remained always one of mutual respect. On reflection, as a mature black woman, she must have understood the tensions of a Southern white boy's emergence into manhood. Because of our differences in age, and because such matters weren't discussed between blacks and whites, the subject of sex never came up. But I learned a lot from her innuendo.

At the fireplace on the winter evenings of those first years, we sat on the floor around her rocking chair while she filled our minds with wonderful stories. Some were a pursuit of wild fantasy, drawn from her psyche, but were heavily influenced by recent decades of a slavery-burdened, cultural exposure to Euro-American ways. Hestle also told us stories of her Saturday-night frolics with her young friends, but she made sure we knew that she never associated with the crowd that carried "frog-stickers" (knives). She never mentioned any love affair or romantic encounter, but did tell us of a friend that ran away from home to Chicago and married a worker in the Swift packing plant. My little brother Elmer popped up one night with, "Hestle, why didn't you run away North?" She looked into the fire that reflected in her eyes and sighed, "Hmmmm." That was her only answer.

One of our favorite stories was about the ghost she encountered one day in Shuqualak on her way to the spring for a bucket of water. Assuring us of her bravura, she described the ghost's appearance in great detail, its movements, and the surrounding scenery.

"I gawd, Mr. Ghost," she began boldly, rolling her eyes, standing to her feet and lifting her hands. "I ain't skeerd o you. What you thinkin bout?" Shuffling on her feet around the fireplace, she told us she was trying to "figger'im out." "He sat his butt down on a stump at the spring and I said, 'What you thinking, ghost-man?'" (The ghost was always male, of course.) "What you thinkin bout? I ain't skeerd o you, Mr. Ghost. Tell me, tell me!" Her voice rose to a shout. Then came what to us was the ghost's anticlimactic reply, a simple but enigmatic response in Hestle's whisper: "Well, Miss, I ain't been thinkin bout nothin! I'm jest sittin here restin. I ain't thinkin bout nothin."

"Thinkin bout nothin." As a boy I was tickled by that phrase, and "nothin" became another of those Hestle words that was built into the Hillman lexicon: "Thinkin bout nothin." When I think about the ghost's answer today, I remember all the aphorisms that we created from "nothin": "Nothin good can come o that!" "He ain't good for nothin." "He'll never mount t'nothin." "Whataya spect from a nothin like that?" Then I muse, smile to myself, and hum Gershwin's "I Got Plenty of Nothing."

After such a story, Hestle slapped her knees with both hands, laughed, and said, "Lawd gawd, Lawd gawd!" reaching for her tin of Tube Rose snuff. She neatly spat into a number two tin can an arrow of brown juice from the space between her upper incisors, one of which was gold. She paused, assessed her audience, and then continued.

We knew we were never to go alone to the cemetery. Ghosts hung out there.

She followed Mr. Ghost with another story, recounting a time when she was on her way back from the same spring. Tiring from carrying a full bucket, she sat down on a big green mossy log that slowly began to move. Showing the whites of her eyes, she stood from her chair and began weaving an elaborate verbal embroider: "I'se just sittin there and thinkin, logs don't move!" Then she sat down again, her eyes getting bigger and bigger. "I gawd, I looked up the path and saw his head. His eyes wuz green, and tongue wuz flappin out. I thought it the Devil, and I got away from there in a hurry!"

By then we were duly scared, but she was a genius at tapering off scary tales with soothing observations and advice. She finished this one off by admonishing us to be careful about snakes. "Don't go swimmin in creek pools where those water moccasins hide, and always wear shoes when ya go to the woods, a rattler may bite ya."

Her voice was melodious, but it had a hint of yearning and despair. Songs were in her very bones. Hestle was always mumbling and humming while she washed and ironed our clothes. And she often sang to us by the fireplace on dreary evenings. Some songs bore the stamp of an oppressed people, but others were songs of survival, hope, and escape. She often sang us "The Flood":

> Well it rained forty days
> And it rained forty nights,
> I'm beggin my Lawd to make my garment white,
> When I get to heaven I'm gonna sit right down
> And ask my Lawd for my starry crown.
> Unh-hnh, unh-hnh!
> Well now, didn't it rain, chillun
> Lawdy now, didn't it a rain fall!
> Some a floatin round the windows,
> Some floatin round the doors
> A beggin ole Noah won't he take on some more,
> When I get to heaven I'm gonna sit right down
> And ask my Lawd for my starry crown.
> Unh-hnh, unh-hnh!

There were many songs about Jesus and the Cross. So real was the one entitled "What More Can Jesus Do?" that when she sang it, I felt that I was looking up at Jesus on the Cross, crown of thorns on his brow, His pierced side gushing with blood, as He was offered vinegar to quench His thirst. "What mo can m'Jesus do / Just what mo can m'Jesus do?"

> Well He died, on a Roman cross
> Well He died, on a Roman cross
> He laid th'foundation, made the way so plain
> What mo can m'Jesus do?

She sang this one on and on with six-syllable introductory lines as long as there was no other diversion:

> Well He died for you and me
> Well he died for sinners, too
> Now he's there with Abraham
> Jacob, Joseph, Mary, too

Then she sang the chorus again, while preparing to shift gears.

She slid sequaciously to others, such as "God Put a Rainbow in the Cloud," and experimented with some that were obviously concocted, winding up with one of my favorites, "Climbing Jacob's Ladder." Tunes to some of these are fast disappearing and remain in the oral tradition of a few aging brains, such as mine. I recently thought of one of hers that not even Google can help me with: "On the Jericho Road."

Mary A. Hestle absorbed the dos and don'ts of our family. She was the only black person in our community and quite well known. Nothing got past her that she thought would disrupt family harmony; no gossip; no clandestine or dishonest "pussyfootin," as she would say. Along with her nimbleness of mind, she was strong of body and would tussle with my brothers and me. We tested her endurance and tolerance, and also her wit.

We often played games. I asked her once, "Hestle, who are the most important people in history?" She immediately said, "Mister George Washington, the Father of our country; Mister Abraham Lincoln, he freed the slaves; Mister Booker T. Washington, that great black man; Mister Franklin D. Roosevelt, who's bringin us out of these hard times; and . . ." She thought a moment, pushed a wad of Tube Rose inside her lower lip with her tongue, and stated emphatically, "Now old snuff man Levi Garrett—he waun't no fool!"

Once in a while I got serious and said, "Hestle, you gotta help me with my arithmetic." "I gawd!" she answered, "I ain't gotta do nothin but die." (She didn't pay taxes.) To get in the last word I always spilled out: "Yes you do, Hestle. You've got to live till you *do* die!"

As the Depression deepened in 1934, my parents decided to return to the farm and to commute to any teaching job they might find. A house was soon under construction at the old Thaddeus Green homestead, forever after known as Thad Hill to friends and family, and which is still deeply embedded in my cranial recesses. Father also built Hestle a cottage out of the same lumber, locating it amid the pines on an incline about fifty yards behind our house.

Hestle's house became a haven for us children when we wanted to escape from our parents' demands. There was no indoor plumbing for either home, as running water wouldn't come for years. The federal Works Progress Administration (WPA; renamed Work Projects Administration in 1939), a part of President Roosevelt's program to revitalize rural America, eventually constructed beautiful outdoor toilets, which Hillmans and Hestle used in common. We drew water from the same pitcher pump. Facilities to wash clothes—a large cast iron wash pot and clothesline—were all nearby. Farther away stood a large sturdy table, built with two-inch-thick hardwood boards. Hestle thought this was her domain, but Father and Mother used it for activities such as meat cutting, cleaning, and canning fruits and vegetables, and as part of the smokehouse complex.

The Hillman family remained closely knit after the move to Thad Hill, but work habits changed drastically; we were now farmers. Father and the three boys went to field and forest. Mother, after completing her housework, filled in by helping to chop wood and pick cotton and cucumbers. But Hestle never went to the fields. She was occupied full time with cooking, yard maintenance, washing, and ironing. We all worked together to improve the beauty of the homestead and Hestle's cottage, planting gardens of camellias, rhododendrons, and azaleas, with an occasional coniferous shrub (*Cedrus deodara*). We were unconcerned about world problems, war clouds, and Hitler, whom Hestle dubbed "the Devil."

Hestle's social life was limited to contact with our family and to friends on her visit to McLain on occasional weekends. Although there had never been black people in rural Neely, as this was never a slave-owning region, at cotton-picking time Father often employed several blacks from McLain to assist us. But there was little contact between them and Hestle. She felt superior to cotton pickers.

In 1937, however, when Hercules Powder Company began dynamiting and removing pine stumps, a relationship developed between Hestle and a worker for the company. He was "top stump blower." During summer month weeknights, we children did not have to be told what was going on in the cabin among the pines. The facts of life come early on the farm. Late on most afternoons, when workhands boarded the truck for home and left without Sam, we knew that Hestle would be scarce that night. Would there be black babies on our farm?

During those seasons of work, school, and dreaming, I became her "Scamp," a nickname of affection. "Scamp," she would say, "bring me some Tube Rose when you go to Mist Sam Green's." This was a mom-and-pop grocery where McLain blacks congregated, especially on Saturday nights. There were special jobs that she trusted only me to do: "Scamp, will ya help me prepare muh possum?" I always assisted her in killing and dressing the possums we boys occasionally caught while hunting. They had to be penned and fattened (possums, like buzzards, eat carrion) before we prepared them for eating. Usually Hestle baked them with sweet potatoes. I ate possum with her, but mainly to say that I had *eaten possum*. One-upmanship on my friends. A claim I still use.

Next, it was "Scamp, yuh daddy wants them hog guts ridded and I need yuh help." She meant chitterlings. This was a rare request by Father, because few people liked the dish, one that was greatly influenced by African-American custom. The process involved cleaning and preparing the small intestine of the hog, then boiling it to tenderness and frying it. As with possum, Hestle knew how to do it all correctly. She fed me chitterlings once, unfried, but I don't remember taking a second helping, or ever eating the dish again.

When I left for college in 1938, the second child out of the nest, Hestle's work with the family began winding down. She left for McLain, perhaps figuring she must ally herself with the blacks there. There was no going-away party. A cousin told me she went to

Louisiana on the strawberry-picking circuit, before settling into a cottage south of town, which my father arranged. It was unrealistic, given all the circumstances, to expect an aging, single black woman to remain in our rural household at Thad Hill in such isolation.

Mother was still teaching. Father was persuaded to run for Greene County supervisor, and was elected. All their children were in school. For the first time in more than a decade no one was to be seen by day on Thad Hill. Hestle's friend Sam had departed to other parts of southern Mississippi.

Maybe Mr. Ghost would keep Hestle company, but she wasn't about to let him try. The dimes on her ankles, which Redhead would inherit along with the amethyst ring, would take care of Mr. Ghost. He was probably still at the spring contemplating "nothin." Father arranged a nice plot in the McLain cemetery so she could be buried with her "people," as she called them. She died in the early 1950s.

In this ambience and local society it was totally inadmissible to say publicly that one loved a black person. But love Hestle I did, and respected her as a human being. One day when we were alone I dared ask her the question: "Hestle, whatcha gonna do when you get to Heaven?" Contrary to some doubt among local churchgoers, I believed that when we all died and began the journey to heaven, surely, she would go with us. Not blinking an eye, she retorted sardonically "Well, I hope there won't be none o them gossipin folks who are always runnin down yuh daddy."

I never doubted that Hestle had a soul like mine, but that was a subject we didn't discuss. Yet, she couldn't sit at meals with us, or, when unescorted, enter the front door when not at work. She sat behind the stove and ate and listened, reacted, and participated in our conversation, eating the cornmeal mush with the hands that had prepared it. As to front doors, like parlors, they weren't used in most Southern homes anyway.

What the "A" stood for in "Mary A. Hestle" she never revealed. I have no photograph, but her countenance is clear in my memory. While combing my recollection for incidents surrounding Hestle's brief years with the family, I thought: *Specific origins, genealogies, histories, and final resting places of black people were of little general interest in that rural backwater.* My experience was different, and I know Hestle was the major reason for that. Her body and soul graced our household. I am sure she perceived our racial bias, but she abided all the same. Like Faulkner's Dilsey, she *endured*, and walked away proudly to a better life.

The last time I remember seeing her was when I was on a break from college. She admonished me, "Scamp, now don't ya go up there and get too much book-learnin." I assured her I wouldn't, but she countered, "If you get too smart for yuh breeches, I'm a comin after ya, Mist Jim!"

Her use of "Mist Jim" startled me; no more "Scamp." I responded accordingly: "Yes, Mary!" and I threw my arms around her. The word "Hestle" just didn't sound right anymore.

Uncle Bo

"JIM. JIM!" HE EXCLAIMED PLAINTIVELY as he pulled up his shorts hurriedly to hide his hot rod. "Jim," he begged, "you won't tell nobody bout this, will you?" I was on my way back from feeding hogs on Sand Ridge and had stumbled upon him and a high school dropout in Lovers Cluster, a patch of bushes behind the field on the Old Mobile Road. It was a favorite spot; I had discovered others "at it" while passing by this lovely nook.

"No, sir!" I assured him. I understood his amorous proclivities, even though I was only eight.

Uncle Bo was always one step ahead of respect, two steps ahead of a real job.

Born in 1906, Bo grew to hate his given name. His mother wanted him christened Robert Edward after Robert E. Lee, the great Confederate general. But his father had a friend, Eugene, and persuaded his wife to make the switch to Robert Eugene, which became Bobby Gene. Only his mamma could tolerate little "Gene" for more than five minutes, and knowing of his lack of love for his name, she began calling him "Boy," which was soon shortened to "Bo."

At the turn of the century, birth certificates hardly existed in rural Greene County, and he was never officially recorded. His name, nevertheless, appeared in the family Bible; otherwise it was just "Bo." Those who wanted to saddle him with first-name handles were brushed off by his inborn legerdemain. If anyone ever used "Bobby Gene," he quickly cut them off with "Don't call me that!" Later in life he incorporated Bo into all his legal matters. Once a special delivery letter came to Neely post office addressed to B. G. Hillman, only to be returned as "unknown."

It was, indeed, the best of times in Neely, and Bobby Gene was to the manor born. In Southern households, a father's doting focused on the youngest female. However, in this case, Eugenia was pushed aside by her younger brother. Perhaps Bobby Gene had usurped his sister's privileged place in the family hierarchy while at the same time rejecting her name. Or maybe he simply hated being called by Eugenia's name.

In short order, such deference to Bo melded into tolerance; tolerance gave way to teenage permission; and permission ultimately became adult support. Charles Hillman's local empire flourished in the boom days around World War I. Prohibition, or what we called "the Noble Experiment," made no impact on Bo's finances, but there were other ways to spend his money. To pull off his carousing, Bo spent it widely at Greene County's few fancy haberdasheries, such as Rounsaville's. After he showed up in church wearing a bow tie and straw katie, people began calling him the Beau Brummell of Neely. In the flapper twenties he courted the daughters of farmers as far away as Hattiesburg and mythical Vinegar Bend across the Chickasawhay River in Alabama.

But the container of my Grandpa's fortune really sprang a leak in the 1920s with Bo's discovery of check writing, and with his ability to flawlessly sign his father's name. When he wasn't writing checks on Grandpa, Bo could convince "Pa" to purchase anything to support his lifestyle. That included buying a horseless carriage, one of the first in the village. So, when he came home from Churchwell Auto with the latest Model T Ford, it was: "Watch out! Here *he* comes!" Free-ranging chickens beware. Even hogs and other animals were in danger on the roads.

Being his father's driver and handyman helped him avoid plowing mules and the cotton field for a while. Although he was able to hold farm work at bay, he did manage Grandpa's several properties. Harvesting timber provided occasional spending money.

Grandpa's support fed his son's indulgence, and that indulgence inhabited a restless body and mind. As his "young buck" persona grew in the community, many old-timers wondered whether he would be a Hillman or a Green, the high-strung, hard-drinking Irish who came up the rivers to Greene County. But in reality, few were critical of Uncle Charlie's offspring. Just about everyone liked him for his ability to entertain. His favorite antic was to mimic a famous silent movie actor, for which he was soon dubbed with the nickname "Buster." A charming adolescence characterized Bo's entire life. He never grew up, and the lack of interest in the world beyond Neely doomed him to insularity and a closed society.

Bo had entered school a year late, was slow in academics, and always tried to skip formal class work. Eventually he made it to high school and, with cousins Herman and Guy "Railroad" Green, composed three-fifths of the local basketball team. Mr. O. U. Sullivan, of the infamous Sullivan's Hollow caboodle in Smith County (think Hatfields and McCoys), came as principal to Neely High School in the mid-1920s. During Sullivan's first week the three set out deliberately to test him. First, during recess, they drew a crowd by singing "My Old Kentucky Home," mocking Sullivan's high-pitched voice, like he sang during daily chapel. Then they played hooky, intending to meet at Herman's house in the afternoon. Sullivan headed them off on the railroad track that passed in back of the school.

The next morning, he called them into his office, took off his belt. "Weep no more, my lady," Sullivan squeaked to himself as, one by one, he gave each a strapping. Bo laughed each time he repeated the incident. When he heard about it, Grandpa walked over to the school, confronted Sullivan, and told him, "Hands off my boy, you Smith County bastid! Or you'll be back where you came from quicker'n you'd like!"

One of the teachers whom Sullivan employed was a Miss Emma Jane Lowry from Hattiesburg, who became involved with Bo's education, although she taught the lower grades. My mother, new in Neely High School that year, taught him English. (During this time, Mother got to know his real character. And Bo, thereafter, always looked pained whenever Agnes's name came up. An appropriate analogy is that she was the hawk and he the chicken.) But her attempt at teaching him to conjugate verbs was futile. Today, I wonder how much my mother assisted in the conjugation of Emma Jane and Bo. While still in high school, Bo convinced the twenty-five-year-old Miss Lowry to marry him.

Emma had been accustomed to an upscale farm life in Pearl River County, with occasional visits to New Orleans. To offset the loss of that lifestyle, Bo promised to build her a "Pink Bungalow" on property his pa had given them as a wedding present, implying they would live there happily ever after. She loved him far beyond his deserving, beyond the comprehension of most, and married him for "better or worse." It was often the latter. Sadly, it had all begun as a grand ruse to assuage his aching hormones, and to prove himself worthy to the community. Beau Brummell had come to life. Bo had veneered his reality with his dreams.

The bungalow got started, a simple cottage just across the public road from his parents' Big House (later burned) and just up the road from Neely village. Charles Hillman footed the bill for the bungalow—not pink but yellow in color—which remained unfinished because of the Crash in 1929. I remember crawling all over the loft looking for holes in the roof when the big rains came. Once I found a keg of home brew that Bo had hidden, and from which he quaffed when nobody was around.

Depressions like that of the 1930s are uncommon, but Bo treated life as if there were no Depression, surviving by his wit. At my father's insistence, he signed up with the Federal Emergency Rehabilitation Administration in the early FDR years and bought a mule that was always outfoxing him. Mules are like that. One day Father and I were passing by a field where he was plowing and asked how things were going. Bo lamented: "It's the first hot day we've had and she's givin it to me already."

A garden saved his family, like it did everybody in those days. And it was Emma who brought home the check—sometimes a $40-per-month warrant—to be discounted for cash by those with money. Bo was too undisciplined to hold down a job with the Works Progress Administration (WPA). Or any real job for that matter. Once, he took a position as muleskinner for one of the oil companies, laying pipe from Texas to the East Coast. Tough work. At noon on the first day, he assessed the job situation and the effort involved and told the straw boss, "I won't be back after lunch." Bo told Father and me that night, "Danned if I'm gonna work like a dog the rest of my life."

This one half-day's employment got Bo his Social Security number. He began drawing Social Security at the minimum age.

Grandpa's death in 1935 played havoc with Bo's gravy train, and he had to look for new props on which to lean. Enter my father. Proving his astuteness once again, Bo persuaded Kim Daughdrill, a brother-in-law who lived near us at Thad Hill, to trade properties so that he might be near his brother. He idolized Bud and came to be even more dependent on him. He obtained a pickup truck and began to horse trade, which became a feverish activity as times got better after World War II. But the Prodigal Son in his nature never changed. Father excoriated him for his irresponsible actions one day, only to "kill the fatted calf" the next.

Once, Bo came to our house with a truckload of fat cattle, laughing, and bragging how he had made a great deal, a "Jake Rubenstein," he said, referring to a mythical peddler who always got it for you "wholesale." Father took one look and said, "Where'd you get them animals? They look like Old Man Dan Roberts's stock." Bo confessed, "I told Mr. Roberts that you said it would be okay to pick them up." Father ordered, "Take em back, right now! Don't unload em; take em back!" My father was scrupulous about people taking advantage of backwoodsmen and rural families. In his mind, Bo had degenerated into becoming a scalper.

My most intimate recollections of Bo—I always called him BGH to myself—were during my early teens. I was essentially his flunky on winter Saturday jaunts to the Leaf River swamp, and a companion to more pleasant environs like the Brushy Creek swimming hole. Somehow I felt he looked up to me, although I was twelve and he was thirty. Maybe he admired my intellectual and studious nature. As we rode through McLain in his Model A, he would say, "Jim, jump out and get me a can of Prince Albert." He smoked but didn't drink. I became a different type of challenge for his cunning. He knew that I knew about all his shenanigans and pettifoggery, his sexual deviations, and his horse-trading chicanery. I certainly was a dependable buddy, and an assuagement to Agnes's resentment about his mooching off her husband. Uncle Bo was equally at home hunting squirrel and trapping wild hogs, bartering mules with Farm Security Administration bureaucrats, or surreptitiously seducing any female who looked his direction.

"Jim, I bought a cow over at Pumpkin Center. C'mon and help me load her." It was common knowledge that only old people and a few scattered blacks lived in the woods across Atkinson Creek. But Bo knew an unwed mother, Molly Jacobs, who owned cattle.

We drove up to the house and Bo began clearing his throat and spitting. Chuck and Lum, her two boys, wandered out front as he dismounted and commanded, "You boys run over there to the pasture and drive them cows to the barn; Molly and me will settle." It took about thirty minutes for us to round up the herd. When we had penned them, Bo and Molly emerged from the back porch. Both appeared *quite* "settled."

One of the weirdest of his ploys was when he was caught under the schoolhouse in Neely with the young sister of the wife of the new basketball coach. To evade the clutches of the coach and the law itself, Bo played "crazy." He faked insanity and began to speak in tongues and to talk with Jesus. He escaped to Emma's old home in Hattiesburg (where he continued to chase women), and it was six months before my father and I went by night to fetch him back to Neely. Fortunately, the coach's one-year contract had run out and the entire family had left town. Bo's sanity returned, and within a year he was back to selling the same old soap.

I took Bo's indiscretions and apparent hormonal needs to be natural; he was an over-sexed Peter Pan who substituted fun for work, and whose parents and siblings, including my father, his "crutch" after Grandpa's death, could never manage or regulate. Nor could his wife and family, or the preacher, have much effect on him. His thinking was seldom above that of a teenager, and perhaps that is why I understood him, sex drive and all.

He tricked me many times, but never in matters involving Aristotelian virtue. I went along with him under the pretense and promise of his fictitious reward system (usually "two bits next Saturday"), but I could never reject him. Such was the hold he had on me through Charles Hillman, my grandpa, and his beloved brother Bud, my father. He used me, but never maliciously, to fudge on life's roll of the dice that had made him just *Bo*, when *Bobby Gene* might have been a *Somebody*.

His habits varied little with the years, and Emma's death presented no barrier to his gallivantin. Under the pretense of feeding Bud's hogs on Sand Ridge, he would pass old haunts and reminisce. Well into his sixties, he met and married a teenage cousin and life began anew. But he never stopped visiting the Lover's Cluster until he got too old to get out of his pickup.

The last time I saw him was when I dropped by Neely on a trip to New Orleans. He was in a rocking chair and could hardly walk. When I drove up in a fancy rental car, he recognized me immediately. Ambling to the front yard gate, he looked me straight in the eye for the first time in his life, threw his arms around me, and sobbed loudly, "Jim, darling boy, you're just like him. Bud'll never die till you do!"

Humoring a Mule

IN MY EIGHTH AND NINTH YEARS I spent time during the summers helping Grandpa with many farm chores at Old House. I enjoyed helping him draw water from the well, chop stove wood, select collards for supper, make a brush broom from gallberry bushes, sharpen hoes with a file, and slop the hogs. But I enjoyed even more watching him work with mules. He seemed to be able to read their minds. When we were alone at the barn, Grandpa entertained me by slipping an ear of corn through a stall door to a mule, all with one amused eye on me.

I was learning the fundamentals of farm life. And I felt closest to Grandpa, and most grown up, when we plowed together. I recall a time we were in the cornfield near the barn when suddenly he began talking about mules as if he were giving me a lesson in life.

"There ain't no ruse, no trick, no angle, nothin ever done by a human bein on the farm that a mule ain't already thought of first, and used years before ya. They're wilier than a hog, but not as smart," he mumbled. "I been plowin em since I had to raise m'arms to reach the plough handles, and should know. I learnt more from em than from most men, but wouldn't trust one any mor'n I would a man, neither. One day they're slobberin all over ya for an ear o corn, and the next kickin yo guts out for no reason whatsoever. Now an' then ya wanna shoot em, but catch y'self, knowin you can't do without em. M'dad tried oxen for fieldwork when he come over here from Alabama, but they're too slow and dumb. He also tried horses, but they eat expensive oats and cain't stand the heat and flies. So we're stuck with these crossbreed bastids, and nobody can make a crop o anything without em. This'n here ain't bad. Old Mattie is the best I ever had. Outwork any man all day, and at sundown wants to frolic. And she ain't no colt!"

Plowing corn with a 1930s Georgia stock.

Grandpa emphasized *colt* and continued: "Watch them blades o cornstalk, Dick, they'll cut yo face like a razor. And walk just a little farther forward so you won't catch so much dust. Yeah, this'n is special; had her for five years, and she's never missed a day; summer 'r winter. Special she is, heah me? Bought'er with another'n, blacker and littler called Maude, but that'n ain't half the mule Matt is. Bought em as a pair for loggin, but that other un can't pull her side o the tree. Main problem is that only I can muzzle and hitch er. Everybody else is too scared to try. She knows that, too. Turned on Charlie Brown, and kicked'im in the nuts. I had to take'im to see McLeod. So, you be careful around this here mule, boy. I'll teach ya how to handle er."

With that promise, he paused, and we made another round of plowing corn in the field across from Old House before we would "take out," the local expression for quitting time.

The routine for me in early May after the school year had ended was to go to Grandpa's and help on the farm. He and the mule plowed corn. I listened, observed, and followed, barefoot in the next furrow, always with a row of cornstalks between us. My nostrils filled with the smell of the earth, the corn's chlorophyll, and mule sweat. I was primarily company to the grandfather I loved and admired, but I was also a ready arm to assist him with any job that an eight-year-old could handle. "Fetch me a bucket o water from the well, and bring the gourd dipper," he would command.

There was no market for timber, as the Depression had already set in. Charles Hillman had to rely on working his own land. Chores abounded for my pair of young hands. I pulled weeds, sometimes until my hands bled. I scraped grassy debris from the shaft of the plough and heel-sweep or the turning plough. I did it all. Grandpa, like most farmers, used a rather primitive single-horse cultivator that hadn't changed much since the Middle Ages. Sometimes I carried an old towel or a worn piece of cotton garment so he could wipe the sweat from his face. Or, I toted dogwood branches or other broadleaf bushes, with which he vigorously fanned himself and the mule at each row's end. When horseflies were bad, I carried a tree frond to swat the insects from the mules.

The salesman had led Grandpa to believe that Matt and Maud were sisters, and would perform the same. Uncle Charlie should have known better, since used-mule salesmen were a cut below secondhand car salesmen. Maud never reached her promised potential and died an early death. Matt had to go it alone, and it was as if she was aware of that. She was a super mule in every sense: work, play, mischief making, cunning, aggravation, and charm.

Not everyone in Neely respected mules like Grandpa, however. In what Aunt Nora called a "scanal on earth," Riley Grant, Jonas Boxer, and some other drunk rowdies cut off the tails of four mules, including Jon Eakes's "Old Puss." The farmers and their families were at the Methodist church during the annual revival, what we called the "protractive meeting," deeply immersed in what they thought to be the Lord's wishes for their lives. Perhaps in time the farmers forgot the cruelty, but if the mules were like Matt, they never would. Mules have long memories. Matt's brain was no exception.

"Come ere, Dick, I wanna teach ya how to harness a mule," Grandpa called one morning from the barn. Before daylight, I normally took Matt to water, shucked five ears of corn and put them in her trough for a breakfast, before heading to Grandma Ginny's kitchen for my own breakfast. Matt had long ago tested wills with Grandpa and come out the loser, learning from the experience of several whacks with a stick across her ears. Grandpa's size, voice, countenance, and demeanor made all the difference when dealing with her.

"Remember, Dick. Never blindside a mule!" he started, as he walked around to Matt's head and patted her shoulder. "First, bridle her," he continued, slipping the leather straps over her ears, "and then put the bit between her teeth so that she'll adjust it in back of er mouth, behind er teeth. Okay, let me see you do it."

He handed me the bridle and I accepted it measuredly. Matt pricked up her ears as I approached her head. Thinking I could bribe her, I pulled an ear of corn from my overalls and offered it, but she wasn't buyin, and gave a warning whinny. Grandpa said, "She's got your number; got you buffaloed, boy. Here, gimme them reins." I backed away as Grandpa gave her a knuckle to her nose bridge, and she dropped her ears and uttered a chortle. "Offer her the corn now," he said. I did, and she grabbed it with her massive teeth, after which I slipped the bridle on her. I had won a tactical victory but not the war.

"After rubbin'er neck down and cleanin it, next ya put on the collar." Grandpa hefted the leather oval over Matt's neck. "Be sure it fits so it won't rub a sore. Now the hames—these pieces of metal and wood have been around a long time with plow mules and oxen so be sure y'fit em right. Tie the hames string tight, and see that the traces are well hooked to the hames with no kinks in em. The traces are ready to hook to the singletree. Be sure to check the back and belly bands. And the last thing ya do is look er over from top to bottom to see she don't have no injuries." With that he proceeded to hitch Matt to a singletree and the plow. We seldom muzzled our workstock. Ours were all single, one-mule cultivators. For Grandpa, it was one on one, man and mule.

At the end of the day, I had to water, wallow, feed, as well as inspect the mule's body. Charles Hillman's mules always had to be led to water in the fresh spring at the head of the branch between Old House and the Carr Place. Grandpa admonished, "Wait there til she gets enough, boy. You'll know she's full when she lifts her head about the third time and starts nibblin grass on the bank o the spring."

Grandpa cautioned me to always keep my eyes on Matt's eyes. "Be sure to take her to that wallerin hole and let *my* mule roll over twice

before you get er up. Y'heah me?" I allowed her to roll in a familiar
spot of soft sand. The cool sand seemed to provide tonic to her skin.
Matt took up to fifteen minutes to wallow, before she rose on her
haunches, stood and shook the dirt off, rolled her eyes toward the
barn, and thought about dinner.

Matt got preference when it came to feeding. I gave her generous
portions of hay and corn, as Grandpa always gruffly reminded me:
"Be sure *my* mule gets forty yers o corn, and be sure all th'shucks are
off em. Big yers; and feed *her* befo ya feed them othern."

Matt was both a constant and transcendent force during my childhood with my grandfather, and she became my bridge to him after
he died.

My father inherited some of Grandpa's farm property, including
Matt. Soon and inevitably, we could see that she longed for her
master and the comfort of that home. The problem was that all
this was now gone. Grandpa and Old House were no longer the
Gibraltar-Mecca she had known.

She liked to escape from our Thad Hill, and we always had to
chase her as far as Neely and the barn at Old House, corralling and
bridling her in some corner before leading her back to our farmstead.
This happened over and over. "Whoa. Whoa! Matt. Daddy, come
quickly, she's gone again," I would yell, as she jerked the rope out of
my hand with a quick flick of the head, her ears pricked up to their
wild form. She would run through the barn gate, jump a low wire
pasture fence, and head for the road to Old House.

Adding insult, she refused to let anyone ride her. I could read
Matt's thinking clearly, written between those alert eyes. I was certain
of what she was thinking during those treks back to Thad Hill, and
away from Charles Hillman's ghost: *Homo sapiens is so dumb! I can
do whatever I please with these children.*

While leading her back one day, I decided to put down in *my*
words what *she* was thinking:

> Y'aint dealin with hogs when y'dealin with me
> Hogs're caught in a pen while I gallop free,
> Other farm animals they're such fools
> Ain't got half the sense of mules;

Kickin my heels high, frolickin free
No gee, haw, haw; no haw, gee, gee,
Free o' them boys–they're easy t'shake,
Outta this barnyard, I'm on the make.

When my brothers and I went off to college, then into World War II, my father was left to hold things together. Most of the farm eventually went fallow, so there was little left at Thad Hill to justify Matt's keep. And she was aging. In deference to Grandpa, Father dared not turn her over to the rendering plant for the war effort. It was beyond question to sell her, or exchange her for money. That would have been a dishonor to Charles Hillman's spirit. He finally loaned her to a neighbor, "saw-sharpener" Charlie Breland. Charlie got Matt, and the high-pitched sound of metal-on-metal must have been music to her ears.

She lived well past her thirty-fifth year, a very long life for a mule. From time to time, when visiting Mississippi, I caught a glimpse of her. She had grown thin and submissive, outfitted with blinders and hitched to a simple wagon. It was a metamorphosis beyond Charles Hillman's moral acceptance. I could hear him say, "Unhitch my dan mule, take her to the barn, and shuck her a trough full o corn."

What We Ate
Back Then

ON A HOT AND HUMID JUNE SUNDAY IN 1934, Aunt Liz invited us for dinner. The day was typical and routine—preaching, then eating. The females busied themselves cleaning up and washing dishes before moving out to the porch swing and oak settee to fan and to gossip. Men and boys retired to the shade of a large oak at the far end of a backyard that bordered briar and wood at the old Byrd Place. Everyone had shared in the heavy after-church dinner. Fried chicken, mashed potatoes and gravy, a mix of okra and butter beans, green beans, collards, cornbread sticks, and biscuit as the main course, washed down with sweetened iced tea. Then pecan pie with whipped cream for dessert. There was the usual tobacco smoking and chewing, but cousin Preston wasn't participating.

I watched as cousin Preston methodically folded the ring and small fingers of his right hand across his palm, leaving middle and index digits unbent, free to perform an ancient remedy for overburdened stomachs. Sheepishly, he turned away, moved to the backyard fence, leaned over, poked the extended fingers down his gullet, and proceeded to throw up everything Aunt Liz had so carefully prepared for us. We dispersed back to the house. Possums and yard chickens took care of the cleaning up.

Most of us accomplished similar stomach relief, but with tidier consequences and less violent measures, such as bicarbonate of soda and other "sour stomach" concoctions. Although he carried a nickel snuffbox of Arm & Hammer in his shirt pocket, a finger was still the tried-and-true prescription for cousin Preston.

In our southern Mississippi culture, it was all about eating—the sensation, the pleasure (and sometimes displeasure) of stuffing our stomachs with the food that the Lord had provided, He who had "blessed the hands that had prepared those victuals." We knew about food if not nutrition. Its production involved simple agriculture, horticulture, and animal science. Procuring food from markets was another matter, its digestion and ultimate utility yet another. The modern cosmology of nutrition and diet and the art of cooking was yet a lifetime away for us.

Ours was a small subsistence farm; we sold little of what we grew. Most of it we either ate or fed to our animals—including corn tops and grasses. Cotton and cucumbers were the crops we consistently planted for sale. But the cuke market was marginal, almost nonexistent, and there were times during harvest that the word went out from the plant in Wiggins for farmers not to bother picking them. I didn't like the stoop labor of cucumber growing and now find it amusing that "stoop labor" became a dirty term. Working cotton, cucumbers, crosscut saws, and crookneck hoes, with back bent, was all I ever knew.

Other markets were tough as well. Once Uncle Till Hathorn decided to plant an acre of squash on his small farm at Neely, in the hope of peddling it in McLain, about seven miles away across Leaf River, which had to be negotiated by mule and wagon. When time came for the squash harvest, he left before dawn and spent the day in front of McLain's artesian fountain. Most of the town's 125 or so residents had no money, and toward sunset not a squash had been sold. Till, a man of determination but also of reckoning, headed home. As he crossed the bridge again, he said "Whoa!" to the mule and proceeded to dump about five hundred pounds of squash into the river.

The predominant part of our diet came from plants, which we consumed directly. Our principal source of food came from a garden set apart from the cultivated fields. The garden was, by Southern tradition, a woman's enterprise, and ours was strictly Mother's domain. She managed it hands-on and worked it as necessary, often commandeering help from children, field hands, and even passersby. But these she never trusted with the selecting, picking, and preservation processes. Father seldom entered the garden, except to see that she had planted turnip greens and mustard greens and collards for the winter.

Mother planted other vegetables in early spring, some even in summer, and cultivated and tended them accordingly, mainly beans

Gardening collards in Gulfport, Mississippi, ca. 1925.

and peas, leafy vegetables, and tomatoes. She directed us in planting black-eyed peas, crowders (yellow and purple hulled), cowpeas, and English peas. Generally speaking, beans you snap, peas you shell. Often, in midgrowth, the hull of the pea will neither snap nor yield its seed easily. Once, while we were shelling peas for "putting up" in jars (we never "canned" anything), one of my young schoolmates, Byron Smith, said to my mother, "Miz Agnes, I don't mind shelling these peas and I don't mind snapping them, but I sure do hate them neithers." He referred, of course, to the tough-hulled pods that could not be easily shelled or snapped. Henceforth, a "neither" became Hillman household jargon for a contrary person who couldn't make up his mind or who refused to take a position on a controversial issue.

Butter beans, a type of Lima bean, were the most popular of all the beans and peas we grew. We ate them fresh, preserved them in jars, or dried them for future meals. Other beans, like kidneys, pintos, and black beans, were not a part of our culture. Mother usually cooked leafy vegetables in a large iron pot. "Pot likker" was a by-product of greens that she boiled with pork fatback, a favorite of aging males and preachers. Maybe the preachers enjoyed vicariously anything called "likker" in our Victorian environment.

The Hillman garden always had a variety of root crops: beets, turnips, radishes, onions in all forms, and Irish potatoes. Tomatoes were basic and were eaten regularly, fresh and preserved. We also grew okra every year. If there was one vegetable we considered almost indispensable, it was "okry." It was not only the soul food ingredient critical for Creole dishes, gumbos, soups, and vegetable mixtures, it also stood on its own as an important dish: steamed, fried, frittered, even pickled. No decent restaurant in New Orleans and Gulf Coast country dared not serve an okra dish.

Crop fields on the farm supplemented our garden. These fields never exceeded ten acres, and bushy areas and forests often surrounded them. They were small compared to those in some parts of Mississippi, like the Delta. We grew corn in these fields, a basic food necessary for our dietary well-being. It was of no special variety. We didn't plant corn specifically for human consumption. Our eating it was incidental to the corn we grew for hogs and mules, which we dried. We picked our fresh corn off the same plant from which we later harvested the so-called field corn. Our favorite way of eating fresh corn, in addition to boiled corn on the cob at mealtime, was to roast it. Mature ears were roasted in the oven, or over an open fire for between-meal snacks. We called them "roast'n ears," and we needed a strong set of teeth to gnaw the roast-toughened grains from the cob.

But most of the corn my family ate came in the form of cornbread and grits, after the ears had been shucked, shelled, and stored in the crib. A weekly ritual was going to the mill with two sacks of corn: one for meal, the other grits. Especially inviting was going to the crib on a wet Saturday morning in winter. Under the supervision of my father, we piled the ears in three heaps. The select ears went for seed, to be planted the next spring. Seed ears had to be long, straight, and large, with rows of grain perfectly aligned and without blemish. That first pile of corn was sacrosanct. Often seed ears were exchanged with a neighbor for an equivalent amount of their corn, as farmers had learned by long experience that planting one's own seed corn year after year resulted in genetic deterioration. Continually using the same variety brought on small irregular ears and nubbins. Nubbins were undesirable runt-ears of corn, and the word "nubbin" was considered demeaning. If you really wanted to belittle someone, you called him a "nubbin."

The second pile of corn was for meal, and the third for grits, which could include inferior grains, since they were going to be boiled and softened anyway. There was no avoiding grits in the Hillman household. They were pervasive. At the gristmill on Saturdays, Mr. Bill Lambert ground the corn, first setting the mill mechanism, or the cogs, to yield coarser bits for grits, then a much finer setting for meal. His toll for grinding was a quart or so per peck of the corn ground, or about 15 percent. We never owned a hand or mechanical corn sheller, and my hands were calloused from shelling corn off the cob.

We had competition for our corn. Woodpeckers, blue jays, and crows helped themselves if we didn't constantly guard the fields. Scarecrows were worthless. Raccoons came by night. Particularly destructive was a weevil that infested the corn after it was in the crib. We tried many home remedies against weevils, even snuff, or powdered tobacco, scattered on the crib floor, but never any arsenic. Rats and mice were rampant, but we had cats, snakes, and rattraps to deal with them.

Among the cornrows, sometimes after lay-by, we planted watermelons. Some of my most exhilarating experiences as a child happened when we discovered a "volunteer" watermelon on a frosty morning in late October among the dense field growth of cornstalks and weeds. We always busted it open then and there with our fists and devoured its heart, but little more.

Sweet potatoes, or yams, of African origin, ran a close second to corn for carbohydrate energy in our diet. Father devoted plots of "new ground" to them, acreage largely turned over to hogs for finishing in October. (The hogs' rooting exposed stumps and tree roots to the elements in winter, resulting in less-obstructed soil with smooth tilth more receptive to the plow.) Sweet potatoes were not labor intensive, except at planting and harvest. We usually planted them on days too wet for plowing.

Since we always harvested large quantities of sweet potatoes for family use, banking them was necessary. Potatoes are bulky and heavy, so the bank was always located in a convenient place usually not far

Bud and Agnes eating watermelon, ca. 1925.

from the barn or the house. Ground for the bank had to be well drained and level and about six feet in diameter. We removed several inches of dirt and replaced it with pine straw and leaves to make a soft, dry bed for the potatoes and protect them from moisture below. At the same time, we placed a pole (usually a wooden shaft) in the center on which a roof eventually rested. We then piled potatoes on this carpet to form a conical shape. No particular amount was required for a bank, but usually ten or fifteen bushels (forty to sixty pecks) of clean, dry potatoes seemed about right. To complete the process, heaps of straw or leaves were evenly distributed as a cover, and slats or boards were placed close together over them.

A third mainstay of our diet was sugarcane syrup (we never said "molasses") and honey, which were always on the table. Sugarcane was an annual crop of the Hillman clan, and it took several acres to provide our syrup needs, at least twenty-five gallons per year. We made two types: Old Blue Ribbon, a lighter syrup, and sorghum, or blackstrap. One of my favorite childhood activities was syrup making, an event that took place every fall. It brought together diverse elements of the community. Loosely speaking, syrup was our salvation.

Aunt Cynt (Cynthia) Bradley was the local syrup maker, and she accepted payment in kind (one-fourth of the syrup) for her services, which included providing the cane-squeezing grinder-mill, the cooking pan-oven, and her time, but did not include the mule to pull the grinder. My brothers and I sat at the mill and fed cane into the massive cogs as the mule circled in its harness to power the mechanism. Juice flowed from the machine by a funnel to a large barrel, and we dipped it out with a bucket at appropriate times to take to a smaller barrel at one end of the oven.

Converting sugarcane juice into good syrup takes a delicate touch, and Aunt Cynt was without equal. She held the secret to cooking the juice properly, and on a good day she could produce thirty-five gallons of syrup. The juice was released from a spigot into a pan atop the oven. Aunt Cynt hovered over the process, sweet steam rising around her. She removed the scum, impurities, by skimming it off with a square copper ladle and placing it in a hole dug near the oven.

We took care that cattle could not come and drink this sweet liquid. It was fatal to bovines; though I have seen hogs get drunk on fermented cane skimmings. We had fun maintaining the flow of the soon-to-be syrup by pushing it along with wooden T-shaped paddles. The syrup finally flowed into a new gallon can at the lower end of the pan, ready to be poured onto cornbread or biscuit. But the best part was when we lifted the paddle from the pan, wiped a bit of syrup off with an index finger, and licked it clean.

Honey was a luxury, but Mother preferred it to syrup. Like syrup, honey had its light and dark consistencies, each with its own

Crushing sugarcane by mule power to make syrup.

distinctive taste. Grandfather placed beehives on a number of his small farms around our village, from which came the light clover-type honeys. The old Turner Place on the margins of Leaf River swamp was one such small farm of Grandfather's, where a tenant lived only occasionally. At one time Grandfather owned thirteen beehives at that ancient house, but lack of care and pests wiped out the bees during the Depression.

Robbing bees was a task I looked forward to in early summer, an activity that took our minds off menial and boring chores. Grandpa took honey from the hives near the farm fields, and he let us help him cut the large combs from the built-in recesses of wooden slats in the hive. It was good practice never to take all the honey, as the bees needed a full supply on which to survive the winter. For me, going to the Turner Place for honey was special, because the drive there meant meandering through the woods on narrow trails in our Model A. Leaves from overhanging tree limbs brushed against my face as I rode standing on the running board. We also occasionally got honey from a "bee tree."

Discovering bee trees and extracting their treasure is a story-world of its own. We called them bee trees, but in reality wild bees made their honey in many vacant spots or containers, such as tree stumps, a tight nook in a hay barn, or an old log, but never in the ground. Robbing a real bee tree was exciting, not just because we got the day off from plowing, but also because Father insisted on asking a neighbor, Mr. Felder Breland, for help. To get at the honey, we often had to saw down a tree, and his expertise and strength were necessary. We children took great delight in watching "Felder," as we called him, go through an elaborate dressing and smoke-making routine, preparatory for the job, talking to himself and others all the while, and building bravado by insisting "Bees don't sting Felder Breland!" After we felled the tree and sawed into the hive, Felder rushed in with a smoking torch, veiled face, and gloved hands, muttering, "Just you watch Felder Breland git this honey!" Raking bees from his hands as we egged him on, and chanting, "Bees don't sting Felder, bees don't sting Felder," he dug the dark, gooey stuff from the recesses where the bees had stored it.

Pork, chicken, beef, and mutton—in that order—supplemented our diet of grain, vegetables, and fruit. Father would say, "We need to kill a pork," or "kill a beef," or "kill a mutton," always using the name of the meat, not the animal. Hogs provided the largest share of our meat dishes, which included the offal, the backbone, souse or hogshead cheese, and chitterlings.

That unique Southern dish, chitterlings, a favorite of my father and our helper, Mary Hestle, required special preparation. Many a time did I help Mary with "ridding guts." Immediately after the hog's slaughter, we turned its small intestines inside out to scrub the rough, thick organ with brush and vinegar water. After several rinses we cut this long, ropey hog gut into two-to-three-inch pieces and boiled them thoroughly. The odor was strong, reminding one somewhat of the barnyard from which the animal came. We seasoned some of the chitterlings with salt, pepper, and onion and served them with beets or turnips. The rest we fried in deep fat, often covering them with Tabasco or Worcestershire sauce.

As a change from pork, our family was fond of mutton. We never used the word "lamb," regardless of the animal's age. The Hillmans had grazed sheep on public and private lands for more than a century. As with hogs, there was nothing scientific about their management and care. We slaughtered them for special events or holidays. In late spring, as I arrived home from college, there was always "a mutton for Jim," my father's expression analogous to the fatted calf for the Prodigal Son. I was obliged to participate in the ceremony, which took place down the pasture slope in a clump of trees near the branch where water was available.

Our slaughter of cloven-footed animals followed centuries-old procedure. In this case, we hung the sheep by its rear legs with rope, using a singletree, swivel, and pulley to hoist it to an upside-down position a foot or so off the ground. Slashing its throat in this position assured that as much blood as possible escaped. We skinned, gutted, beheaded it on the spot, and cut the carcass into quarters. The offal of sheep was of little utility to us, and we carried it into the woods for vultures to enjoy a decent meal.

We ate chicken year-round: fried, roasted, or, in the case of older birds, stewed. My dad had a taste for fat pork and was not fond of chicken, one reason being his disdain for its eating habits. If chicken was served too frequently, he would say, "I don't want no dadgum chicken again before . . ." and specify some specific future date. Ours were so-called yard chickens that grazed freely around the house, barn, pasture, and cow lot. People who today demand cage-free eggs or free-range birds probably have no idea about the scavenging nature of chickens. Chickens, like possums, are omnivores, eating everything available. We put birds for consumption in a coop and fed them grain for a couple of weeks to "clean em out," as Father would say.

My younger brother and I liked to compete for the role of chicken executioner. On these days, our mother took a chicken from the coop, tied its legs together, and hung it from the limb of a dogwood tree in the pasture. She then handed a hatchet with a sharp blade to the "lucky" boy, who severed its head and darted quickly aside to escape the blood, which flew far and wide as the headless chicken flapped, wiggled, and writhed. Many a chicken breathed his last in the copse behind our house. Today, I still wonder what induced two God-loving farm boys to find such seeming pleasure in beheading chickens, in slashing sheeps' throats, and in stunning hog or cow.

We rarely ate beef, because it was too expensive. And the lack of refrigeration was another barrier to the slaughter of large animals.

We had a few cattle of beef type, mixed breeds that ranged the woods freely. When we did "kill a beef," it was usually a community affair, and neighbors negotiated among themselves as to when their turn came to kill and to share.

Father insisted on keeping a dairy cow or two, Jersey or Guernsey breed, if possible, for rich milk and butter, which he perceived as important to our health. A pitcher of milk and two eight-inch-in-diameter, inch-thick pones of cornbread were standard fare for supper. Milk, with five percent or more butterfat, and butter were always on the table, and Mother placed several aluminum or porcelain pan-containers in quiet corners with screens to protect them from houseflies.

No refrigeration meant sour milk, cream atop, and nonfat solids floating in liquid below. We churned the cream, producing butter and buttermilk. The nonfat "blue john" wound up as clabber, whey, or in the slop bucket for pig feed. Clabber, that harsh-sounding Gaelic term, had an interesting usage about our village. If you really wanted to insult someone, you could just call him "clabber-headed," which was worse than calling him an imbecile or idiot. Almost as bad as calling him a "nubbin."

During the Depression everyone hunted and fished, in season and out, and we occasionally ate deer, turkey, squirrel, quail, and dove, even possum. Rabbit was never an accepted dish, although we shot many in the bean fields and pea patches in spring. We did, however, eat wild squirrel quite often, shooting them every Saturday in winter from November through February, mostly in the Leaf River swamp on my grandfather's property. At about age ten, I was a special companion to Uncle Bo, and we had a prearranged, noiseless hunting routine. Our usual plan was to rise before dawn and drive to the swamp to "still-hunt" squirrel.

Still-hunting meant that we walked while communicating only by motion of hands and arms. Within minutes we heard the first squirrel bark. Bo motioned me to a particular tree, and I clung stiffly to its trunk, looking up into the oak canopies for movement. Soon an oak nearby was alive with the little animals, and I pointed them out to Bo, who began blasting away. On a typical day we went home with seven or eight squirrels, enough for supper for both families.

After skinning and gutting the squirrels, we removed the eyes, ears, and feet. Mother steamed the entire lot, four or five squirrels, until tender, and then dumped the carcasses into a pot of rice, which was already cooking. Seasoned with onions, pepper, and parsley, the squirrels simmered together with the rice until well blended into a soupy stew. Sometimes Mother prepared squirrel dumplings.

The thought of eating possum makes some people squeamish, but during the hard times of the 1930s many explored the possibility. My father gave Mary Hestle permission to prepare possum on occasion, principally for her own use, but my brothers and I often joined her for the experience. We captured possums mostly on night hunts after the dogs had treed them in a wild persimmon or other tree where they were foraging. Father insisted on penning them for at least two weeks, during which time they were fattened on table scraps and vegetables. The preparation for cooking was not unlike that for squirrel, but the cooking process itself was very different. Mary liked to place the skinned possum on a steel platter and roast it slowly in the oven. When asked, "What does possum taste like?" I reply: "Like possum! Greasy as hell!"

We caught fish—perch, bream, catfish—in many creeks and occasionally in the Leaf River, all before the era of catfish farming. I remember that we ate tiny perch whole, head and all, fried in deep fat. Fishing, however, was poor because of poachers. Even if a family controlled certain wooded or river property, as did my grandfather, poachers kept fish and wildlife populations greatly reduced. It was not until the 1960s, well after World War II and the exodus of people from rural Mississippi, that hunting and fishing returned to what they had been at the turn of the century.

Despite our poverty, both my father and grandfather considered hunting and fishing a waste of time. They weren't real work. Was it a Hillman hang-up or Puritanical vision? Not likely a Victorian constraint, as animal slaughter, even occasional abuse, was never condemned. We rarely fished, except on some Saturday afternoons or when the ground was too wet to plow. My parents valued only the time young boys spent in the fields plowing or in the woods sawing logs. Too much "play" might be a sin. Father had a standard argument against fishing: "Son, you don't wanna spend yo time fishing. Just look at old Parolee Todd. She sits all day on the banks of the Leaf

River with hook, line, sinker, and worm, and doesn't catch nothin. You don't wanna be like that."

Our most plentiful fruit was the pear, a so-called sand pear (*Pyrus pyrifolia*). Until a fungus invaded them in the late 1930s, large pear orchards dotted the landscape along rural roads all over southern Mississippi. My grandfather had such an orchard at the Moody Place. Pears were grown for itinerant truckers, home canning, and hog feed. In 1934 we had a bountiful harvest. I spent hours picking pears, climbing the large trees and pitching each pear to someone on the ground, who placed them carefully in a ten-quart galvanized bucket. After depositing them in croker sacks, we lugged them to the barn and sold them to hawkers who had driven north from Mobile. All for the unbelievably low price of fifty cents per bushel of sixty pounds.

The fruit wound up in Mason jars, because this variety of pear, being coarse and grainy, is best made into preserves. Since the sand pear has almost disappeared from southern Mississippi, it brings a premium price. I have a cousin who preserves several pints when the crop warrants, which happens about once in three years. She uses the preserves as an inducement, along with figs and blue-ribbon molasses, to lure me back home. When I answer the phone in October, an annual call, and Cousin Ruby is on the other end, I know what's coming: "Jim, I have some pear zerves for you. When ya comin to get em? I ain't got no figs for you this year. Too many mockingbirds."

We easily grew figs and certain other Mediterranean fruits, but all were subject to insects and birds. Grandma Ginny had fig trees and made us chase off the birds with our slingshots. She was careful to say, "Don't kill the mockingbirds," which were sacred, though no one knew why. We also grew plums, pomegranates, and mulberry. Ginny had two large quince trees, and her quince preserves were always my favorite, especially on a buttered biscuit.

Wild fruits and nuts grew everywhere but not in sufficient and reliable quantities. Blackberry and huckleberry made very good preserves. We picked berries in midsummer, grapes at summer's end, and nuts in the fall. We also picked chinquapin and hickory nuts. The lovely little chinquapin fell victim to a fungus, *Cryphonectria parasitica*, known as chestnut blight, and is now gone from our woods. Beech mast grew in the swamp, but only hogs foraged upon this tiny nut.

Modern scuppernong arbor.

The vines of the native muscadine, or bullace, wound themselves profusely along the fencerows, and we used the fruit for jelly. The scuppernong was its domesticated equivalent, although scuppernongs were light colored and tended to be sweeter. Like most Southern men of property, my grandfather had a backyard arbor, which grew from a single scuppernong vine that he planted when he built his house. We ate scuppernongs fresh, but Aunt Nora Carr baked a wonderful pastry called grape-hull pie from the fruits. I was about four when Aunt Nora first offered me a piece, and I thought: *How funny, a pie from scuppernong hulls.* It was tart and less sweet than most fruit pies and quite different from mock cherry pie, which is made from grapes. The pie must have tasted good for me to have remembered it for eighty years now.

We bought only a very small portion of our food in the Depression years. These days it is all supermarket and restaurants. Once, the largest single item we purchased was wheat flour. "Self-rising," a local generic term for biscuit flour, came in twenty-four- and forty-eight-pound sacks of loosely woven muslin, which Mother ultimately turned into homemade garments, principally shirts for the males of the family.

Mother used wheat flour for making biscuits every morning. Her daily preparation took place in a large wooden bowl into which she poured a quantity of self-rising flour. In the middle she made a sizeable depression and poured in melted lard by her own measurement, milk, or buttermilk, as needed, then proceeded to mix it all into a consistent dough for baking. Tins were lightly oiled with lard to prevent sticking. The usual baking numbered about twenty-four biscuits, each measuring three to four inches in diameter and an inch thick. It continues yet to amaze me that three growing boys, their dad, and two women could consume such volumes of biscuits.

We occasionally bought unsliced "light bread" loaves (we called any bread not made out of cornmeal "light bread") and other bakery items, such as buns and cinnamon rolls, but these were all luxuries. Rice, sugar, coffee, tea, and condiments, along with some canned items, normally topped our shopping list, but the mix depended on when we had the money. Canned meats and fish were the best buy. We could rarely afford fresh fruits, such as bananas, oranges, or apples. Seeded raisins on the stem came in wooden boxes labeled "Sun Maid" and were sold by the pound, usually at Christmas.

Everything was a nickel: a loaf of bread, a quart of milk, a half dozen eggs, a box of crackers, a Coca-Cola, a box of salt, and so on. A customer usually ordered a "nickel's wurf o'cheese, a quarter's wurf o'sugar." Twenty-five cents bought two No. 2 cans of salmon. (We mixed it with yard eggs for supper or added water until the salmon was soupy, then warmed it and poured the mass over helpings of steamed rice.) Five dollars' worth of groceries filled the back seat of our Model A.

Our local Neely merchant, "Uncle" Albert Harvison, sold food staples from large containers, one-hundred-gallon wooden (staved) barrels or drums, and cheese from massive hooped molds. Occasionally, usually on holidays, a stalk of bananas graced a dark corner.

He dispensed flour, sugar, dry beans, peas, and other grocery items after sacking and weighing them, usually in small quantities of five pounds or less. Often a pickle barrel and a five-gallon jar of pig's feet, or knuckles, sat on a rough wooden counter. Stale food in boxes and cans lined the shelves. Prepackaging and refrigeration were still decades away. Most of these gross containers were trucked up from Greer's wholesale warehouse in Mobile, Alabama. Uncle Albert, a garrulous, portly man, wanted you to think he could get anything when nobody else could. He had a saying: "Greer's got it, and I can get it!"

Uncle Albert could get food from Greer, but how could we get it from Albert? The answer: money, which was in short supply where the head of the family of one-third of households was unemployed, and where social-welfare foods were yet nonexistent. I remember when the first truckload of federal government commodities was dispatched to Neely community in the mid-1930s. Hungry people ambled about the schoolhouse after dark, uncertain why the truck was there. Many refused at first to sign up for free food, for to do so classified them as "paupers," and their pride was all they had. Finally, a few broke the ice and signed a certificate that they were without assets. Our family was not eligible for free commodities and, like most others who had a farm or garden or relatives with either, we turned to the land for survival. Although growing food on the farm was unpredictable, we never went hungry. But we never got as much "sto-bought" food as we wanted. Nevertheless, we were better off than those who depended on the weekly commodity truck. Indeed, most local people thought and dreamed in terms of more and better food but had neither garden nor farm, and few could afford even small mercantile purchases.

These days, I am well fed, well nourished, and full of vitamins. I inhabit the proverbial "Fat City." I choose for morning refection a tea from my selection of Upton varietals, an exotic blend that will put me in the mood to contemplate the problems of the day: a special brew for body, mind, and spirit. After a cup of a classic Assam or first-flush Darjeeling, I begin a ration of John McCann's Irish Oatmeal. During its lengthy cooking, I retrieve the *New York Times* and the local paper, delivered daily to the front door. While the oats are steaming, I drink a glass of organic apple juice, take my pills, and enjoy a papaya that has been flown in from Mexico or Brazil. I spread my buttered muffin with Tiptree quince or guava preserves from County Essex, England. Welcome to my palatal Xanadu in the Arizona desert.

My years have bridged strange culinary worlds. During childhood I spent most of my daylight hours directly producing, preserving, and consuming what our labors wrought. I planned farm schedules for next season and worried about executing them. I was continually anxious as to how my poor parents were going to put food on the table.

Maybe I have grown fat and indifferent, not worrying these days about what's for supper. My major concern no longer is food—its availability, its quality, its nutritional content, its palatability, and its presentation. Like millions of others, I have the problem of choosing what *not* to eat, and how to choose food that is compatible with my lifestyle and health needs. There is abundant time to feel anxious about the lives of those millions today who don't have even a portion of the food that I had when I was a child.

For most twenty-first-century Americans, "What's for dinner?" doesn't mean, "Will there be any food?" but instead, "What will be our choices?" I've now entered another world of maturity and old age: taste buds grossed out, an appetite for food conditioned not so much by the senses as by the necessity for health and physical comfort. The thought of going to supermarkets to choose among mountains of unpalatable products repulses me; even "organic" turns me off. Emotionally, I have great difficulty in identifying with the lack of sweat in the current agribusiness world. I sometimes wonder how I have moved from a life of subsistence farming to such soulless consumption of food, eating what I have not earned by the sweat of my brow.

Sex on the Farm

"WHA DEY DOIN! WHA DEY DOIN, DADDY?" he shouted. "Pecker, pecker, pecker! Wha dey doin, scriddlin? Scriddlin, Daddy?"

The right side of his brain was busy picturing the scene in the pasture. The left side was occupied with processing: what's going on between these two animals? Both lobes combined picture and information in an attempt to articulate what was in his head. His three-year-old tongue fell short of words, but his biology was mysteriously at work.

Cattle were grazing here and there; chickens wandered about looking for tumble-turds (dung beetles), grasshoppers, or fresh cow manure. A sow and shoats lay in a midpasture wallow; Lamikin and Ramakin, his pet lambs but pests to his Grandpa, clipped grass and weeds. And the work mules, Maud and Mattie, whinnied as they rubbed against fence posts in a far corner near the woods. Toward the other end of the pasture at Old House, atop the most celebrated pecan tree in Neely, a lone crow squawked a complaint.

But his attention remained focused on the action between Old Dick and the other one. He ran to his father, jumping up and down, waving his arms and screeching excitedly, "Wha dey doin? Wha dey doin, Daddy? Pecker, pecker, pecker!"

Old Dick, the bull, having fought off the competition from several opponents, proceeded to service the cow, and his "long thing" dragged through the grass and soon disappeared, except as an image in the boy's mind. Suddenly, all became calm. But a sharp voice barked, "Be quiet! I'm gonna tell yo mamma. She'll wash yo mouth out with laundry soap!" And, with a threatening gesture, his father pointed toward Big House and said, "Go tell yo Grandpa to come down here!"

The boy and the old man soon emerged from the house. He was still excited. Anxiety blanched his young face, and puzzlement filled his head. Charles Hillman, taciturn, mumbled through his mustache about "coffee getting cold" and "that dad-danned crow," slipped a square of Blood Hound from the breast pocket of his overalls, tore a chaw from it, and with right thumb and forefinger carefully stuffed it into the recesses of his left jaw. They waded through the bitter weeds (*Helenium amarum*) and wiregrass that grew thickly around barns and fencerows. Carefully crossing the cattle guard, they quickly returned to where his father stood observing the two bovines.

The bull, head down, moved slowly, making soft base-utterance guttural sounds, slobbering at the mouth, licking the nose, and in between licks tasting the air with his tongue. Brisk air registered the hot breath of the nostrils, as biology linked the body to the next rutting. *What day is it? Pleasure, pain?* No such registration in Old Dick's indexing. A dull emptiness filled a massive horned skull.

The female stood still a few yards away, chewing a cud placidly, a little bowed in the back from that poking of her innards by that long thing, and was looking at some distant object, but with a brute gaze. Anyone very familiar with farm stock could easily read her gaze: *That's over. That bastard's off my back. Now let's return to our routine pastoral existence and serve our masters, those carnivores, who think they know everything and the meaning of everything, including the timing of my next heat.*

Both lobes in full gear now, the boy watched the two adults attentively. They whispered asides, mumbled, conjectured, kicked the dirt, spat tobacco juice, while deliberately making the day's plan—the business about which his daddy had driven up from the Gulf Coast that weekend. "I'm sure she'll take," the old man said, adding, "Several more are comin in, and Old Dick will have his hands full. He's up to it. I feed him good. I promised Albert Harvison he could bring that new Santa Gertrudis cow over tomorrow."

Father responded, "Pshaw! Old Dick ain't even got started yet, Pa." Shifting the subject, he added: "While I'm up here, I think I'll take that listed sow over to Louis Breland's Duroc boar and see if she'll stand still this time. Hard to tell, whadda ya think?" Grandpa grunted assent. "Them McKenzie boys, Les and Jay, will help ya take them over there. They know how to handle Maud and Mattie and the wagon. Take her in that hog box behind the barn, and be sure to fasten it good. Don't let Louis charge ya. He owes me a breedin.'"

The boy's brain, even more alive now, was alert and calculating, and had made the connection between the men's references to bull and cow, and sow and boar, so he excitedly asked, "Daddy, daddy, can I go, can I go, can I ride th'wagon, please. Le'me go. Daddy, le'me go watch'em!"

Les and Jay were fun. They had jawbreakers and always carried slingshots. "Le'me go, Daddy." No father could resist such persistent begging.

Was this a request from a small boy to be part of the activities of his paternal idols? Or a Freudian subterfuge by a sex-savvy child? Was his real purpose to ride the wagon, suck hard candy balls, and to shoot birds? Or was it to observe animals play, sniff each other's "check points," paw and scratch the earth, groan and grunt?

Even at three, he was not unaware of his "thing." Daddy and Grandpa had one; they peed with it in the bushes. Little girls didn't have one. Why? His family was mum on the matter, and the pervasive Puritan culture assisted in keeping any such tool out of family and public discussion. Nothing made sense, yet his biology was working.

"Pussy," he said to himself under his breath, and hung his head, knowing that it was an ugly word. "Pecker" and "pussy." He had heard those words from Howard Green. Uncle Bo said that "long thing" of Old Dick was a pecker? What did it do? Peck?

At that moment his father answered, "Yeah, sonny boy, you can go with'em." But in the same breath, he admonished him to keep his mouth shut and to stay in the wagon while they were there.

Les and Jay geared the mules, loaded the sow, and the four were off to the Breland place, where they pulled up in front of a small wire pen. A big red boar paced the turf. High on the wagon, the boy had a ringside seat for the show.

Junior and Hazel were playing house. (This interlude was decades before Elvis's seductive song "Baby Let's Play House.") They were under the high porch at the Big House, that part of the space beneath the massive structure where Grandpa had constructed a playhouse-space for children's diversion. They didn't realize that any-one could be watching. The boy thought: *Daddy built me a playhouse in Pineville, but I didn't play house like this!*

He watched with the unsullied brain of a three-year old. His eyes wandered toward one of Grandma's pet cats, but his focus kept returning to the "mama and papa," and this new kind of game, "house." They weren't playing baby dolls.

He remembered the scene of Old Dick in the pasture yesterday. He thought: *People do that, too?* It was hot on his brain. He watched as Junior, who was a year older than he, pull out a stiff little thing, pull up little Hazel's dress, wrestle her down, and crawl on top. He could see her mooneymod and everything underneath the dress, which was now over Hazel's head. Junior was trying to put the thing between her legs, to no avail because she wasn't cooperating.

The boy jumped out of hiding, yelling, "Whatcha doin! Whatcha doin! Whatcha doin t'Hazel? Pecker, pecker, pecker! I'm gonna go tell Grandma right now!" He ran off, letting go of his own stiff little mooneymod.

Junior was only copying what he saw hogs do in his front yard, or what his dad and mom did at home. Or what Mr. and Mrs. Cox were doing under the sheets.

People like the Coxes, itinerant laborers in rural Mississippi, who lived in close quarters in small houses, seemed unaware that children watched everything. Thinking, perhaps, we didn't understand, they "had at it" right before our eyes. Lack of privacy assured children box seats to the playhouse theater every night.

And the play wasn't always between mamas and papas. A weather vane for amorous proclivities, Uncle Bo wore the title "Neely's ladies' man" without debate. We hunted squirrels on Saturdays, and butch-ered the occasional hog. When we removed the "thing," I thought: *How gross!* Bo's conversation with me was always guarded, because he suspected that I guessed his biological urges.

I remember that he took me hunting before daylight on Saturdays, and we had a regular stop. He would tell me, "Jim, stay in the car; I gotta see Jody about a hog." Curiosity led me to peek through the window to see Bo playing house with Jody's wife. I later found out that Jody worked on weekends and that he had no hogs.

Without fanfare, blocks of my sex education derived from the exploits of my Scotch-Irish relatives. Since we didn't have TV, radio, or magazines with sexual motifs (except in the doctor's office), I learned a lot about sex through my imagination and the conversations between my father and grandfather, and granduncles Dave, George, and Leake, even though they were cautious when young ears were around. Culture, custom, and tradition always assured flavoring the serious with some frivolity. "Scriddlin" had to be funny as well as juicy.

Listening and learning from the process—*synousia*, the ancient Greeks called it—I was slowly becoming a part of the clan and adult community.

On Sunday afternoons, Hillman males rotated gathering on one another's porch to talk about their farms—a conversational thread here and there, mostly relating to animal behavior. After several hours a garment of significance would be woven for the workweek ahead. But the ultimate aim was to make a crop, to *produce*. Calves, piglets, lambs, and biddies.

They also updated each other on how their crops were doing—corn, cotton, sweet potatoes, and sugarcane—but would never have thought of a cornstalk or a "tater" vine as having a sex life. Yet, sex it was. *The Secret Life of Plants*, and more.

Masculine talk was fixed on the proclivities of animal biology, gender, and mating. Males unobtrusively smacked their lips when thinking about sexual consummation. Idle chatter revealed their irrepressible imaginations about human behavior substituting for animal behavior.

In such gossip, people were always the first subject. I once snatched a whisper from Uncle Dave to Grandpa: "Charlie, ya know dan well that Homer's ruttin Old Ethyl!" He suspected that I had heard, and the talk shifted quickly to animals: "I might hafta rest Old Dick," Grandpa retorted, "Bo said he's gettin tired; too many o them heifers." Ultimately, all conversation led to bulls and cows, boars and sows, rams and ewes, sometimes even roosters and hens. Chicken sex talk was at the bottom of any list with my father.

That sex was pleasure had to be hidden; it was the culture. After all we were a church community. Perfunctory talk was about as close as Old Washington church permitted. Adult men could wonder about

Joe Hooker and his relationship with his ewe-sheep, but would rarely speak about it. Yet the children knew all about the sex lives of Adam and Eve, David and Bathsheba, and Solomon and his thousand concubines. "Goody!"

Somehow we skipped Solomon's Song with its up-front "kisses and wine." I learned early from Sunday school about Sodom, Lot and his daughters. The sin of Onan was once mentioned in a Bible study group but, like Achan's sin, it was too complex to dwell on. Love and sex subjects had to be black and white.

In fact, "sex" became almost a code word for sin. Chalk that up to closet Victorianism, or Puritanical thought, but not to ignorance. Perhaps it was an organized conspiracy among rural machos and low-grade preachers to keep rural women under their thumb of influence. Is it any wonder that some of those holy mountebanks were praying with (preying upon) the church sisters while their husbands were off at the sawmill or working on the new pipeline project?

Knowledge was creeping in; biology at work. On the farm I picked up the rudiments of sex without having any idea about its physiology, social meaning, or purpose. "Seed" seemed to be a key word. "Sex shows" by animals planted a seed in my psyche and childhood persona. Sublimated images were alive and well in my noggin. Lots of seeds in there. I soon discovered that life itself was linked to the sex act.

As I grew, I acquired more evidence, looked life in the face, and watched nature's doppelgänger itself in fecund fashion.

My parents weren't burdened with explaining to me the facts of life. That began behind the barn observing farm animals, indeed birds and bees, even relatives. When I noticed Uncle Jeb nuzzling Aunt Kate's neck, I thought it was like Old Dick sniffing his mate.

Mother focused on the romantic nuance. It was an art. She began such conversation cautiously, with a glance of the eye, a nod of the head, or a clearing of the throat. Even the position of her fingers, as she knitted. Her practice was to proceed delicately, and to conclude when adults were silent or when children began asking questions. If questions from us children got too suggestive, Father administered an elbow to the ribs, or an under-the-table kick on the shin.

She was emphatic: "Don't say that! It is filthy and vulgar; the Jacksons use it and I won't let you be like them." Looking me straight in the eye, she said, "Thoughts of the gutter are unbecoming a gentle-man." She went further and suggested that such language meant that the user was ignorant, and couldn't think in proper English.

My parents were practical, but never quite explicit, about sex. They were part of the culture and were repressed when speaking openly about such intimacies. By default, they let the farm animals and horny uncles do all the talking. There was plenty of that. Apparently, they believed that we absorbed the facts of life on our own. My father's best advice was: "Keep that pecker in yo pants!" I remember one occasion when we were riding in the Ford pickup in the woods and the topic came up. He blurted out, "Son, if you're gonna scriddle don't do it like dogs on the public grass; go to the bushes, or where people ain't watchin!" That was my first and only lesson from him about sex. Had he not had a sense of humor to poke fun, however, I would have remained even more ignorant about it.

In Mississippi animals were free to roam about, graze and root, def-ecate and copulate at will in public, and were often a public spectacle. Unfettered, they wandered about churches, the village store, and private, unfenced home yards performing their biological functions. Men and grown boys often stopped to observe, women and children moved on. Was that a vicarious wishing game? Hogs seemed to enjoy it most, with the top-hog, or boar, grunting, mouth agape, tongue hanging out under his snout, appearing to doze during the ceremony.

One day in Pleasant Hill school I watched two hogs outside in the schoolyard. Ellen Byrd, two desks away from mine, observing the rutting overture, wrote me a note: "Hey Jim, look out the window at them hogs; look at that old boar's peter. " Mrs. Williams intercepted the note, and each of us got a good lecture after school. She told my mother, who was teaching in another room, and the incident made its way home. Mother, with her dry Irish humor, recounted the incident with delight to my father. "Guess what our little Jimmye got in trouble for today."

Later, I watched from the library window at Avera as two hounds enjoyed each other. The dogs got "hung up" and remained linked until the bell rang at three o'clock. Children seemed embarrassed, but gawked intently as they walked slowly to the school bus. I didn't mention the show at supper.

This was the only kind of sex education we learned at school. The lack of such information coupled with the failure of parents to talk about sex left children vulnerable. This vacuum forced children to seek answers in stories repeated by naughty boys and "smart alecks." At the outdoor toilet at Avera school I was introduced to a wealth of raw language and sex talk.

Girls and their anatomy became a major part of boys' conversation. I heard every word but, embarrassed, managed to stay aloof. But quickly, I picked up the language: He "topped her," "crawled on er," "popped her." Girls were "had," "laid," or "made." A new word, "sluttin," appeared one day.

I got plenty of exposure to vulgar language and a picturesque description of sex organs from older boys at outdoor toilets. Percival Bragg even liked pulling down his overalls and showing his odd-shaped penis to others and me. I thought, somewhat anxiously, *What is he goin to do next with it?* Cousins Jake Green and Bo Williams had vulgar mouths and liked to embarrass me with filthy conversation. One day when we three were behind the barn, Bo said, "Jim's a goody-goody and doesn't know how to do this," and he pulled out his penis and started to play with it. I was a bit startled. I had heard about self-abuse but thought it to be a term used by pious hypocrites to scare little boys. I felt the same after an episode in the toilet one day when my "thing" hardened and an exhilarating feeling followed between my legs. *Whoopee!* I thought.

From this pre-teen braggadocio, I had a full vocabulary and picture album of why God and Milton made so much of Adam and Eve.

My childhood became replete with daily reference to sex relations and birthing phenomena; but the adult conversation around me seemed constructed to avoid clarity and specificity. Were the two connected: male-female and babies? But unlike the toilet-mouthed boys, the language among my adult male role models was laced with euphemism. "Bud, yo bald-faced 'pided' cow found a calf yesterday near the spring in that head behind the Old Carr Place," Uncle Bo said, adding, "Looks like she's all right but I didn't take time to see whether it's a bull or heifer." I immediately thought: how did the cow "find" the calf? Was that how calves came; did cows go out looking for them?

"Bud, that old muley-headed Jersey dropped her calf in them bushes down behind the hog pen last night." I thought this was strange since Grandpa had said that Louise Byrd "dropped another'n, number seven, a girl." *From where did it drop?* My child's mind thought. *And did it get hurt?*

"Do you suppose it's Old Dick's?" Father asked. "I doubt it, don't look like his'n," Bo added. "One o them young bulls might have got to her first, they were jumpin everthing but billy goats, and Old Dick was tired last spring. Pa let everbody in Greene County bring their sluttin scrawny heifers over there for him to jump."

It seemed that babies arrived from some mysterious place. A cow "dropped" calves. A sow "had" pigs; a dog had puppies; a cat "brought home" kittens, or "came in with" them as if the mother cat had been out visiting and ran into some strays. A mare "woke up with" a colt as if she had been asleep, dreamed, and presto, there was her baby. She "lambed," she "foaled," or she "calved," "came in" as the case may be. Rabbits "produced" bunnies, quails behind the barn produced covies.

Angels brought my little brother, and the stork my baby cousin, Jack. But Dr. McLeod "delivered" our little redheaded sister, Lora Jean.

I had no idea of how this took place. But I was rapidly solving the puzzle. Watermelon seeds go in the ground, they sprout, grow, and new watermelons come. I watched as wee kittens emerged from the back end of our mamma cat and thought: *a seed must have been planted in her.* Was Old Dick planting seeds?

Then the seminal moment: As we were once eating Sunday dinner, Father matter-of-factly said to Mother, "Did you notice the preacher's wife this mornin? She must have swallowed a watermelon seed." There was silence.

She's going to have a baby.

That was it! I had unraveled the mystery. By age seven I had discovered where babies came from.

God and Politics

Old Washington Baptist

Silent and amazed even when a little boy,
I remember I heard the preacher every Sunday
put God in his statements,
As contending against some being or influence.
—*Walt Whitman, "A Child's Amaze"*

"OH! WHY NOT TONIGHT? OH! WHY NOT TONIGHT?" the small congregation wailed plaintively at the end of a week of revival-meeting preaching, singing, praying, and not a small amount of indulgent eating. "Oh! Do not let the Word depart!" the voices admonished in unison but in an unconvincing tone. Brother Black, the sweat from his balding head reflecting light from the large kerosene lamps, superimposed his voice over the singing. There was no choir. "Jesus is calling! Jesus is calling! Do you hear him? Heed Him! Sinner, come home, come home. Jesus is calling! Won't you hear His voice? Don't let the Devil talk you out of it. Tonight, accept Jesus. Tonight, tonight. You may walk out that church door and never have another chance. Today is the day of salvation! So step right out into the aisle. Others will let you through. Walk right up here and give me your hand. Jesus is calling—sinner, come home!"

The pleading became more urgent. But from the audience there was obvious equivocation. Bodies shuffled, shifting from one foot to the other, throats cleared: a subdued and somewhat embarrassed, remonstrative whispering. Eyes shifted about the small sanctuary, but no one moved toward the altar. Drama, struggle, and resistance characterized the typical revival of my youth. These were its expected ingredients, relished by some, tolerated by most, aphrodisiacal. All this was ad nauseam to this youngster.

"I feel the Lord's spirit here," Preacher Black cried. "Every head bowed, every eye closed. Please, now, listen to the voice of Jesus in your heart." One couldn't hear much from Jesus above the persistent whine of the preacher and the pianist. Brother James, who was directing the singing, changed songs to "Only Trust Him," a more strident invitational hymn. This harangue followed an hour-long sermon, and continued while we sang (twice) all four verses of "O Why Not Tonight," then every verse of "Almost Persuaded," "Jesus, I Come," "Jesus Is Calling," concluding with "Just As I Am," the old tearjerker made famous decades later by the Billy Graham Crusades. I was relieved that this year we never got around to "Rescue the Perishing." All the same, we sang these revival hymns slowly (unlike the normal Baptist practice of rapid alliteration of melody and omission of the third verse) while Preacher Black punctuated the music by pleading with us to "Step right out, now. It may be your last chance. Who knows what might happen before tomorrow? Tomorrow may never arrive for you. Only trust Him. He will save you, now!"

Nobody was responding. After all, fourteen children and several adults had already been saved that week, professed their faith in Jesus and after baptism by immersion in water would be accepted as voting members of Old Washington. "Accept Him, now! Accept Him now!" Brother Black appeared desperate. The sweat was pouring off him now. "Let's pray again. The Lord is telling me that there is someone here tonight who needs Jesus, who needs to make a decision." Now he was using the old ploy of implying that there was a specific person in our midst and that our prayers should be focused on that *sinner.* But to me it seemed rather obvious there was no immediately identifiable target, no virtual sinner. I was thinking: *This guy doesn't have to hitch the mules before sunup tomorrow or else he'd shut up and we could go home. Everyone knows we all need Jesus, but right now I need to hit the hay. I'm tired of hearing preachers yelling and babies bawling.*

Inducing the sinner to make a decision for Christ transformed noticeably in my early years from a predominantly emotional, arm-twisting, pleading, even threatening type of appeal to a more rational and calm sales pitch: "Don't you want to accept the Lord?" and "Wouldn't you like to consider joining the church?" These, instead of asking the unregenerate the blunt question: "You don't want to spend eternity in hell, do you?"

That night's audience was composed mostly of women and children, a just-married couple, another courting, and a few latently penitential backbenchers, all of whom I knew had already found Jesus and had their names written in the Book of Life. However, I wondered about two with half-pints in their back pockets who had had the "Damascus Road" experience but now seemed on the low road again with their smoking, cursing, and drinking.

In our local Baptist communion the euphemism "joining the church" gradually took on the meaning of taking one's stand with those who thought in terms of not only being for or against sin or against some imagined outside evil, but as being absolutely sure of salvation: once-saved-always-saved Baptists.

We were different from the Methodists, who believed in a social gospel where salvation came from church association. In our case we became voting members of Old Washington church only after accepting Jesus and being baptized in the creek. Then, we didn't talk anymore of salvation, finding Jesus, and elementary Bible-school stuff. You were "in," counted among the faithful, and dropped for the most part from the worries of preachers and their minions. The professional revivalists and huckster-lay-salvationists tended to leave you and your family alone. They fed on new and raw sinner's meat, the unregenerate. You were saved, and the implication for the moment at least was that life's problems were secondary; you should be thankful to God and happy. That night, every person present knew every other, knew most of their social habits, their church manners, maybe some of their innermost thoughts. Ours was just such a closed village society. Revival meetings tended to reinforce this tradition.

I wondered just whom Brother Black was talking about. By now I was squirming a bit. *Could the preacher be talking to me? Was I the object of so much commotion and concern?* I hadn't yet been "ducked," as we said, referring to baptism. But I didn't intend to succumb to Brother Black's high-pressure tactics of selling Jesus like liniment and medicine at the county fair. Who else could he be haranguing the tired crowd about other than little twelve-year-old Jimmye, already in high school but not "saved," a bright and promising pupil for him to brag about "bringing to Christ"?

"Jimmye, don't you want to go forward?" a woman next to me asked, with a nudge. "Quit punching me on the ribs!" I muttered.

I resisted becoming a statistic to prove the success of our revival meeting, an addition to the preacher's portfolio of baptisms. Counting saved souls like a hunter counts coon and possum pelts, recording them with marks on the barn door. *Who else could he be talking about? And how did he, an outsider from Hattiesburg, here for only a few days, know so much about our hearts, our lives, and our needs?* I had deduced early on that baptism was serious business, and that the reasoning "everyone does it" was insufficient. Such sacred propositions must have all doubt removed. Besides, everyone knew that, like all preachers and politicians, Brother Black was a hypocrite.

The audience was becoming restless, on the verge of exhaustion. Only a few of us were calm, steel-willed, inured to the hard sell, tolerant of the emotional excess, and unmoved. A number of girls were in tears. Some older boys looked to the door, and there was more shuffling of feet and disrespectful whisperings. Occasionally one or two slipped furtively out into the dark.

Most of the tired souls were just awaiting the "Amen" when they could hurry out into the warm evening, light a cigarette or allow the night breeze to relieve them of Brother Black's irritating appeals. As the congregation hummed the last strains of "Just As I Am," he finally retreated to the pulpit and gave a benediction. Outside I heard Jake Farley and Elbert Williams break into a local ditty:

> If ya wanna go to heav'n I'll tell ya how to do it:
> Just grease yo'self with mutton suet,
> Slip right outta the devil's hand
> Right over into the Promised Land—
> Makes it easy; good an' greasy!

It was all over. The revival balloon had released its hot air into this August night in 1935. A drone of hushed voices infused the humidity as people left the church, most afoot. No new souls had been saved tonight, but a few had ventured forward to request the preacher's prayers, several others to ask for strength and support lest they lapse again into undisclosed sin. I noted that some were the perennial "joiners," hangers-on, weak-kneed, those who depended on such gatherings for an emotional lift in their dull lives. For the most of us, it was back to our petty routine in an economically depressed

Mississippi village. Back to plowing and picking cucumbers for me tomorrow, revived and exhausted. Back to the quiet of the field where the only noises were horseflies buzzing around the mule's head, and chirps of mockingbirds and cicadas at rows' end. Obviously, sin would abound, but grace would much more abound. In spite of Brother Black.

Next year Brother Floyd from some church in Mobile would give it *his* best.

Annual revival meetings at Old Washington Baptist were rooted in a tradition going back to eighteenth-century pietism found in Dutch Reformed, Lutheran, Methodist, and Presbyterian churches. Baptists, however, appropriated and perfected the essence of the religious revival technique and used it extensively in rural Southern congregations. They replaced the concept of revivalism with revival and the "revival meeting," a planned event, not just a spontaneous religious gathering held in a tent or a brush arbor. This was the centrifugal force behind the growth of Baptists in the South.

These weary souls accompanied the bodies of my ancestors. They were pioneers, adventurers, fortune seekers, and others, many on the lam, who began trickling into Greene County, Mississippi Territory, at the beginning of the 1800s. Trickle became steady flow just before the Civil War, and the numbers increased toward the end of the nineteenth century. Homesteading, free land, and space were not the sole objectives of these itinerant masses; just as important was the search for the New Jerusalem, a Promised Land.

Anger-driven, fatalistic, pathos-filled, most had little but God to bind them together, and after defeats at Shiloh, Vicksburg, and Cold Harbor there crept in doubts even about God. Nevertheless, in the beginning they came up the Pascagoula and Leaf Rivers from the Gulf of Mexico to Salem (Leaf), Scotland (Vernal), Old Washington (Neely), and across country from South Carolina, Georgia, and Alabama, fording and bridging the Chickasawhay River to Old Avera, Adamsville, and Leakesville, arriving by oxen or mule or wagon train, but often afoot, seeking havens for survival and for hope.

Inheritors of the promise of religious freedom, descendants from decades of the followers of Calvin, Knox, and the Huguenots, simple practitioners of the doctrine laid down by Roger Williams, independent preachers emulating Jonathan Edwards and Dwight L. Moody, Congregationalists, ecumenicists, those who elected pres- byters—the lot. A few Catholics, and fewer Jews, but no heathens. Scotch-Irish origins, mostly. These individuals and their families, a ragtag band, put down stakes where either fortune or subsistence afforded, and began to thank God. *For what?* some of their descen- dants are still asking.

The bones of one of the earliest pioneers, Rachael Moody, née Shuler, born in 1776 in the Orangeburg District, South Carolina, lie atop Boise Bluff at the juncture of Courthouse Creek and Leaf River. She was my ancestor. No doubt other bones also lie below that same clay soil. As a child, I often passed her eroding gravestone while accompanying my father on hog-hunting expeditions. Father always said there was a chapel nearby, an early church structure of pine logs used by the first settlers during early Mississippi statehood.

After the Civil War, which some fought in the name of God, a wave of Confederate veterans joined others seeking an intermediary to God other than Robert E. Lee and Stonewall Jackson. One of these soldiers was my great-grandfather Pinckney George Hillman. An itinerant farmer, part-time logger, ultimately he felt the "call" to preach. There wasn't a vocation of full-time minister those days in Greene County, nor money for such. Pinckney and the family later moved to Old Washington several miles distant, where he helped build a small Baptist congregation. He died during World War I and now rests in Old Washington cemetery, soil donated by one of his sons, my grandfather.

Old Washington Baptist Church began around 1845, and for a hun- dred years or more had no full-time pastor. A loose, transparent, social structure similar to that in all frontier Baptist assemblies accompanied a simple congregational form of church government. Each organized group was not only self-contained, but was constituted of individual members who through prayer and meditation thought of themselves as uniquely God-directed. No historical and ecclesiastical baggage, no intermediaries between God and man, no organized structures, no boards. No bells, incense, and other worship appurtenance to please the senses other than thought, mind, and intent.

Pinckney George Hillman grave.

The spiritual security of the baptized-by-immersion believer meant everything. Once saved always saved. Faith in Jesus became the all in all to salvation. The soul stripped down to its bare minimum, an ability to commune with God. Only this was necessary. It was more of individual salvation than community of believers; the "cloud of witnesses" mentioned in Hebrews was secondary. Such individual believers, once elected into full fellowship of the local congregation, became church members and had the vote to prove that God had answered their supplications. They couldn't read the Bible, but they knew what the Lord intended.

In retrospect, the frontier faith of these transmigrated Europeans was path-breaking. The culture that was forged from this human admixture ultimately formed what became known as Southern culture, or more condescendingly, the Dixie mentality. God and religion was at their life's center, and was there by preordination. Many had visions and answered prayers to prove it. The successes of Calvin were signs of the inerrancy of his ways. Justice and grace were rationalized as sacraments. An indomitable spirit that knew no time-space boundaries, no achievement limitations reinforced the pioneers' egos. After all, they were "the elect."

The emergent individualism, with its burnished residue from the faith of my forefathers, remained a part of my own spiritual heritage, try as I have to divest myself of some of its tenets. Inevitably such thinking fragmented a lot of Baptist churches. Splinter groups abounded. Trying to make sense out of the then-and-now of my family's religious evolution and heritage made me wonder if God might be confused. Splintering caused church fights and cliques, and even families at Old Washington became divided. (Coincidentally, during this time, slavery was not the divisive issue here that it became nationally, or even in other parts of Mississippi. There were few blacks in these wooded precincts.)

In the early 1900s, the original congregation split into churches named Old Washington Baptist and Old Washington Missionary Baptist. Solomon himself could not have settled which had the right to be called "the original church," nor could he have rationalized the bases for their theological differences. Such inanities and insoluble issues are part of the forces that turn people off of organized religion. (In this case it was strong differences of opinion between the families of Pinckney George Hillman and James Francis "Tinner" Green, concerning whether or not Christians should evangelize the "uttermost part of the earth.") What matter anyway, now that most of the communicants and disputants, and many of their descendants, rest in several acres of cemetery between the churches.

God wanted the heathen converted, but there was not unanimity on which ones should be saved first; nor did they agree on what Jesus meant by "Jerusalem, and in all Judaea, and in Samaria, and unto the uttermost part of the earth. . . ." Similarly, "all nations, beginning at Jerusalem" meant one thing to one faction but another point of geography to those of a different persuasion. Isolation, reinforced by an attitude of "Let's take care of our own first," meant that William Carey, that great eighteenth-century English missionary, wasn't going to be the model for poor frontier subsistence farmers. There were no bishops or pope to settle differences; so the general result was schism.

Some of the nastiest feuding as I grew up was between Baptist church folks. But fights also arose between those whose differences were more about social issues (like whom children chose to marry) than they were about church doctrine. Aunt Candice, one of my father's older sisters, announced, "I'll go join them" when the "Missionary bunch," as my father referred to them, split off from the original congregation. She ran away to marry Frank Kim, and joined the Landmarkers. Landmarkers were particularly disgruntled about what "Nashville, Louisville, and Atlanta are doing to us." (Nashville printed all of our religious literature; Louisville produced our seminary-trained preachers; and Atlanta was where the mission organizations were centered.) "We don't need none of that stuff," Uncle Mark Green announced, "just the Word o God," as he held up his Bible one day in an agitated session.

Until Old Washington Baptist Church split into Old Washington Missionary Baptist Church and the Baptist Church, the greatest crisis seemed to have been over at Buck Creek Church where they wanted to know what to do about a member who had deserted the Confederate army. Some deacons wanted to remove him from fellowship, saying, "Should we 'church' him?"

These Missionary Baptists, like the Landmarks, Hard Shells, and remnant Campbellites, believed there should be no supra-organizational body. Over the years self-serving biblical exegetes revealed bases for even further disagreement, which resulted in competition among the congregations for local prestige, power, allegiance, and even commerce. Saving souls became secondary to gossip, family intrigue, and with whom you affiliated. Inevitably, people tended to choose sides, often along bloodlines and family ties rather than upon doctrinal belief, reminding me of what Saint Matthew said about "a man's foes shall be they of his own household."

But the fledgling assembly at Old Washington remained linked with the Baptist hierarchy. They had started with the Pearl River

Association, one of the oldest organized church enclaves in the state. Then came Providence, Ebenezer, Leaf River, and Greene County Associations, in that order—all affiliates of the Southern Baptist Convention, the Rome of Southern Baptists. Old Washington wasn't always represented at the regional associations. A small cluster from the greater Hillman family, nevertheless, had been part of the development of the Mississippi Baptist faith from the outset, and down through the decades someone from that thread of souls could be counted on to keep the church doors open and care for the needy, widows, and orphans.

Elder Pinckney George Hillman preached the opening sermon to the delegates of Leaf River Baptist Association at Sand Hill Church, Greene County, in October 1896. He and his son Charles remained active as church delegates from Old Washington for another several decades. Old Washington Baptist continued its status in association with the Southern Baptist Convention, officially changing its name to Neely Baptist Church in the early 1970s.

After the Civil War, Mississippi villages struggled to maintain an identity, and history books are sprinkled with names that became ghost towns and churches that disappeared with them. Yet a corps of institutions survived, and arguments about the interpretation of God's Word and intent continued unabated, ultimately resulting in a church on just about every "fork of the creek" in Greene County.

Surveying my spiritual and secular landscapes, what appeared obvious to me was that deep behind the overworked, gentle personage of Jesus Christ, there loomed the unmoving, passionless countenance of Plato's god. This god cannot suffer, and is embellished with some aspects of the Stoic ethic. Rigid rules of "right and wrong," derived from Neoplatonic bases, were keys to Southern understanding of Judeo-Christianity, which emphasized the God of the Ten Commandments. There was little tolerance for sin, as defined by the local and temporary church hierarchy, as in our pastors and deacons.

We believed that sin precipitated terrible personal misfortune, sickness, and death, as well as collective bad circumstances such as hurricanes and floods. Most disasters were a manifestation of the justice of God as payment to sinners. (This is the same belief system that prompted Jerry Falwell to claim that the 9/11 attacks were

God's punishment of New Yorkers for their sins.) Distributive justice, however, was available at the altar of Old Washington. Church members distrusted concentrated secular power, but they were suckers for religious hucksters who doled out Jesus.

The Baptists' stand against a central authority and foreign commitments provided a convenient argument to express a states' rights political doctrine in a religious context. This rugged frontiersman philosophy gave cover for the provincial Southern individual to forget external things in order to concentrate only on matters between himself and the Lord. An individual's rights became as sacrosanct as the worth of the single soul. The village church was a cozy nook in the woods to ignore the problems of the Old World, even the legacy of Jeff Davis, and to commence a new isolated, independent existence, both spiritual and secular, in the Promised Land. With this belief system firmly entrenched, hard work, prayer, and worship could overcome troubles even as horrific as the Great Depression, even if one had to swallow hard to accept FDR and the New Deal. Social programs and community integration spit in the face of their God-given individualism. Such was the nature of our Southern faith. And such was the nature of my parents' faith, and their parents before them.

Family tradition meant that I attended *the* Baptist Church. (The Missionary Baptists had appropriated the name "Old Washington.") On Sunday mornings we drove along the gravel highway toward one of the three boxlike sanctuaries that dotted the Neely-McLain road. Ours sat among the pines, with a big water oak out front, next door to Neely school.

Later we returned for evening services. I looked forward to Training Union where I could get my teeth into the Bible and participate in a discussion. Many older teenagers, however, skipped this part of the service and slipped off next door to have sex at the teacher's home, which was built high off the ground. I felt uneasy discussing Saint Paul's Second Letter to the Corinthians while thinking about what was going on under the porch next door. My cousin Charlie claimed he had discovered used rubbers there.

The Missionary Baptist Church sat on the same side of the highway, across several acres of cemetery stones, under some giant red oaks. A quarter mile farther south on the west side was the Methodist

Protestant, or MP, building. No more structures were necessary, as there were no known Roman Catholics and no Jews. The few Presbyterians went to church in Leakesville if they were serious about their denomination. The Holiness congregation, we called them "holy-rollers," met in the house of a church member or for their revivals in a bush harbor during warm weather. I enjoyed going down there to watch Brother "Foots" Ball speak in tongues, which always sounded just like the cursing he directed at his mule when plowing.

The mix of religious constituencies in the entire county has always been about the same. Recently I was reading the "Devotional" page of the *Greene County Herald* and counted sixty-six churches, predominantly Baptist (thirty-eight), some Methodist and Presbyterian, but increasingly Pentecostal and Church of God. There are even now Catholic and Mormon flocks. I spotted a "Cornerstone Full Gospel" group in Neely. The names of some of these Baptist congregations evoke biblical lands: Antioch, Canaan, East Salem, Mount Olive, Mount Pisgah, and Zion's Rest.

The congregations at all three Old Washington churches worshipped in a similar pattern, though our church was more structured because we didn't want to be like the missionary Landmarks. When we visited another local church, we usually chose the Methodists rather than the *other* Baptists, as there was perennial bad blood. My parents were opposed to changing church membership too freely, but they did visit other churches as a gesture of community harmony. In Neely, one never changed church membership except out of spite.

We children hated to go to the Methodist church because Brother Nicholas breathed hellfire and damnation for at least an hour and a half. "Be ye redeemed. . . . Be ye sanctified!" he would yell about halfway through the sermon, loud enough to wake the cattle in the barn across the road. But I never felt pressured to walk the aisle as I did when Brother Black preached at our revival. Eventually, as Nicholas ran out of steam, the young ones would fall fast asleep and his monologue would continue through the early afternoon hours. Such sessions led my father to quip, "Th'ain't many souls saved after the first twenty minutes!"

Although we attended the Missionary Baptist services only as a last resort, we repeated stories about them until they became part of the folklore. There was the one about a visiting preacher who, after an exalting, stem-winding introduction, got so flustered he couldn't remember his text. Embarrassed, he asked Brother Robinson, the regular minister, to come to the pulpit and help him find it. For years afterward in the Hillman household, whenever someone couldn't find an answer in some book, we would yell, "Find my text, Brother Robinson. Find my text!"

Their preacher was a frequent no-show, especially during the cold, rainy, winter months. Brother Forrest, a lay Landmarker, always seemed unperturbed when someone invariably "volunteered" him to fill the pulpit. Quick to his feet, he agreed to say "just a few remarks." In a twangy, slow, unintelligible drawl, he repeated the saga of Gideon and the brave three hundred. Forrest detailed the Israelites' historic altercation with twenty thousand Midianites, quoting from scripture: "And they stood every man in his place round about the camp." Every minute or so for the next hour he repeated some incident of that saga, such as when the Israelite soldiers scooped water with their hands on the run. Then, he thundered the admonition: "Let every man stand in his place around the camp!" On one Sunday night he said it twenty-six times, or an average of a little more than once per minute. I was counting.

The original church buildings in Old Washington village were strikingly similar, having been built about the same time, between the end of the Civil War and the end of the century. In each case, over the years, small Sunday school rooms had been added on the rear, but the interiors were much the same, with a musty smell and sand on the floor. I hated the hard benches. Everything was spartan, no seat cushions or kneelers, and no cooling or heating because electricity hadn't yet reached Greene County.

A piano stood at the rear of the structure. Two aisles led up to a small platform encircled by a low railing, upon which rested the pulpit and some occasional chairs for the visiting preacher, choir director, and chairman of the board of deacons. Spiritual power emanated from that elevated spot. God spoke through the preacher. Sinners were struck by verbal lightning. There was no holy of holies, just a space where shout or whisper resonated from any part of the pine timber sanctuary.

Architecture can tell you volumes about spiritual experience. Our church buildings were simple and accessible, with plenty of space, and were painted white but with no cross and no other symbol on the short spire that rose from a boxlike bell-less belfry. We sang "Little Brown Church . . ." at Sunday school, except that our church was white. The preacher warned us that crosses were graven images, and *Catholic*! (Although over the years, I noticed every time I visited that the cross was creeping in, first behind the pulpit, then on the steeple. *Pinckney George must be trying to rise up from under his slab*, I thought.) Church bells were also suspect. We never locked the large front doors. Though the building didn't evoke the emotion of a Chartres Cathedral, there was something about the ambience. I've visited St. Peter's in Rome many times, but never felt closer to God than at our little family church house.

Old Washington Baptist, like most village churches, had a quarter-time ministry, meaning that the preacher came only once a month. We elected our deacons, but few people cared enough to politic for the job. Power was largely symbolic. There was a treasurer but no formal budget for lack of contributions. Ours was a hand-to-mouth spiritual enclave. Sunday school superintendent, pianist, Baptist Training Union (BTU) director, and others were volunteers.

On nonpreaching Sundays we met for Sunday school in the morning and Baptist Young People's Union (BYPU), later called Baptist Training Union (BTU), in the evening. We opened with prayer, sang a hymn or two, then divided into classes. Sunday school, always short on men, was where teaching and indoctrination began. Good, dependable teachers were difficult to come by, and the Sunday school superintendent was forever having difficulty persuading people to take on the job.

Some teachers, however, became possessive, even fossilized in the job. Mrs. Eckles thought of the sixty-plus-year-olds as "my class." Jealousy, suspicion, and rancor abounded, and on one occasion when someone suggested a change of her room, she complained to the deacons that she would quit. The following year (after twenty-six years of her tenure), her own class began considering another teacher. The gossip fallout almost caused a church split. Mrs. Eckles abruptly quit the class, stopped her tithe, and withdrew from church membership.

She pouted for years, blamed my mother, but Mother wasn't even in the class. Serious business, this instructing the Lord's handmaidens.

Men were not big on Sunday school, considering it to be for "women and children," but some condescended. These would douse their cigarettes, disassemble or stomp on the butts, or cast their Brown's Mule or Spark Plug cud into the hedge behind the church. Then they would follow their wives into the sanctuary.

Their motivation wasn't always pious, as some found the church a convenient place to discuss business. God didn't seem to mind. Several sent wives and children home, then gathered around a Model A Ford to argue the policies of Theodore Bilbo, Mike Connor, Hugh White, or some other Mississippi politician. Huey P. Long of Louisiana was a favorite, and FDR, who was rapidly becoming their savior. Hoover was always bad news. I remember one ditty: "Our Father who art in Washington, Hoover be thy Name, took away our Lucky Strike and gave us Golden Grain!" (Golden Grain was the cheapest form of tobacco; some said it was tobacco factory sweepings, others that it was little different from horse manure.)

After the politics, it was home to see "What mama's scrounged for dinner." One of the men might speak up: "Next Sunday's Third Sunday, preaching, ya r'member?" Another, as he cranked his stripped-down Model A: "Yeah, and the Lord's Supper, and baptizing. The preacher finally got old Frank!"

Sunday evening service or Training Union was more informal and sprang up as a way to occupy the local youth. We sang hymns spontaneously as people called their favorite page numbers. BTU was devoted principally to "giving parts," which was a presentation of materials taken from Southern Baptist Convention literature. These exercises consisted of reading scripture or a biblical story, then sharing its interpretation. I liked to defend my ideas, and all my life found this experience to be excellent for thinking on my feet. After BTU, there was time for a romantic interlude before we headed home. Young ladies were instructed, however, to beware of the boy who wanted to "walk you home alone."

Every Third Sunday was filled with excitement: that's when the preacher came. After Sunday school, families assembled in the churchyard, and veteran members hurried to their pew lest some child or visiting interloper occupied their seat. Baptists didn't believe in owning seats; there was never a name on a pew. But beware if someone were ignorant or bold enough to sit in Uncle Charlie's fifth-row bench near the window.

From Grandfather's window, the cemetery displayed its ancient and modern headstones to the beautiful pine forest beyond. Under those slabs of concrete lay the remains of his immediate ancestors, siblings, daughters, and grandchildren. The rest were friends because Uncle Charlie had few enemies. The rival Landmark Baptist Church, where one of his daughters and her family worshipped, was in full view. I often wondered what he was thinking when he looked out that window. More than likely it was: *Why do people fight when they could hunt hogs?*

The service began with the Sunday school superintendent giving his report. Brother Herbert was a middle-aged farmer-introvert whose matted red hair always needed washing. Apparently he loved being in front of an audience, and was always on time to announce the numbers after the congregation was seated and quiet. He had dropped out of school early, and his English was bad, but like many country people he was good with numbers. "There was a hunert an lebem in Sunday school this mornin," he would announce. We Hillman children made fun of him with all his "sebems" and "lebems."

Then the singing began, usually led by Uncle Neville, which warmed up the congregation for the preacher. "Nevilles" was a dull songster, and even duller man. His penchant for singing was perhaps a cover for his inability at conversation. He could barely carry a tune and alternately tried to sing bass and tenor, which confused everyone. "Skip the third verse," he would whisper to the pianist, but the audience ploughed ahead in confusion anyway. He coveted the job and was highly jealous of it, but today he's as forgotten as those third verses.

We sang a minimum of four songs between Sunday school and preaching, with one or more involving "the Blood." "Nothing but the Blood," "There Is Power in the Blood," "Are You Washed in the Blood?" I found it curious and weird to sing these songs when we slaughtered so many animals on the farm. Blood was rote. We sang "Amazing Grace" so often it became dull and we made up our own words. I remember little Aubrey Jacobs whispering to me one

Sunday: "Amazing Grace, how sweet the taste / When the polecat peed in the possum's face."

An offering followed. Two or three deacons, always men, literally "passed the hat." Albert Hall with his Panama hat, called a "straw katie," and Neville with his musty fedora, were dependable money handlers. They walked up and down the aisle as people deposited their nickels, dimes, and quarters, the children their pennies. I distinctly remember Albert gazing at me once as I shook my head with a plaintive look of *maybe next time*. Many of the coins—there was hardly ever a bill—were sweaty and soiled, and I sometimes thought that Indian heads took on an additional smell from the hats.

I was old enough by then to wonder about these deacons. One was a horse trader, buying animals from unsuspecting neighbors and selling them at the auction yard at an exorbitant markup, modern-day money changers. Another was sleeping with a friend's wife while the poor guy was away on a construction job. There are few secrets in a small village church, even among children.

As the preacher occupied the pulpit, we got comfortable and attentive. New mothers opened bodices to give junior his "titty." In the summer, sweat poured from everyone. Turkey-wing and dogwood-branch fans waved, accelerating when the preacher spoke of Lazarus and the rich man Dives, intensifying with his description of the consequences of a sinful life and the destination of that person who didn't accept Jesus. Sermons were usually built around a parable of Jesus, illustrated liberally with examples drawn from Saint Paul's epistles. They never lasted less than an hour. My favorites were the sermons Brother Moulder preached about Balaam's ass in the Old Testament, and the episode of Paul and Silas in a Macedonian jail. Uncle Bo always made fun of Moulder, saying, "He forgot what he preached last month. All he has is one text: 'Sirs, what must I do to be saved?'"

We celebrated the Lord's Supper only two or three times annually, at the discretion of the preacher and deacons. Welch's grape juice and Nabisco saltines constituted the elements. The saltines were broken irregularly, and children always reached for the big pieces. We sometimes sipped from a common fruit jar, but Mother and Father warned us not to drink after certain people. Normally, however, the elements were passed up and down the aisles in an odd variety of little glass containers and a dinner plate.

Baptists practiced "closed communion." Unless you were a member of a recognized Baptist congregation, a duly baptized-by-immersion believer, you were not welcome to the Lord's table. When the Lord's Supper was announced at Old Washington, usually a week in advance, non-Baptists either did not attend that day or departed church when communion began. I knew that I shouldn't invite my Methodist or Landmark playmates to church on Communion Sundays.

The "invitation" followed the sermon, at which time sinners were given the opportunity to get saved and, of course, to join the church. After we sang the final hymn, everyone scattered to his and her chicken and dumplings, collard greens, and banana-pudding-vanilla-wafer dessert.

Religion played an important part in our family life, but it wasn't dominant. We didn't exactly leave the Lord at the church building on Sunday, but neither did my family saturate our lives and daily activities with constant reminders that we were Christians, that Christians should or shouldn't do this or that. Nor was it suggested to the children that with every eventful decision we should ask, "What would Jesus do?" Neither parent was a dogmatist; both were quite practical about religion: it was created for Man and not the other way around.

At home, other than saying a blessing or an occasional reading of scripture, we didn't have much religious ritual. We didn't overplay the Jesus card outside the church; that bordered on sanctimony. Holy Rollers and Pentecostals did that. My father made us wary of any person with "too much religion," especially if one "found Jesus" suddenly during Revival. "Watch that guy—he's got religion," he would caution us without mentioning a name. "Guard your henhouse when he's prayin.'"

Although our culture measured most of our dos and don'ts, Father and Mother had some ideas of their own for our moral conduct and ethical decorum. The Ten Commandments and the Sermon on the Mount formed their base.

Father's hang-up was the Sabbath, the fourth commandment. Even though it is given more space than any other admonition written on Moses's tablets, I never could figure out its relative relevance to us. I reasoned that after going to Sunday school and church, even

Sunday night service, one should be free to enjoy the rest of the no-work day. Father thought differently, and was adamant: "No fishing, no baseball games, and no hanging around Callie Creel's store."

But Father did permit us to accompany him on Sunday to Uncle Jeff's and Aunt Veen's over in the woods on Atkinson Creek at Pleasant Hill. There, after dinner, my father and uncle sat in the swing under a large water oak and swapped yarns, chewed tobacco, and spat for two hours or more. (Tobacco, of course, was not considered a sin, even on the Sabbath.) We children entertained ourselves by wading barefoot in a branch of the creek or throwing sticks at mockingbirds in the fig trees. (No slingshots on Sunday.)

Father also took us to bait and feed wild hogs near Bear Branch, sometimes giving chase if a fat porker appeared, apparently giving little thought to the Lord's Day. I soon figured out that religion and piety were not the only thing behind his insistence on our Sabbath observance. He was a social animal, needed company on Sunday. I was always there to accommodate him. It wasn't all wasted time for me. Sitting in the Ford pickup, I got to be present with my father, one on one, man to man, and to gain a special education, particularly about the physical and cultural geography of Greene County.

"Jesus worked on the Sabbath," we argued. "He gathered corn with His disciples." Not to be outflanked by our biblical knowledge, but showing his vulnerability, Father summoned, "That wasn't real corn, just roast'n ears. All right, go on out in the yard and pitch ball to each other, but don't go play at Neely. Heah me, now?" With such incidents we gradually eroded the orthodoxy of the rigid "rabbi" within him.

I also figured out that Father had a more mundane and practical purpose for his Sabbath sanctimony, one that simultaneously fulfilled God's wishes and his own. If the children were well rested on Mondays, more acres could be plowed, more cotton and cucumbers picked, sweet potatoes dug, corn harvested, and paper wood and logs sawn. Expending too much energy on baseball, messing around and cluttering our minds with foolishness, even fishing—all these competed with work on the farm.

If father was hung up on keeping the Sabbath, I had issues with the other commandments, like covetousness. I could hardly discern the difference between strongly desiring something and coveting it.

Was it a matter of ownership? Don't covet thy neighbor's stuff, his maidservant, ox, or ass. I didn't like the Bible's inclusion of the word "ass" in the commandment. My neighbor's ass! A little prudish, I wondered if the finger of God had actually written the word "ass." A nasty term for me. Why didn't the Bible use the word "mule"? Was it because mules weren't asses, only half-asses? I could abide that, because a "half-ass" was something undesirable anyway.

Besides the Sabbath services at Old Washington Baptist Church, we attended Wednesday night prayer meetings. These were not big on our family agenda, yet they were not wholly avoided. We had to be seen at least occasionally at prayer meeting. Choir practice came on the same night, and I often wondered if this wasn't a way to get people to church on Wednesday nights. Decades later these became church suppers and social gatherings.

We Baptists seldom prayed on our knees. This was for the Roman Catholics and Episcopalians. We reasoned that the Lord could hear us regardless of the positions of our bodies.

Occasionally, the Old Washington flock felt it necessary to ask for special dispensations: the Lord's help for healing someone, to help save a particular "sinner," or for bringing rain. My parents taught me that prayer was somehow linked with toil, something one did all the time, and that a special occasion was seldom needed. One shouldn't run to God with trivia, but some people had lives so full of prayer that we considered them saintly. My grandmother Ginny was one of these. People often said, "Aunt Gin's life is a prayer book."

One summer after a severe drought the congregation of Neely decided to have a special prayer meeting for rain. There was an especially large attendance, including children and one mentally retarded young man named Moddy. Every member—Baptists never used the word "communicant"—was asked to pray, as the Lord led him, for "showers of blessing." When it came Moddy's turn, he, like the others, prayed hard for rain. But while he had the Lord's ear he decided to expand the request. It was past suppertime and food must have been on his mind. He boldly requested, "Lord, things shore are bad over't house. Please sen us a barrel o flour. Lord, sen us a barrel o sugar. And Lord, while you're at it, sen us a barrel o meal and nother with grits in it, a barrel o salt, and a barrel o pepper." Then, sensing that something was out of place, he suddenly reversed himself, adding loudly, "No, Lord, fergit it. That's too damn much pepper!"

Our family never took meals without "the Blessing." We didn't call it "grace." This custom, brief as it was, constituted about as rigid a ritual as any other religious practice in our household. It was tradition for most Southern families. Even in restaurants. However, in our case it became increasingly memorized, shortened, and routinized. Father's prayer consisted of a few mumbled words, but we children had an even briefer thanks that we surreptitiously muttered: "Bless the meat, damn the skin; back your ears, cram it in!" Then there was the Pa Kettle blessing: Gazing toward the ceiling, we uttered humbly, "Much obliged."

One Thanksgiving dinner, Father asked cousin Cranford, who had recently heard the "calling of the Lord," to invoke a blessing on the turkey and trimmings. Apparently mistaking the dinner table for the pulpit, Cranford's supplication went on and on, drowning out our growling stomachs. With eyes wide open, we wondered if Cranford's hearing was bad. Our minds drifted and we thought, *Would the end never come?* We were saved by Uncle Bo, the irreverent pseudo-apostate of the Charles Hillman clan. He interrupted the monologue with a loud voice from the back of the room, "Shut up, Cranford! Let's eat!"

My parents viewed feeding the preacher as a holy duly. Everyone called this "having the preacher," which meant not only feeding him but housing him and his family for an entire weekend. My mother and father wanted the family to have an opportunity to know and appreciate the "vessel of God in our midst," as he was sometimes called. His service to several rural churches was in addition to a full-time job, usually in a city nearby. The congregation looked forward to actually having an ordained preacher in the pulpit, someone to break the weekly monotony of just Sunday school and singing. We particularly wanted an alternative to certain self-appointed laymen "expounding" on scripture we already knew too well.

Ours was one of the few families that could afford to house and bed the preacher and his family from Friday through Sunday night. The Hillmans' turn came about twice each year. On those Saturday visits Father took occasion to educate our bearer of the Good News on the facts of farm life and other mundane matters around the homestead. Father enjoyed walking around the barn and grinned when the preacher stepped in cow manure. Our guest usually drank it all in with wonder and innocence. Mother was great at entertaining the wife, especially if she was of a literary nature or interested in gardening. Spiritual benefactions appeared to be part of the deal, and usually time was found for the minister to counsel us children, delicately approaching the subject of "the Lord." Had we thought about and sought Him? Had we *found* Him?

We were more at ease discussing both spiritual and sexual matters with anyone other than our parents. For most of my years of wondering and inquiry, the minister supplemented very nicely my parents' own attempts to broach the discussion of matters of faith and practice. There was never pressure to "walk the aisle for Christ." No selling from this pastor. I always liked visits from Brother Moulder because of his three lovely daughters. My eyes were fixed on the auburn-haired twelve-year-old who wore a constant smile. (I always thought she was directing it at me.) Unfortunately, their arrival meant that we children had to stay with neighbors. But in my imagination, lying there on unhallowed pillows, her face was just as beautiful as if we were under the same roof on Thad Hill.

We were always concerned about the minister's welfare, even on Sunday when we had to continue the regular farm duties. My family, together with the congregation, filled his car with leg-tied chickens, eggs, canned pears, black-eyed peas and okra, honey and syrup. Brother Moulder, who was our quarter-time preacher for years, always responded with grace and always seemed pleased to be at Old Washington. Third Sunday became special. But it was not the same with every preacher, as some were misfits and bores.

Aside from church, much of my religious experience came from reading the Bible and religious literature such as Sunday school books and the hard-knuckle Training Union manuals from Nashville. These, and a copy of Grimm's fairy tales, were the principal books in our possession. There was a giant book of Hurlbut's Bible stories, a world in itself just in its pictures. It contained more than a thousand pages of Old Testament saga and New Testament salvation: man's origins, life and death, war and peace, love and hope, redemption and resurrection. Everything in between. You needed no further education than what came within the pages of Hurlbut and Grimm.

We had no library. Learning to read at four, I knew some Bible stories at six and began reading the King James translation soon thereafter. Mother shared her consuming interest in Romantic and Elizabethan literature with me, and the sound of her words brought life to this version of the Holy Scripture, which became, and still remains, my preference. My appreciation for words, phrases, and poetry, primitive at first, began there. Words, phrases, place-names, and ideas like *Garden of Eden, cedars of Lebanon, waters of Babylon, Mount of Olives, Sea of Galilee, wild beasts of the field, birds of the air, boars of the forest, fishes of the sea, Egypt, Sinai, Moriah, Jezreel, Ophir, Nain, Jerusalem, Tarsus, Ephesus, Rome, tree of life, salt of the earth, the Alpha and Omega* . . .

I didn't know it then, but Mother's penchant for Elizabethan English would whet my appetite for Shakespeare. Coupled with high school Latin and a good English teacher, Mrs. Backstrom, it grew. I would come to believe that language is what separated people from the animals, and was that which kept us from being just another biological son of Adam. In the same way, foul language dragged us back to groveling with the swine.

"Elmer just said 'goddam,'" I reported to Mother with triumphant glee. Little brother Elmer at four was my junior by three years. To further impress her with the seriousness of the incident, I repeated the curse loudly and with satisfaction. "He said it four times, 'goddam, goddam goddam goddam.'" Mother bristled and became flush of face as was her custom when one of us so flagrantly broke the commandments. "I'm not gonna let you curse like those Smith children," she said. "Bring me that gallberry brush broom, Jimmye." I ran to where she pointed at the storeroom shed by the side of the back porch, smiling all the way. She selected several stalks from the broom, two to three feet in length. "Turn around," she said to me, and proceeded to switch my legs vigorously. "This is hurting me more than it is you," she said, which I never believed. Elmer received only a stern warning. Mother was a strict observer of the third commandment and often threatened to wash out our mouths with soap and water. We could use the word "Lord" with impunity, but "God" was not to be mouthed.

Following long tradition, Old Washington had an annual revival meeting. Our revival meetings were scheduled church calendar events for the specific purpose of saving the souls of sinners for Jesus and adding numbers to the church body count. Those already saved had corollary benefits: a re-warming of the congregation's spirit of brotherhood, or turning over a new leaf in a person's life. We called it "rededication," which was for the so-called backsliders. Baptists, already saved, could not be lost again, but a good re-treading helped.

Our revivals were not institutional diversion or individual enter- tainment, but were the spiritual and focal point of church every summer. It was serious business to enroll names in the Book of Life and to ensure that eternity was spent with Jesus. We believed that Heaven and Hell, as described by the early church fathers and Dante, were geographic locations in space. Saying otherwise could get you "churched." We weren't Amish, but we sure could shun a misfit.

Weeks before the appointed date, we held special prayer sessions, sending supplications into Heaven that the Lord would bless our effort with a "bountiful harvest." The names of Brother Cranford, Brother Black, or Brother Williams were brought to the "Throne of Grace," and the excitement was comparable to a Sharkey and Schmel- ing bout. Prayers specified a few particular sinners by name, laggards, lukewarm members, and downright nonbelievers—all who needed to be saved, baptized, and join the church, or their faith rekindled.

Old Ben Doggett never yielded to salvation inducement from the pleading crowd, never budged from his apostasy. Yet when he died soon after the revival of 1936, I didn't hear anyone say, "He's burnin in Hell right now."

We held revival services twice daily, morning and evening. Mostly women and children attended morning services. I went with Mother, and it seemed that we prayed for everything from "Genesis to Revela- tion," and for everyone from "Yaller Rabbit to Vinegar Bend." Some who were caught up in the moment knelt on the floor—no prie-dieu or prayer rail for us. But generally, long prayers were un-Baptist- like because dinner was simmering on the stove at home. (Morning services also gave preachers the opportunity to learn which housewife baked the best chicken for Sunday dinner.) Everything concluded about dinnertime, and going to church sure beat farm chores.

On the first Sunday following the opening week of revival, we had dinner on the ground, a polite reason for gorging yourself. "All day preaching and dinner on the ground" had become a cliché even before my time. It was a ritual no less real, however, and important to the revival motif, the institution of revivalism itself. The rural Baptist hierarchy spoke of prayer and preaching, but food and eating was always in the back of their minds. This day came as close to a feast day (without their admitting to the Roman Catholic term) as is outlined in the calendars of Judaic and Catholic traditions. "Dinner on the ground" was a feast day for a church that didn't recognize any saints after Saint Paul.

Brother Black always prepared a special sermon for dinner-on-the-ground Sunday, half the audience of which were not church members. His remarks were built around special stories like the Israelites wandering in the Sinai Desert and being fed manna from heaven, or of Jesus's feeding the five thousand. The homily was very simple, eating food, but I always wondered if we were going to wander in the desert for forty years before we got to eat. After the invitation, there was a mass exodus to the tables under the oaks.

This was a special Sunday when a captive audience of hungry people, irrespective of church affiliation or individual belief, could attend church, suffer the morning sermon, resist the temptation to be saved and to join the church, and yet be first in line for dinner. Some, in fact, didn't even enter the church. But Mother, among others who thought the preacher was too soft on freeloaders, would confront these vagabonds as they assembled at the tables, saying, "The least you can do is go listen to Brother Black before you run here for my chicken!"

Each family that could afford it would bring a basket or box of food. It was an organized potluck, although we never used that word. The ladies took charge, laying out chicken and dumplings, baked ham and boiled pork loin, boiled eggs, baked sweet potatoes, collards and turnip greens, butter and lima beans, okra, black-eyed peas and green beans, cornbread and light bread on long tables covered with starched white cloths. There was enough variety to evoke surprise and pleasant comment. "Emma, where did you get bananas for your pudding? I thought the grocery truck hadn't come by yet." Or, "Nora, you've outdid y'self this year with your black walnut cake." Aunt Nora often baked a cake everyone called "Nora's Special," a three-layered vanilla-flavored, icing-covered mass. Her recipe was a secret. We made a dash to get a piece of it before piling anything else on our plates. But she always saved a slice for me wrapped in a piece of brown paper, saying, "Jim, I kept you back a piece. If I'm not here, it'll be in that basket under the table." On one occasion, however, the ants got to it before I did.

Dinner-on-the-ground took two hours, as we made time for stories and gossip, for chewin, smokin, and dippin. "Why didn't Ben Doggett make a decision," someone might have asked. "He was close to going forward."

Non-churchers, widows especially, took advantage of every revival to fill themselves and their children. "Did you see Froggie and her bunch, Aunt Lou and that crew? It's probably the first good meal they've had since the Methodist revival." Mrs. Vernon came to every feast with her six children, ranging in age from five to thirteen. She must have felt guilty, because she confessed to my father: "Mr. Bud, I done joined all the churches, but don't know *what* I believe." My father later said, "She would have joined the holy-rollers if they had revivals."

What's a widow and hungry offspring to do, and what is the church mission but to feed them? If all this meant a bit of hypocrisy on the part of the down-and-out, listening to hellfire-and-damnation sermons without any intent to commit and to be a part of a congregation, so be it. There were not just a few of these, and their numbers grew in the 1930s. They would drag themselves from revival to revival, community to community, and one sensed that their next move would be to demand a change in the menu.

With diminished interest in revivals after World War II, dinner-on-the-ground went out of style. In the 1970s I remember seeing some old rotting tables under the oaks near Old Washington church, and the scene made me think of Aunt Nora's Special.

Two weeks of revival meeting concluded with one last canvass for souls. Baptism services were duly scheduled. Catholics were sprinklers;

we immersed the saved in the creek. Cousin Glenn, who had worked on the Mississippi River levee near Lake Pontchartrain, told me that most New Orleans Catholics drank, smoke, and swore just like everyone else. "Jimmye-boy," he told me. "I don't think nary-a-one of em is saved!" *Maybe saved from being Baptist,* I thought.

Our ceremony took place either at the Brushy Creek swimming hole, or at a bend in Atkinson Creek near Harvison Bridge. My own Baptist bar mitzvah happened at the bridge site on Atkinson creek in 1936 when I was thirteen. I had made a decision after talking to my mother. She had said, "Don't you want to get baptized this year, Jimmye? Look at all those others. Maybe you should talk to Brother Moulder." Moulder, my mother knew, never made me feel cajoled, coerced, or like I was being sold a bill of goods. He wouldn't give me some high-powered evangelistic pitch to tick me off his list. I finally did visit with the preacher and assuaged the fears of my parents who were concerned that I wouldn't make a public display to their satisfaction. Their concern about my salvation was a mystery to me. I thought it was obvious to everyone that I loved the Lord.

There never was an exact moment when I "got saved," and it didn't matter to me. I was more concerned about my earthly prospects than heavenly. I had never felt insecure about my spiritual underpinning. Nor did I feel "elected" in a Calvinistic sense, either before or after immersion. I worried much more about my poor father and mother. Night after night they went to bed tired; day after day they woke up anxious and distressed about putting food on the table.

Years later, I read Elaine Pagels's *Beyond Belief* and was surprised by our similar thinking. Pagels asks what happens, or doesn't happen, when a person undergoes baptism. She then suggests that it isn't the same for everyone. Some go into the water and come up saying, "I'm now a Christian." Others experience a mystery. I was in both groups.

A small choir sang "O happy day that fixed my choice" as one by one we stepped into the warm, flowing stream in our Sunday clothes. Following Ruth Green, I cautiously waded barefoot up to my waist into the deep water, which felt much colder to my feet. Preacher Moulder stood on a high spot of sand in the middle of the stream, taking the hand of each candidate.

I watched Ruth rise from the water and felt relieved that she didn't seem distressed. I gave Brother Moulder my hand, and he placed his left hand between my shoulders as I looked across the creek at my parents among the oak and dogwood. "Jimmye," he began, "I baptize you in the name of the Father and the Son and the Holy Ghost," at which point he placed a handkerchief over my mouth and nose and levered me backward into the water. I came up unsurprised, as we had swum in this hole many times before. Moulder muttered, "Buried to sin, raised to new life," and handed me off to Brother Neville, who gave me a towel to dry my face and hair. A small blind of sheets had been arranged on a creek sandbar for the girls, while the men and boys went off into the bushes to change clothes. My skin was moist, and a summer breeze along the creek gave me a sensual, peaceful state of mind.

My baptism left no doubt that I had deftly escaped the devil's snare and wouldn't be going to Hell after all. I had avoided torment and the writhing of lost souls in the Fire, as described by Brother Black and many others. An eternity of weeping, wailing, and the gnashing of teeth had given way to hope on a pleasant afternoon. I could smell the musty swamp and latent dogwood blossom. Brother Moulder left for Hattiesburg with a carload of live chickens, and we returned home to Thad Hill.

Along with my spiritual guarantee, it was also a surety that the next day would see me back in the field picking cucumbers and in the cotton patch with a hoe; or behind Old Mattie, heel-sweeping weeds from amongst the corn.

I never gave much attention to the formal ceremony of baptism at Old Washington. Farm work seemed more of a sacrament than being "ducked in the water." Baptists never used the word "sacrament" anyway. We had other names for the sacraments of reconciliation, priesthood, confirmation, and eucharist. I later learned extreme unction was available for believers when we were dying. But what was it? I knew that someday the angel Gabriel would blow his horn and we would proceed to join that caravan of ancestors who awaited us on the golden shore. When the congregation sang "When They Ring Those Golden Bells" at funerals, I imagined the beautiful pealing amongst the mysterious seven stars and seven candlesticks of Saint John's Revelation. Michael and his angels had fought the dragon, Old Satan, and had prevailed. I never thought much about my own mortality.

"Call Mister Rile," was the command when the body lay still, sheet over the face, and the soul had flown. It was the expression people were all too familiar with. "Call Mister Rile." Rile Dixon, a small, wiry man, always wearing a mustache and sweat-soaked hat, was the village gravedigger. Rain or shine we could depend on him and his helpers to "shovel the dirt" as the saying went, and to be sure the gravesite was recorded with the appropriate church secretary. Over the years, he buried bodies from three generations. He always dug a grave the afternoon before. He was not closely affiliated with any one church, owed no favor, nor was owed, and people respected him, an able assistant to the undertaker. His payment came in kind, and I remember my dad gave him a half a shoat for digging Grandpa's grave.

In our community, it seemed that one of the churches was always burying someone. Several of these were my childhood friends, like beautiful little Theda Myrl Breland, the cause of her death no more known than the reason God chose her. It almost devastated Neely school when Rufus Goff died, probably of pneumonia. He was a bit older than the rest of us, our indisputable leader, and drove the school bus over the treacherous road to the Forks of the River. Who would God send to drive the bus?

Pneumonia, tuberculosis, appendicitis, and farm accidents were the prime killers before the sulfa drugs and penicillin came along. Lightning killed two of my cousins, one of them Hinkle Green. Hinkle, while at work one day on the Texas–New York gas pipeline, had made the mistake of getting under a tall pine during a thunderstorm. Lightning had badly burned his body, and there was no viewing at the funeral.

"Miz Agnes, somebody's dead," Mrs. Cox, my mother's helper, would say. "Don't know who it were, but I seed the ol Hugin truck go by this mornin." Hulett was the source of much conversation, because if the undertaker was on the road someone was definitely dead. Gossip began when the hearse passed, but nothing definite was known until Mr. Rile was contacted. This could sometimes lead to rumors of people dying who weren't dead: as was the case with old lady Lottie Keyes, who had two bastard kids, lingered on forever, and died several times. (Lottie had a peculiar vocabulary all her own. For example, to receive government relief you had to get certified for need. Once my mother asked if she was going to sign up for the commodities, and she answered, "Yes, Ma'am. But first I gotta go to Leaksville to get circumcised." My mother almost dropped her teeth.)

"Oh, she been dead," Pete Fairley said every time Lottie's name was mentioned. "She been dead."

Most people hesitated to say that someone was "dead," to speak in terms of finality. Instead, they might say, "The Lord has called him" or "He passed away" or "God took his soul," "He's gone on to glory," "He ain't with us no more." In the case of children, it was, "The angels came and took him to heaven."

We rarely saw the hearse from Hulett's funeral home, because it was too expensive. For those who were too poor to afford a mortician, Hulett had burial insurance policy premiums, which could be paid in part with chickens, eggs, or syrup. I remember Mrs. Cox telling my father, "Mr. Bud, I think I'll drop that old burial policy. It ain't done me no good no way." Father, at a loss for words, said only, "Probably, Ethyl."

Bodies were usually laid out in the home and carried directly to the church. The corpse had to be in the ground before its smell overpowered the homegrown flowers that decorated coffin and parlor. The stale aroma from the flowers often became pervasive. I still associate cape jasmine, the most common flower, with death and funerals. Its strong sweet odor masked the emerging scent of rotting flesh and turned me against wanting to attend funerals.

I came to terms with death early: dead cows, dead hogs, and dead mules. I thought: *Is a human being any different from the Blue Boar?* I remember the stories Mother read to me of Hades and Styx. Did Charon ferry Grandpa Charlie across the river? Everyone found comfort in talking of Heaven, especially during times of loss, but such things didn't concern me as I gazed on the dead person's face.

Whether or not they were church members, most every person around Neely wound up in Old Washington cemetery. They had Christian rites, even though some were passive nonbelievers. The job for the minister was to preach them into heaven. The blackguard doubters and the church-going darlings got equal time. The standard reading at funerals was from the fourteenth chapter of Saint John, and I had memorized all four verses: "Let not your heart be troubled. . . . In my Father's house are many mansions. . . . I go to prepare a place for you. . . . I will come again . . . and the way ye know." The word "mansions" always fascinated me until one day the Sunday school teacher said it meant "rooms." "Mansions" meant rooms. Jesus lived in just a room? Is that all I'm gonna get?

You could distinguish between the poor and those families who were living above the margin by the flowers rather than by the casket. Poor families and friends could not afford wreaths but instead made their own from local gardens, twisting cape jasmines around a length of baling wire. Some insisted on an expensive, shiny casket with soft, quilted lining. They spent all their savings, even went into debt, for this one moment in church and what they called a "decent burial."

When a well-to-do uncle of mine died, he was laid out at a funeral parlor in another city. His son, who lived in California, came back to Mississippi for the ceremony and didn't like the choice of casket. "This is too cheap for my Daddy," he said. "He ain't gonna be buried in no wood box and I'm gonna do somethin about it!" He borrowed money and had his father's two-day-old corpse removed and placed in a solid copper coffin. Charlie's type could have been the grist for an entire chapter in Jessica Mitford's *The American Way of Death*.

Most all funerals were public, the casket cracked open for a last good-bye. We sang songs during the viewing and people lined up, passed by the casket, and touched the lifeless face. It lay against a silk lining, cheap powder dusting the puttylike form, hands across chest. That process became increasingly abhorrent to me through the years. It wasn't just because they were dead. I seemed to have comprehended that, long before my parents explained what it meant when "Aunt Veen has gone to be with the Lord." They were dead and attempts to make them look otherwise were grotesque to me, even misleading. "Don't she look natural?" or "He don't look like hisself," and a thousand other remarks or thoughts. *How are the dead supposed to look?* I thought.

Perhaps it was here that I began to wrestle with what later became a serious interest in phenomenology. Souls went to Heaven. I could accept that and leave the rest to my imagination, though Heaven always seemed to me to be very boxed-in, a potentially boring place with everybody being happy all the time, singing and shouting *hal-lelujah!* How could I be myself, and retain my individual personality?

The viewing was the longest part of the ceremony, and often included loud outbursts, emanating from deep, emotional uncertainty about Earth and Heaven. Hymns of comfort assuaged the pain and loss. The melodies had a way of soothing and comforting the individual as well as binding believer to believer, assuring them that when "the roll is called up yonder" they would be present to reunite with that nonbreathing person who lay in front of the pulpit. Favorites at Old Washington were "What a Friend We Have in Jesus," "Rock of Ages," and "The Sweet By-and-By." I always liked "Near the Cross" because it had those poignant last words from a refrain that only Fannie Crosby could have written: "Till my raptur'd soul shall find Rest beyond the river."

I understood that the river was the Jordan, of course. Heaven lay beyond, the New Jerusalem, victory, a day of rejoicing in Abraham's bosom with God and His angels, eternity, peace, talking with Jesus in hushed tones. It sounded to me idyllic; then why all the fuss?

Most of the weeping seemed real, a releasing of grief and assuaging of tired minds and bodies. But some appeared to be manufactured, "put on" as Mother would say. From those who needed attention, it was a chance to say to the world, "Yes! he is dead but look at me. I'm alive, and I'm still here and important." The volume of noise often varied according to who had died. Like when Will Hathorn was laid out in his fancy casket inside Callie Creel's store. You would have thought everyone in the county knew him personally, though he had lived in Louisiana for years. I don't mean to imply that we had paid mourners, but it appeared to a youngster such as I that love, loss, and grief were expressed just a bit louder for the more well-to-do.

After the funeral, hanging around the graveyard for some seemed preferable to going home, entering an empty house, gazing at an empty rocking chair, and trying to sleep without the loved one in the room. Sometimes people showed concern about the survivors. "How's Aunt Lou and all her kids gonna make it now that Bill is gone?" I worried about what I would do if Mother or Father died suddenly.

Flying into Mississippi from Arizona, tired and emotionally spent, I hastened to Mother's wake. I remember entering the room with all eyes upon me. Cousin Charlie rushed up to comfort me and whispered, "Jim, she ain't dead, only sleeping." I looked down at Mother's most unnatural, artificially-made-beautiful-but-lifeless countenance and blurted out, "She's dead as hell!" And I kissed her forehead.

The next day Mr. Rile's crew dug the hole, and, as she had requested, we sang "Abide with Me" before lowering her beside "Mr. Hillman," her husband for fifty years.

Recently, I visited Old Washington cemetery and noticed an encroachment on the Hillman corner plots. Some of the markers not only didn't bear the Hillman name but they had no death dates, only birth dates. I thought to myself, *Nothing ever changes, even after you're dead. People are always horning in on the Hillmans.*

Yellow Dog Politics

HUDDLED UNDER A KEROSENE LAMP in our parlor one late summer evening in the mid-1930s, the candidate in the soft chair and one of his precinct workers on the floor pored over a handwritten list of names. It was hot, and a dank smell blanketed the room.

Election day was approaching and things were heating up in other ways. The race, already close, was getting closer; each vote was critical. Children weren't permitted at such gatherings, but I peeked out from my bedroom.

Mumbled exchanges between the two figures went on into the night. Names of individuals and families were chosen at random, then came a long monotone, followed by questions, pauses, and muttered crossfire. An air of excited assertion issued from the figure on the floor. Pause, question, and repeated assertion: the conversation went on inexorably until the list was exhausted about midnight. From the other room, I could little mistake the words: "Mr. Bud, I ain't got no better friend. Mr. Bud, I ain't got no better!"

The candidate was my father, J. L. "Bud" Hillman. On the floor was Sam Fairley, a well-known local political junkie who, every four years, sold himself to the highest bidder for "walking money," Greene County style. It was my father's first run at office, and he needed entrée to the Leaf precinct, called "the box" locally, in the southwest part of the county near the river by the same name. The list contained twenty-three voters in that box. Sam claimed to be friendly or closely associated with each one, all the Leaf swing-vote electorate. Leaf was marginal in Beat Five, the district of 350-plus voters, other boxes being at McLain, Neely, Unity, and Pleasant Hill.

Father wound up receiving only five of Leaf's twenty-three votes. He narrowly lost the election, conceding after the results were in from the remote box, Pleasant Hill, with its twenty-five votes, which always was the last to report. (Later, whenever my father was uncertain about an outcome, he liked to say, "Wait till Pleasant Hill comes in.") Leaf reported early, and during the counting of other boxes it became a drag on his positive sums. Votes in his favor elsewhere were insufficient to offset that disaster. This narrow defeat laid the groundwork for refining his political acumen, which eventually led to a long period of county service. His political career came after he had retired from teaching in the public schools.

The election forgotten, Father later recounted with boyish avidity that fateful evening of political innocence: "Sam, do you really think he's with us? How does his wife stand? Will the family come along and who will get them to the polls? Is their poll tax paid? Is money involved? Is he a Baptist?" His response to each name on the list was: "Mr. Bud, I ain't got no better friend in the world." Or, "Mr. Bud, he's one hundred percent, with us all the way, I guarantee ya." The voter was in Sam's pocket. "I ain't got no better!"

Father came away from that unexpected defeat disappointed but gained an aphorism that got many laughs that reverberated down through the years. If we were looking for absolute assurance, someone would say, "But remember Harry Truman and his upset of Dewey in 1948?" Then another would yell out, "I ain't got no better!" It became Hillman family lore: "I ain't got no better!"

I acquired a thick skin early and deduced that people must have a sense of humor to survive. I also learned to count votes, to be skeptical of political prediction, and to doubt professional pollsters. Little did I know how much I was learning about the discounting of human expectation. And I hadn't even read about the Battle of Thermopylae.

This campaign also etched on my childhood mind several other observations about politics, many of which have since become general clichés: *Don't get involved with politics; it's a dirty, disappointing business. Never trust a politician; all politicians are liars.* On a hopeful note: *It ain't ever over 'til the last vote is counted.* And my mother's favorite: *Politics makes strange bedfellows.* One particular adage of my father's has stuck with me for a lifetime: "Son, there are two great imponderables in this world: Who will a man vote for when he gets alone in that booth; and, who will a woman marry if given a free chance?"

I suppose his first disappointment with the electorate in Greene County helped give rise to the first; and the marital experiences of his seven sisters, the latter.

After the election, our family returned to normal speculation about the future, something akin to the Second Coming. It was always the same ritual: the wake, the burial, and the resurrection of hope for a different outcome in four years. Without doubt, there *would* be another battle. Egos had been bruised, psyches disillusioned, but the metamorphosis always took place. Personal prestige must now be accommodated. The stakes were too high to turn aside an opportunity to avoid the ignominy of failure. Gossip and rumor ran rampant in the questions people were asking. Specifically, "Why did Bud listen to that crackpot?"

Postmortems held by a losing candidate were simple: brief assessments of what went wrong and what could be done to rectify the defeat. It's a given that there will be a rerun because politics is like sex: once you've had it it's impossible to abstain.

My father sought personal perspective from a few elder statesmen and sages in the Beat Five, despite his suspicion that some counselors had not supported him. Though negative feelings ran high between candidates in a heated campaign, one never cut the possible binding rope of future support from anybody. A nod from a past opponent might mean the margin of victory next time. In Father's case, late in his political career, one of his staunchest supporters was a man who had opposed him earlier, had eliminated him in that first try at office. Often among one's best political friends were one's enemies four years back.

Politicking never stopped in our village. Like many others in Mississippi, it tended to be a cultural redoubt after Reconstruction. Apparently, the competitive urge filled a void in the droll lives of men who had little other means of entertainment. One didn't have to be a candidate to be perennially immersed in Machiavellian small talk and election supposition. Every country store had a "mourners' bench" where men gathered to predict winners and losers. These clusters of adjunct second-guessers, come election time, were ready for the asking to jump on the bandwagon of any candidate.

The interim between election days became a game period, testing the wiles of the candidate against some stranger often at the

Principal J. L. "Bud" Hillman, ca. 1942.

far end of the district constituency. One strategy might be to make
the opponent pose as an economic threat to property owners, or a
barrier to one's social standing, or an imminent danger to the status
quo of the community. Reasons for candidacy were easy to come
by: "Ya gotta run, Bud. Willie is a no-good crook. Buford is incom-
petent, doesn't know what he's doing, and will break the county!"
Revenue questions and tax issues were central, as important then as
now. "He'll raise our taxes," it was said of the phantom opponent.
(Property taxes were the major source of local revenue.) Roads and
transportation ran a close second to taxes. Father perceived this, built
his future campaigns around road building, and coasted to victory
election after election by keeping his constituency convinced that
he would build and maintain new roads. The automobile was then
becoming a part of our rural life. But even for those with only mule
and wagon, this was an appealing political platform.

My father had already retired from a career as schoolteacher and tended to be an exception as a politician. Running for public office was a means of satiating the ego-appetites of little men, giving fodder to the chicanery hatched in their minds over long winters, assuaging the pain of being ignored by the community, a way of identifying with a "cause," however ill-founded. An unknown backwoodsman could attach himself to an eminent personality, county or state leader, and commit himself to a societal role beyond immediate family. Political commitment was an avenue to power beyond church office, civic function, and school committee. It was a path of escape from farm or other occupational routine, a chance at a regular salary for four years, no small matter in the Depression. Some ran to prove their worth to friend and foe, and to themselves. It is safe to say that at least 50 percent of the eligible males in Beat Five had, at one time or other, considered announcing their candidacy for public office. A man's capacity to dream is equaled only by his tendency toward self-delusion.

Women were not a major factor in Greene County politics, a lamentable fact still true of many locales. And, of course, there were no black candidates.

Campaign strategy was never complex. Unlike today, time trumped money. At the state level there was seldom a Republican opposition, and in the primaries no names on the local ballot were of that party. The winners were decided in the August primaries. The polls might have been open in November, but I don't ever remember seeing anybody vote. No one bothered to register Republican. In fact, "Republican" was a dirty word, as many associated it with carpet-baggers, scalawags, federal-appointed governors, Sherman, Farragut, and other enemies of the Southern cause, though in my childhood this dream of plantations and Gone-with-the-Wind romance was becoming more nebulous.

How "Solid South" Democrats of the Franklin Roosevelt era became the "Red State" Republicans of today is not a mystery to those of us reared there and who know the culture. Volumes have been written on the subject. The hard facts are that, just as race and "states' rights" were instrumental in the solidification of the Democrats from Reconstruction until World War II, so race has remained advantageous whichever party claims this as a core issue. Today, "values" (meaning "white values") has become the instrument by which politicians today persuade a registered Democratic electorate of Greene County to vote Republican at the state and national level.

My grandpa used to say, "I'd vote for a yellow dog before I'd vote for a Republican!" These days, the people of Greene County might repeat his very words, only substitute "Democrat" for "Republican." It does remain a paradox, however, as to why voters choose officials who apparently support policies that run opposite to their economic and social interests.

Greene County politics resolved itself in the tactics used by the candidates. Gimmickry and transparent fabrication were tools frequently used. One candidate said he would build a bridge across Atkinson Creek to Uncle Jeff Byrd's place. (We all knew that one project would take half the budget of the district.) He then moved on to the next family up the road and made a similar promise. Promises to cut taxes had little consequence because most of the populace had no property.

Ultimately it became an option—which man did you like, believe in, or trust, not only with the job but also personally? Personal appeal was vital, placing the burden on the candidate to use an intense sales pitch, selling himself, of course, one on one to the voter, usually making promises the bases for which he knew little. Even so, voters cast their lot with the candidate who favored their economic self-interests. This is a far cry from today when, for some abstruse reason, their poor, unemployed descendants are voting for moral-value candidates who would eviscerate the New Deal programs that literally kept their fathers and mothers alive.

My Grandma Ginny often called politics a disease. She thought the devil himself was in the process of pitting one man in the community against another in the privacy of a voting booth. "Why couldn't people come out in public or stand up in church and state who they were for? Let the community leaders decide, or the church deacons, who should run things." She was not infatuated with Susan B. Anthony but never failed to exercise her right to vote, mainly against whom she considered an unworthy candidate. Unfortunately she died before being able to vote for her beloved son, my father. Yet, she had a brother whose political career bore testimony to the intensity and personal dedication of a man obsessed with running for office.

Marque "Mark" Ellsworth Green, my grandmother's brother, was
second-generation Irish, born in 1865, the last child of a pioneer
family. He grew up and homesteaded near Old Washington and
was buried in its cemetery in 1948. The youngest of the clan, for
eighty-three years he was a farmer and itinerant trader, forever restless but especially so after most of his eight children left home. He
came to political ambition naturally (being Irish), but, unfortunately,
the electorate smiled little on his endeavors. Up through the 1940s
he ran many times for state representative, but was elected only
once, on the second attempt. Across Greene County's dirt roads he
strode, often in overalls, denim shirt, and tennis shoes, light Irish
skin, sandy-colored hair, sweating and dust-covered. For years, his
bodily presence moved specterlike across the county. "Go get em,
Uncle Mark," children would say, but their parents had no intention
of sending him to Jackson.

Seeing him walk barefooted in the summer, I wondered how such
a man could bear the public's eye and ask their confidence as their
representative in the state capital. The answer was ego, that irrational
and unsubstantiated belief that his ubiquitous presence in the community really mattered and that he, personally, could make a difference among the eighty-two county representatives in Jackson. Asked
why he continued to stand for office after those numerous drubbings
at the polls, his parrotlike reply in a high-pitched thin voice was, "I
gad, I have never been defeated, only delayed four years."

By God, Mark Green's candidacy was an inevitable harbinger of
political gatherings in Greene County and southern Mississippi every
four years. In retrospect, he was our local Harold Stassen. His was the
kind of ego that drives men to disregard every vestige of inevitable
failure, to plod on in face of lurking doom and social and personal
humiliation in order to gain their self-defined prize: winning. It is
the primordial propulsion of moving protoplasm, laden with psyche,
consciously wanting power, to beat the other, to defeat the enemy,
to be crowned with victory. The Hebrews' Ariel, the Greeks' arete.

Mark Green was elected in 1920, and no one was more surprised
than he that a majority of the electorate had X'd in his name. Between
November and inauguration, he strutted around the county, expecting praise but receiving only disappointment that the people were
more interested in returning to their normal activities than indulging

him and his capricious presence. In fact, some were already planning to run against him in 1924. Even his family, though tolerant, was soon satiated with his temporary claim to glory.

After New Year's, like other elected representatives, he began preparing for Jackson. Few families of that era possessed automobiles, which meant taking a train and staying at cheap hotels during the legislative session. Finally, on the first Tuesday after the first Monday, January 1921, dressed in a J. C. Penney blue serge suit and fedora, Marque Ellsworth Green cautiously stepped into the legislative chamber to explore what victory the voters of Greene County had wrought.

Eventually he met the future speaker of the house, a man from the Delta, Walter Sillers Jr. Delta representatives inevitably carried more tenure and stability than those from the hills. The census gave that region more weight because of its many blacks, who were counted but who never voted until late in the twentieth century. Despite all the forward planning, he immediately felt uncomfortable of station and dress. In the rush he had not bought new shoes and was still wearing cracked, dusty brogans.

Eyeing the attire and underpinnings of another colleague, Mark approached him, asking, "I gad, wher'd ya git them shoes?"

The colleague described how to get to the place. "Better yet," he said. "You're a privileged member of the legislature, and all you need to do is to telephone the clerk down there and I'm certain he'll accommodate."

A man of expeditious action, but no experience with Mr. Bell's invention, Uncle Mark went immediately to his office and picked up the telephone receiver. "Number, please?" the operator asked. Assuming a telephone manner commensurate with his new, high office, Uncle Mark barked, "Nines. Medium wide, and send em up here immediately!"

Unfortunately, his glory was ephemeral and his influence availed little in Jackson. He returned to Old Washington after four annual sessions. There was little to show for his time spent wrangling and arguing and for the limited confidence voters had vested in him. One consolation was that he had made political contacts with statesmen like Mike Conner, which would redound to his lifelong political interests but meant little to the well-being of Greene County.

Moreover, he created corresponding enemies, particularly Theodore Bilbo, an enmity that became legend. This region of the state waned in political power for a long time. Recently, I read that the governor of Mississippi, Haley Barbour, had visited Leakesville, a token appearance and one of the few visits of a major state politician in decades.

Uncle Mark is but one example of a Greene County politician. U.S. Senator Pat Harrison had once taught school in Neely and later in Leakesville. He asked my Aunt Nora, then seventeen, to marry him. I asked her once, "Aunt Nody, why didn't you marry him? Now you'd be in Washington as a senator's wife." Without blinking, she said, "Because he wore his pants too tight!"

Among others, Newton James and Webb Walley had been elected to statewide office. I discovered that all these, and some others, were somehow related to the Hillman family. Mark Green's fatuous meandering across the county, for example, illustrates the reach of a small-town mentality exceeding its grasp, its inability to obtain social and political justice for the people represented, even for those who elected him.

The most sought after elected positions, however, depended directly on compensation. For example, the sheriff-and-tax-collector job was highly prized. It was limited to one four-year term, and an occupant had to sit out four before he could run again. As tax collector, the sheriff had the power to withhold a percentage from each tax take. Men elected in the rich counties could become wealthy in one term. The sheriff also enforced liquor laws; many dealt with the problem by quietly accepting "hush money" from bootleggers. It was said that during Prohibition, sheriffs, preachers, and bootleggers had an alliance. Bootleggers assured the preachers that church coffers would never be empty, while the preachers seldom reported violators to the sheriff, who got his cut as well. I often wondered how it was that certain of my classmates could come to school so well dressed while apparently their fathers were unemployed. Years later it became an open secret: it was the revenue from "liquid corn."

There were lots of stories about the office of sheriff of Greene County, some dating back to territorial days. Jokingly, my father once asked Uncle Till Hathorn the name of the current sheriff, to which Till gave a smiling reply: "It's Old Man Murdoc Walley, Bud, and he's a damn good sheriff at that: he ain't never hurt nobody. Ain't always been that way. You remember when Kenny Wagner killed McIntosh back in 1923, I think it was, when the sheriff caught him moonshining. Now I hear 'Is' Turner was thinkin of givin it a go next time. He should be a good one."

"Is" Turner, as he liked to call himself ("I. S." sounding more sophisticated than his real name, William Lewis Turner), was a member of a pioneer family. He was elected sheriff and later served with Father on the board of supervisors. An incongruous incident happened soon after he took office as sheriff: While driving his new county vehicle, he collided with and killed one of Father's cows. "Were you drunk on some of your moonshine?" my father kidded him. He never lived it down.

On another occasion, Father, knowing he would get a funny response, asked Uncle Till what he thought of the present sheriff compared to those of the past. Rising to the challenge, Till grinned beneath his graying mustache and said, "Well now, Bud, you remember young McIntosh in the twenties made a playhouse out the sheriff's office appropriate for the flappers. Jake Green made a shinny still out of it during Prohibition. Then ol Andy Byrd turned it into a whorehouse, even men from Mobile comin out here for their fun. Now, Old Man Murdoc Walley is just smokin it out. Go in to see him and he'll be a sittin there in his swivel chair with his feet on the desk, his pipe hangin from his jaw. Right! Bud, as I said, he ain't gonna hurt nobody."

The county's most important elective officers were the sheriff-and-tax-collector, all one office, for law and order, and the chancery clerk, who kept land records and assured proprietorship of the land base. A board of supervisors ran the county's business and paid the bills, assisted by elected clerks. Eventually, a county superintendent of education grew to major status, as the population demanded more schooling. State government impinged on the locals through district judges, representatives, and the executive or governor. Ultimately, there was the federal bureaucracy to deal with, but it was not elective.

Formed in 1809 when Mississippi was still a territory, reaching almost from the Mississippi River to Alabama, Greene County was one of the oldest political enclaves in this part of an expanding nation.

Ironically, from the beginning it had little political clout beyond its immediate borders. Perhaps it was this that resulted in a dispropor-tionate emphasis on local elections. With a minimum of interest in what went on outside the district, in Washington DC, or in Jackson, the capital, there unfolded from the minds and personalities of these pioneers a historic emphasis on self-interest, local issues associated with Jeffersonian policy and politics. Nor was Andy Jackson's populist philosophy far behind. Indeed, one pictures elements of the ancient Greek polis at work in these post-Confederate villages.

It was powerlessness at a state and national level, coupled with rigid local control in a poverty setting, that gave rise to the accep-tance by Greene County citizens of federal programs such as those of the New Deal. At the same time, they continually wailed about centralized intervention in their affairs (which remains so today). The price they required for "getting the government out of our lives" was that locals be in control of decisions that affected local matters. An example of this was the farm program of price supports and production control that a county committee strictly managed and coordinated in Washington DC. The County Agricultural Stabiliza-tion and Conservation Committee (ASCS) structure remains intact after more than seventy years in operation. In addition to giving farmers power over the management structure, local control gave individual producers a watching and listening post to prevent cor-ruption and fraud, an opportunity to see that their neighbor didn't get preferential treatment. This kind of transparency is the reason there has never been any scandal in the farm programs.

Before the New Deal came along, only a tenuous chain of alli-ances among old settlers and first families linked geographical areas. After WWII and the onus of poverty had been lifted, movements toward civil rights and slogans about the "liberals in Washington," buttressed by a new wave of conservative religious politicking, turned the old FDR model on its head, and Republicans became not only respectable but also dominant in Southern precincts. Some find it inexplicable that the same people who sent representatives and sena-tors to Washington under the pretense of less federal government intervention never really wanted the politicians to keep their prom-ises. After Ronald Reagan promised to "get the government off the farmer's back," the budget of the U.S. Department of Agriculture skyrocketed to historic proportions.

Officeholders in the early nineteenth century in Greene County were those settlers who had been enterprising and successful, who had the prestige to be elected and the time to serve. Some were not inclined to share their private fortunes by running the county's business and often had to be "drafted" into public service. An example was the family of Peter McLeod and Sarah McCaskill. Their son, Dan McLeod, born 1838, was for many years the most important political figure in the county, holding at one time or other every political office. Lack of transportation and other communication was also a deterrent. A shift in this practice came with the growth in population, changes in technology, and the need for laws and regulation to replace "frontier justice." Protecting one's self-interest became a strong inducement for property owners to occupy public office.

The Brelands, Byrds, Dunnams, Greens, McInnises, McLeods, Smiths, Turners, and Williamses were among the first settlers, and during the next century or more were joined by Hillmans, Walleys, and many others. The public offices bore these names into the twenty-first century. It was Byrd, Walley, and Turner in the sheriff's office and Hillman, Smith, and Williams as chancery clerk. Not uncommon were the names Churchwell, Dunnam, Freeman, McInnis, and Breland. An "in group" at Leakesville seemed always to have an advantage if for no other reason than name recognition, which continued even as the county developed and after nodes of business and population sprang up in other places. At supervisor in the five beats, the same general pattern of old names prevailed. In Beat Five, for example, it was J. L. "Bud" Hillman versus W. S. "Bill" Turner, that first race of my father's, which Turner won in the second primary.

Inbreeding was inevitable, leading to a lack of desire to change the way business took place in the county seat. Weary of the Civil War, its fallout, and Reconstruction, and tired of the trek toward new homesteads, most of these people simply wanted to settle down. The "closed society," a condition described by James W. Silver, had its inception in places like Greene County. Reading about that pioneer life brings on a mixed nostalgia. Living in Leakesville in the 1880s had a certain romance and advantage, but incumbents were inclined to hold onto their elective seats and to resist change.

When I was growing up, methods for running a campaign were subtle, beginning with personal probing, sly hint, and a certain rural divination long before election year. A deliberate ploy was to delay announcing your candidacy as long as possible because you wanted the opposition to show his hand first. Also there existed a certain "clientele" who, every four years, used this opportunity to be parasites. These showed absolutely no preference by party, income, or station and took handouts from anyone. Roxanne Lucas, a widow with three young children, showed no compunction about approaching a stranger for "a dollar to feed my babies," be it in church, at Mr. Harvison's Merchandise, or along a dusty road. In election years she equated all strangers with politicians whom she could put the bite on.

In the spring of election year the competition came to a boiling point, as those intending to run had to make an official announcement by a deadline date. The game of political "hide-and-seek" and "will he or won't he?" played itself out, the public's impatience was assuaged, and the list was published in the *Greene County Herald* each week, just as it would appear on the ballot, until the first primary in August. He who had avoided commitment, for whatever reason, was finally smoked out, and the candidate became fair pickings for those who demanded favors for their vote.

The process reminds me of some periodic event that becomes a time for freeloading, or what we considered "acceptable begging." Every time my father's name appeared in the *Greene County Herald* as a candidate, Lou Pipkins approached him and said, "Mister Bud, could you lend me two dollars till Saturday?" My mother ground her teeth and complained, "Here we go again."

Some votes were expensive. Not a few widows with empty cupboards and pre-teen children approached each candidate across the entire ballot for food, a sack of flour, transportation for a family member to McLain to see Dr. McLeod or to the hospital in Hattiesburg, or a signature on a note at the bank.

Even so, for the candidates, little money was involved in those elections. I am certain that Father never spent more than a hundred dollars on any campaign. It all seems so impersonal now, the "conning" process so commercial and uninteresting. The buying of votes is so mechanized; the hypocrisy so routine it's hardly even hypocritical.

Personal persuasion was paramount in Greene County campaigning. Home visits were accepted, often turning into long summer evenings of storytelling and gossip. Shading of the truth was not unusual, especially if the facts could not be checked, or the source couldn't be discovered. Candidates were everywhere, showing up at barbershops, cattle sales, sheepshearings, school functions, and every store in town. On Saturdays they walked the streets of the county villages. Sunday was for the fourth commandment, no politicking, and at church it was a carefully observed rule that political conversation never took place in the open. Church was for religion, not politics. Nevertheless, the very appearance of candidates at church services made one wonder. "We're happy to have him, but why is Mr. Dunnam of State Line at church today?" The motives behind such appearances were more questionable in times of bad economy, bad weather, bad roads, and expensive transportation.

Then came the political rallies, the picnics, the barbecues, and social gatherings whose principal function was to expose the office seeker to the public. These public displays epitomized rural political interaction in that era, and the people looked forward to them, some for the fiddling and singing, some for the food. However, the candidates were anxious to get their message across. There was no entrance charge and who footed the bill was always a mystery. My grandfather Charles Hillman usually donated a yearling and a shoat for the barbecue.

One such picnic took place under the large red oaks across the road from Old Washington Baptist Church in July 1934. All candidates federal, state, and local were invited. Uncle Dave, Grandpa Charlie's brother, took charge, barbecuing sheep, pork, and beef in a large pit with hickory and oak coals, thrusting a long iron poker at the chunks of meat and turning them during the roasting. It was a slow process because of the size of the cuts. I had been permitted to stay up and watch. The conversation related less to politics and more to hog-hunting dogs, fishing, rifles, and shotguns. No talk of women around an eleven-year-old son of Agnes, but some smut nonetheless. By midnight I had become drowsy, but not before Uncle Dave stuck

Political barbecue (mutton or pork) in 1936.

a sharp knife into a leg-joint of beef, inserted a spoon where the knife had been, and tasted the juices, which looked awfully bloody to me.

Theodore Bilbo, two-time governor (1916 and 1928), and a spell-binding orator, was running for the US Senate and was the leadoff speaker the next day. Uncle Mark Green was Bilbo's local nemesis, having aligned himself with Mike Connor, another politician who had split with Bilbo in earlier tussles. Uncle Mark occupied a front seat during the speech, and toward the end when Bilbo made the provocative statement, "If there is a man, woman, or child here today that I did not do a favor for while I was governor, let them stand," Uncle Mark jumped up and exclaimed, "I gad, Bilbo. You ain't never done nothin fer me!" Ever the clever speaker, Bilbo retorted, "Sit down, Uncle Mark, I built the institute for the feeble-minded over at Ellisville just for you."

On a roll, Bilbo continued: "The poor people of Mississippi never had but three friends, Jesus Christ, Sears Roebuck, and Theodore G. Bilbo!" And so it went that day, a final fling for Uncle Mark before political oblivion, but not before showing off at one of the last barbecue-picnics of its sort.

Huey P. Long had been making noises as governor in Louisiana and reputedly told Bilbo, "Shut up, or I'll come across the river and eat you up!" To which Bilbo replied, "Yes, by God, then you'll have more brains in your belly than in your head!"

Bilbo was elected, as always with a racially tainted, white-only vote, using the age-old gimmickry of "them against us" (the rich moneyed magnates of the North, or Yankees, versus the poor dirt-farmer Christians of the South). He then went to Washington and conscientiously supported the New Deal before dying in national political disfavor in 1947.

Male, Scotch-Irish property owners dominated the balloting in Greene County when I grew up. As with all of American politics, the right to vote was correlated with the ownership of property and with gender. When they met at Philadelphia to draft the original Constitution in 1781, the Founding Fathers limited the franchise to property-owning white men. It took almost two centuries, a civil war, a protracted women's suffrage movement, and several constitutional amendments to slowly extend the franchise to what we have come to accept as today's embodiment of "We the People."

We were still operating under the Mississippi Constitution of 1890. Article 12 spelled out in detail the franchise. Section 240 read in part: "All elections shall be held by ballot," assumed to be written and secret. The article makes for interesting, if not painful and amusing, reading, particularly section 241:

> Every male inhabitant of this State, except idiots, insane persons, and Indians not taxed, who is a citizen of the United States, twenty-one years old and upwards, who has resided in this State two years, and one year in the election district, or in the incorporated city or town, in which he offers to vote, and who is duly registered as provided in this article, and who has never been convicted of bribery, theft, arson, obtaining money or goods under false pretenses, perjury, forgery, imbezzlement [*sic*] or bigamy, paid, on or before the first day of February of the year in which he shall offer to vote, all taxes which may have been legally required of him, and which he has had an opportunity of paying according to law, for two preceding years,

and who shall produce to the officers holding the election sat-
isfactory evidence that he has paid said taxes, is declared to be
a qualified elector; but any minister of the gospel in charge of
an organized church shall be entitled to vote after six months
residence in the election district, if otherwise qualified.

Note that preachers got a special deal, only six months residence,
"if otherwise qualified." One wonders if they had to pay the poll tax,
a sum levied on all males, except those who were "deaf and dumb,
and blind" or otherwise "maimed" (sec. 243). Poll tax specifications
were couched in the same flowery legalese. Cursory reading and
analysis of the written code, and the unwritten words and thought,
leaves no doubt that the writers knew exactly what they were doing.

In the ancient plutocratic Athenian democracy twenty-five-
hundred years ago, citizens were paid to attend assembly meetings
and to vote. Qualifications to vote between the time of the French
Revolution and Napoleon often were so quixotic that many French
citizens stayed off the street for fear of the guillotine. Robespierre
led the way for selected franchise, but eventually paid the price with
his own head. From the beginning in the United States there was a
gradual widening of the right to vote that coincided directly with its
discourse on race and gender. In addition to the property-owning
constraint, a poll tax was added to other barriers in states like Mississippi, keeping away "unqualified voters."

Greene County citizens paid a poll tax of two dollars, imposed
ostensibly for school aid. Every elector had to be able to read,
understand, and give an *interpretation* of the state constitution. I
remember the story of a black Ivy League graduate who returned
home to McLain, and having duly registered and paid his taxes went
to the polls on election day, the first primary. The precinct officer,
with a copy of section 244 ready, met him at the door. He gave a
perfect reading of the constitution and convinced the officer that he
understood it. His "reasonable interpretation," however, did not
please the officer and the small crowd that had gathered. A ballot was
not extended to him. That's the way it was in Greene County where,
ironically, there were not enough black voters to make an impact
anyway. No white voter was ever subjected to such questioning.

(The poll tax was still being levied when I returned from WWII. In 1947 I was married, and my father, who was still involved in politics, registered my new wife, Helen, and me, paid our poll tax (Helen was appalled), and we both cast our first vote.)

Because Old Washington had the largest number of voters, a multitude of candidates floated in and out from under the giant red oaks in front of the schoolhouse. There was no restriction on politicking and proximity to the polls. The candidate himself was careful whom he was seen with. However, political surrogates and flunkies were everywhere, twisting arms, often fabricating stories about the virtues of their candidate, and spreading gossip about the opponents.

Poll taxes were always vexing to voters in poor communities such as Old Washington. It embarrassed people to admit they couldn't vote because they didn't have two dollars. This raised a question: If someone else could pay his or her tax, would the voter consider casting his ballot for a suggested name? As election day approached, candidates assiduously checked the rolls to see if there were individuals who were for you, leaning toward you, or who could be bought and who hadn't paid their taxes. Should there be delinquents who fitted either one of these categories, the game playing would begin.

If a candidate could be sure of a vote in exchange for poll tax payment, this might be a bargain. In a close election, fifty swing votes could decide the outcome. Compared to asking a candidate to pay a doctor bill for a sick baby or signing off on the elector's note at the bank, asking him to pay a poll tax was entirely different. A candidate like my father could instantly read wordplay and body language. All kinds of negotiations took place on or near election day. Bargaining was intense. If elected, would the candidate give the voter a job at road maintenance? Help his graduating child get into college? Assist the voter's wife in getting transportation to see her parents in Alabama? There was great uncertainty in this process. A number of voters were notorious at promising their franchise. Astute candidates were aware that once you start such a chess game, an inexpensive checkmate was never likely.

Such bargaining became more intense on election day itself. My father always started the day in Old Washington precinct, but soon spent time at the other four boxes, Leaf, McLain, Pleasant Hill, and

Unity. At each location he was met by people, such as Price Moody, who hadn't voted, who obviously were holding out for the best deal. Some people voted only at the last moment before the polls closed. Candidates were aware of this quadrennial sleaze, but were helpless to find an honorable solution.

The only way a candidate could be absolutely sure of a vote was to buy it. The candidate or his trusted deputy would, by some nefarious scheme, obtain a blank ballot containing the entire slate of candidates from the highest office, usually that of US senator, to the lowest, normally justice of the peace. Such a list was not lengthy in Depression-era Greene County and was on a single narrow printed form, which could be easily folded and hidden. Said ballot was appropriately "voted" or marked. Away from public view, the deputy would rendezvous with the voter, instruct him on the process, and give him the marked ballot, which the voter would hide on his person and then proceed to the polls. There he received his legitimate ballot, which he slyly put away. Simultaneously, he pulled out the marked ballot and dropped it in the ballot box.

The final act of this drama consisted of the voter presenting the deputy with the empty ballot and receiving his payoff in cash. The voter then quickly disappeared. At this point another prospect, who had been watching from a parked car or other hideaway, emerged at the nod of the man in charge.

The candidate himself was never involved in the dirty work. Negotiation went on as long as there were accommodators on each side. This method of buying votes had to be discreet and was usually limited to the most desperate and needy of candidates and the most disreputable voters. A specific nuance to this process was that no two bought ballots were ever marked alike. That could be too easily spotted. Only the candidate's name was consistently marked X.

Jake Jacobs, who was particularly adept at buying votes (as well as shady hog and cow trading), moved in and out from the bushes behind Albert Harvison's store. He kept his hands in his pockets, fumbled a cigarette, and faked a cough to clear his throat. The look on his face told you that he was up to no good. Only a handful of people committed such scheming; but it only took a few bought votes to swing the election for a particular candidate.

My reaction to selling votes for two dollars was to abhor the actors and to hope that Father wasn't involved. I found the entire process nerve-wracking but entertaining, a local game mixed in hypocrisy and coated with a bit of Southern charm and intrigue that self-corrected any polarization. Community and cultural intercourse have a way of ameliorating old political wounds. That process appears to be far different from the current massive corruption of national campaigns and from the mechanics of commercial political activity, voter registration fraud, and other devices that border on the criminal. Witness the recent elections, where billions of dollars have been spent buying votes. *Yes, buying votes.*

What was once a local political blot in places like Father's Beat Five has become a plague on the national scene. However, Greene County politics, nasty and personal though they often were, never endangered the US Constitution. Correction was self-generated by way of the courts. For example, *Brown vs. Board of Education*. Those elected could not disregard the electorate and pursue policies that endanger the course of history set by our national character.

On election day, voters, candidates, and their families milled about the polling places, aware that four years of toil and sweat and bargaining were being tested behind the stage curtains in the auditorium at Neely School. Fate and entertainment were in abundance, some voters holding cardboard and turkey feather fans, others nursing babies.

Activity became frenzied as sundown neared. Clandestine clusters of would-be kingmakers milled around. Election-day hirelings were busy hauling last-minute stragglers from their rustic abodes around the district. The candidates emerged on the scene to make a final check. "Has Uncle Alec's bunch voted yet? Aunt Froney and Rachael?" Names of people were called who lived in the remotest parts of the district, and the backwoods. "Don't forget Old Man Roberts, his wife, and them girls," Father told Jay Brown, a helper. "Them girls" were four "maiden ladies" who seldom left home. At that time there was no absentee balloting. Nevertheless, there was better than an 80 percent turnout of registered voters in most primary elections.

After voting, many people went home for supper and came back to the polling place for the verdict. It was the biggest event of the year and had the largest community attendance. At an appointed hour, vote counting began by gaslight, with the monitors seated at a large table on the stage of the auditorium, where the booths had been removed. A chairman presided, who stood and called the house to order. He had a clerk assistant who checked and verified his every move. He officially unlocked the box and the count began. He pulled a single ballot from the box, unfolded it, and began reading the names. Two recorders tallied the outcome, a separate tally for each. With the clerk at his side looking on, the chairman in a mild bark intoned, "For United States Senate, Theodore Bilbo, one vote." Each recorder repeated, "United States Senate, Bilbo one vote." Chairman: "For Governor Hugh White, one vote." Recorders: "Governor, Hugh White, one vote." On and on until ballot's end. The process repeated with the next ballot until all votes were counted. My memory tells me there were about 110 ballots at Neely box.

During the evening there was twittering in the audience with every unexpected incident, like a baby's wail inside or the blast of a shotgun outside. Many people entered and exited, perhaps disappointed or excited about how the count was going for their candidate. Large numbers had pencils and paper, doing their own tally in the dim light. Astute counters correlated votes on the separate ballots because it was common practice, and common knowledge, that trades were made between candidates running for different offices. "If you'll help me at Neely, I'll speak to my Uncle Luther at Pleasant Hill to see if his family will go with you; nine votes there, you know!" Finally, when the counting was over, clerk-monitors tallied the votes and the chairman read totals for each candidate.

Neely normally was the last box to report, as the number of votes exceeded others in the district. Pleasant Hill was a laggard, however, and because of its remoteness, district candidates often had someone there to get the totals and make a dash for Neely, ten miles away, where by midnight the other boxes were in and local races were decided. Happy faces often far outnumbered the sad. As the counting proceeded, losers had sensed the coming defeat and had gone home.

The box was sealed, and all Beat Five votes were transported to Leakesville, the county seat, later that evening. The attention now shifted to the county and state totals. The next day the results came by word of mouth.

We had barely finished one election when speculation began about the next four years: Who will run? Political palaver was a way of passing the time. A friend said, "Bud's got it as long as he wants it." Someone else opined, "Surely Uncle Mark won't stand again, he's already seventy." "If Mark Green is alive, he'll announce," replied another. Small talk and gossip went on past midnight for some, but the Hillmans had already left. The biggest conundrum: *How does Bilbo do it?* No one ever admits to have voted for him, but he always ends up with a plurality.

When my Dad won his first race, I remember the sigh of relief that rose from the family and friends gathered in our living room at Thad Hill. Being a young "worrier," I was especially proud that my father had won an honorable victory, and was now assured a chance to correct some obvious malpractices of the county's business. "Bud" Hillman looked especially tired that night, but his famous smile shone through to all. Dry humor and jokes, stories about the campaign and its ups and downs, and the so-called turning points punctuated our celebration. No obvious drinking. I thought to myself, *Mr. Bud, I ain't got no better!* And, I smiled, too.

Greene County will never completely return to that political era of my experience, which appears to have been unique, even to Southern politics. The Civil War, Reconstruction, and economic "panics" punctuated the pioneer world of first- and second-generation immigrants, frontier development, and religious passion. A particular type of political man and political system had evolved in places like Greene County particular to my youth and observation.

After the Depression, pressures were on to move ahead. Inducements were everywhere for the voter to flee rural areas for the cities. There was no turning back from the changes made by Franklin D. Roosevelt. Federal programs such as the Works Progress Administration (WPA), the Civilian Conservation Corps (CCC), and the National Youth Administration (NYA) greatly augmented rural economies and the mobility of youth. (I worked my way through college on NYA money, first at fifteen cents an hour, then twenty-five cents.) Population decreased sharply in Greene County and rural America after WWII, women played a larger role in government, and blacks soon voted in larger numbers.

A complete written political history of Greene County is impossible, not only because of the paucity of records, but also because of their destruction, usually by fire. Single copies of records were kept in the courthouse. The burning of primitive courthouses, deliberate or not, was not unusual, and two log-cabin types went up in flames, one just after the Civil War and one in the 1870s. The courthouse I grew up with was built in 1899, was expanded and a jail added. A magnificent red brick structure with arched windows and entrance, it also burned. Records were kept in the basement of the old jail, but floods brought on by Hurricane Frederic in 1979 destroyed many of those that remained.

One wonders why so many official records went up in flames in rural counties. General Sherman also had a reason to burn things.

Endings

Soft Womb of
Greene County

IT APPEARED NOT UNLIKE A THOUSAND other rural villages. But the place where I was born and raised wasn't anything like them. In fact, it was very dissimilar, because that spot of Earth was the place of my early and peculiar memories. My recapturing consciousness made it different. It was mine, and for all its temporal and later-to-be-discovered imperfections, it remains mine, and my recollections bind me to it.

Southern Mississippi villages are like that: places that variously give birth to reminiscence, retrospection, and often celebration, for those who look back. What, then, are memories except storehouses for our souls' journeys? Their existence via matter and spirit in the world of form permit us to reflect on an earlier life in time. Memories are our virtual selves— we and us. Literally, we-and-us is transmuted to society. By some strange leap of my imagination, I *become* my childhood.

Across the South after the Civil War there was a struggle for survival, family success, and social well-being. Circumstances varied, but it was the white, Anglo-Protestant lifestyle that prevailed. Closed and insular societies, however, carry with them a double-edged sword: On the one hand, the past is never forgotten; its beautiful moments and its ugly face. Paraphrasing William Faulkner, "The past ain't dead; hell, it ain't even past." On the other hand, the outside world becomes foreign.

My recollections here derive from selected personal experiences and observations that identify my childhood with life in rural Greene County. My story does not produce a generalized account; it originates from a single linear experience. If one wants fuller insight into the real "Southern mind," one should first read W. J. Cash, then consult Faulkner, O'Connor, Dickey, Welty, Walker Percy, David L.

Agnes Hillman with baby Jimmye on porch of Big House, ca. 1923.

Cohn, or Hodding Carter Jr., and wind up with James C. Cobb's *Away Down South*. I make the painful observation that my account is one of the last to connect those who lived during the Civil War and those remaining in the twenty-first century. So few of us are left.

We arrived at Unity Baptist Church for the seventieth reunion of my Neely High School class of 1938. I studied the crowd to see how many faces I could recognize. Watching their movements, I spotted a few same-age survivors: grayer hair, hearing aids, and wrinkles, cautious body movement, and blank stares. More sat than stood. If you knew them as I did in the 1930s, you would immediately recognize their countenance, which, like a fingerprint, never changes. I read the minds of two ladies in loud flower-print dresses across the room: *What's Old Jim doin back here? Someone tol me he wuz dead.*

Rita Daughdrill Clark and Alpha Turner Stanford were our hostesses and managed the "Memory Table." I picked up a copy I had never seen of a picture of my father when he taught briefly at Neely. Among the piles of old letters and photographs stood a framed newspaper article about Ed "Too Tall" Freeman, who had attended the reunion in 2006. It told of his winning the Congressional Medal of Honor for his valor at Pork Chop Hill in Vietnam. I remember his father, Ed senior, and his uncle, "Am" Freeman, who lived up on the railroad stop at Garner, next to the Hamm brothers, Frank and Elam, who were all friends of my father. They lived so close together, I never knew who were Hamms and who were Freemans.

Cousin Cal Hillman, a war hero in the South Pacific with his own collection of medals, had already come and gone. Son of Benjamin F. Hillman ("Bear Ben"), Cal is an expansive personality, and later by phone wove again his favorite story about the time in the 1920s when we all were on the train platform at Denco and a passenger had to jump onto a moving carriage because Denco wasn't a scheduled stop. We called it the "Mud Line," and from an ancient train schedule in my files, I see that Denco was twelve minutes from Neely. Cal's brother Randolph, or "Randy," paid the ultimate price in the North African Campaign in 1942 and never had an opportunity to reunite with all the graduates of Neely High.

There was a brief business meeting, and individuals said four separate prayers for old-timers gone, for soldiers in foreign lands, for our teachers, and other public servants. I had traveled the farthest, from Tucson, Arizona, and was asked to say a few words, which were carried in the weekly *Greene County Herald*.

Baskets of food were unloaded and spread on the tables. Glazed hams drizzled on the serving platters. Fried chicken, piled high, tumbled from aluminum trays. Steam rose from vegetables of every configuration—collards, black-eyed peas, turnips, and corn on the cob. And it seemed like every berry in the world had been baked into a pie.

"Darlin, you just gotta try some of my chocolate cake!" one lady said to Tom, my grandson, whom I had persuaded to leave Bard College during spring break so I might acquaint him with my village and Mississippi culture. Tom had lived most of his life in the Yankee north, and this was his first visit to Greene County. He became an instant hit with the women, who kept calling him "Darlin," "Sweetie," and "Honey."

Each reunion meant fewer bodies than the year before. The list of living graduates has dwindled since the school closed in 1958. When I graduated, five high schools dotted Greene County, and now only one remained. Neely High, along with its beautiful gymnasium built with the largess of Charles Hillman, crumbled into disuse long ago.

Although I hadn't seen him for decades, I recognized W. T. "Willie" Lejohn, still buck-toothed, smiling but stooped and with receding hair. I can still picture him in sixth-grade declamation class, sputtering William Cullen Bryant's "Robert of Lincoln": "Bob-o-link, bob-o-link, Spink, spank, spink, Chee, chee, chee," with spit flying everywhere. With prompting from my mother, who would forever repeat the incident and giggle, Willie added, "Miz Agnes, I think the lark was also saying, 'Laziness will kill you! Laziness will kill you!'"

Betty Ann Morehead was still beautiful, blonde and blue eyed with an evanescent, come-on look, even in her eighties. She told me she now lives in New Orleans and has a dozen grandchildren. Married for a while to my possum-and-coon-huntin cousin Cranford, she quit him when he repeatedly came home and jumped in bed smelling of polecat. I understood her reasoning, having smoked out many a skunk with him while listening to the GM&O night train whistle through McLain. Nor did Betty Ann like it when he decided hunting wasn't worth his time and accepted the Lord's call to preach. The Lord had neglected to consult *her*.

"Welcome home, Jim. You remember me, don'tcha?" I looked at his eyes, mouth, and head shape for a clue. Embarrassed, I guessed, "You're a Walley, one of them Ben Walley boys, ain't ya?" He didn't seem to mind my mistake. "Nope, I'm Clyde Cooley." "*You* can't be Clyde Victor! *Clyde Victor Mister Cooley?*" I said. We laughed, then began to reminisce about how he picked up the nickname, which resulted in his attempting to formally introduce himself during class as, "I'm Clyde Victor. Mr. Cooley."

Just a few of the twelve of the 1938 class were at the gathering. Alas! Jean, Winona, and Zelline, all Byrds, Dunnam brothers, Alton and Lehman, and Harold "Preacher" Breland were absent this year and forever. Where are Leo Fike and Deloy Smith, old faces from other years?

My fascination for origins and cultural and family history always drew me back to these gatherings. My older brother, Bill, never attended a reunion. Brother Elmer, who was on the Neely basketball team and won the state championship in 1941–42, attended only when I came for visits. He died in 2004 and according to his wishes was buried on his own farm in the next county rather than in the family plot in Neely. Sister Jean went to school in McLain and was a "foreigner" to Neely folk but did occasionally frequent the Unity gatherings. Grandson Tom, at six feet four, no doubt reminded people of Charles Hillman and other tall Hillmans, many of whom now lay in Neely's Old Washington cemetery.

As some lips were quietly moving, I calculated the subtle gazes and imagined what was passing through some of those rural cerebra: *Old Jim up and left the South; thought he was too good for us; he coulda been Guvnah if he hadda staid home.* My mind dizzied, flashed back, and began living the golden moments of youth and exuberance at a place that for generations my forebears had made home. *And, old Jim understands.*

Alpha Stanford invited us to visit her country home, her grand-father's "Old Place." The longleaf, heart-pine house still stood on its original foundation of liteard stumps, each one mossy green but solid as stone. The Alex Ball farmstead, at least 150 years old, was a typical settlement of those who swarmed into Greene County after the Civil War. It reminded me of Charles Hillman's "Old House" of my childhood. Barns, cattle sheds, hog pens, and sheep paddocks, even the old well and the "two-holer" outhouse. It all looked just like the places people lived in when I traveled with Father as he worked summers for the federal farm programs during the FDR administration.

Alpha regaled us as we boarded our rental car to look for Old Highway 24, the route to the Grand Avenue Inn, our bed-and-breakfast in Leakesville. She insisted, "Come back next year and stay as long as you like."

My mind was set a thinkin about others who had accompanied me on my Greene County tours: wife Helen, daughter Brenda, and granddaughter Louisa; and friends Herman Kohlmeyer of New Orleans and Ken Lamberton, my Tucson scribe.

Ya'll come, ya heah! Southern hospitality, Greene County manners. I'm reminded of the Satchmo quip about jazz: If you gotta ask what it is, ya ain't never gonna understand.

It is Sunday and I have just attended St. Michael's Episcopal mass. Looking out the den window to our patio, I see a grapefruit tree laden with fruit. I listen to television news describing a local school problem, followed by a political discussion on a faith initiative. I think: *I had never seen a grapefruit before college, and it was 1942 before the Rural Electrification Administration brought electricity to our home. Church and state intermingling were a no-no in my youth. YouTube has arrived, and Craigslisting is upon us. Will the printed media soon be extinct?*

Change has been a constant factor, beginning with my adventurous years in a one-room schoolhouse and on our subsistence farm. After escaping the drudgery of plowing a mule and sawing paper wood, my pursuit of knowledge was predictable from my parentage, and somehow I felt excited about every turn in life: Learning about Yankees and Catholics; loving my Jewish roommate in college; observing the progress of racial integration and affirmative action; and an increased access to the educational process, universal suffrage, and the election of the first black president have all buttressed my optimism about the prospects for a fairer society.

There was little time in my childhood and youth to reflect on high social ideals and egalitarian motives, or on calculated intolerance and hate. The 1930s Great Depression blotted out most thought except that about survival. I learned that when crises arise, even the rich and high-minded of societies become subject to prejudice, and political leaders begin looking for scapegoats. Somehow my young and uncluttered brain concluded that human flaws derive principally from centuries-old family or religious bigotry and community grudges, and are culturally ingrained. Preying on another's insecurity was never my game.

So-called closed societies (them versus us) get that way for a reason, and I deduced early that the principal reason is fear. Fear of the outsider, fear of the unknown. But fear can be assuaged and eliminated, not by flight from one another, but by nothing less than a common will to listen to the old verities emanating from the human heart.

It is clear that the insularity of a small community like Neely protects residents from outsider influence. By the same token, doors can be closed from the outside; bias works both ways. A New York friend of mine once joked, "Jimmye, how'd ya make it so good? You were born a farmer down in rural Mississippi . . . and a Southern Baptist. Did you even go to school?"

I remembered a conversation between Charles Hillman and his son, my father. In response to Grandpa's derision of a neighbor, my father said: "Pa, you can't condemn a man for being born who he is. But with some luck, and a bit of fightin, he can rise above the crowd. He may even challenge the preacher and the sheriff, but he's gotta take the consequences." Looking at me, he continued, "Be careful, scalawags are everywhere."

I learned that I had to cope with institutional prejudice, and fight the necessary battles to assuage my conscience without breaking the law. This took a lot of effort. I refused to be intimidated by the elite, intellectual rich or embarrassed by the fact that I came from a humble background, had Confederate ancestry, and grew up among rednecks.

I don't want to personally assume all of Southern society's perceived liabilities. The circumstances of my youth, family, church, school, politics, and culture were in most ways an asset. Pressing against the resistance of custom, and fighting a certain stereotype, has enabled me to stand out against the broad human canvass in answer to Faulkner's call to "endure and prevail."

By the time I left the farm at fifteen, I had a sensitive nose for sorting what's absolute and what's relative; the phony, the real. Indeed, change comes slowly. *Tantae molis erat, urbs condita.* My parents put me on the train at State Line for college in September 1938, with a steamer trunk of used clothes and five dollars. Father's teary admonition was, "Boy, as quick as ya get up there, ask them for a job." "Them" were very good to me.

After eighty-eight years I look back and discover that the piney woods had prepared me for the world.

About the Author

JIMMYE HILLMAN WAS BORN IN 1923 and grew up on a subsistence farm in southern Mississippi. He received his PhD at the University of California, Berkeley, and has been associated with the University of Arizona in Tucson, where he served as head of the Department of Agricultural Economics for thirty years while doing groundbreaking work in agricultural and trade policy. He is now professor emeritus. He has also served as executive director for the National Advisory Commission on Food and Fiber under President Lyndon Johnson and as consultant on US-Japanese agricultural trade policies during the Reagan administration. Hillman's other honors include: Research Fellow at Jesus College, Oxford University; Fulbright Fellow, Lincoln College, New Zealand; and an honorary doctorate from the University of Ceará, Brazil.

CPSIA information can be obtained at www.ICGtesting.com
Printed in the USA
LVOW06s1957021013

355093LV00005B/16/P